SELECTIONS FROM PHILOSOPHERS

EDITED BY
MARY WARNOCK

Plato's Epistemology
and Related Logical Problems
by
Gwynneth Matthews

Aristotle's Ethics
by
J. L. Ackrill

ARISTOTLE'S ETHICS

ARISTOTLE'S ETHICS

J. L. ACKRILL

*Fellow of Brasenose College and
Professor of the History of Philosophy in the
University of Oxford*

NEW YORK
HUMANITIES PRESS

Andrew S. Thomas Memorial Library
MORRIS HARVEY COLLEGE, CHARLESTON, W.VA.

First published in 1973 in the U.S.A.
by Humanities Press
450 Park Avenue South
New York 10016, N.Y.

Printed in Great Britain by
Robert MacLehose & Co Ltd Glasgow
All rights reserved

ISBN 391 00281 3

This edition and selection
© J. L. Ackrill 1973

FOREWORD

Aristotle's Moral Philosophy

For twenty years of his life – in the mid fourth century B.C. – Aristotle was a member of Plato's school in Athens. His very earliest writings, lost except for a few fragments, were dialogues in the Platonic manner. Probably even these writings were critical of Plato; and by the time he came to write the works of his maturity the distance from his master was considerable. The Platonists firmly believed in two worlds – a real world of Forms, separate from the illusory world of material things. Values were not to be found *in* the world but beyond it, in the perfect realm of real existences. In Aristotle's ethical writings reality *is* the world in which we find ourselves. His aim as a moral philosopher is to discover what makes a good life for man. The good life will be the life in which a man, as far as possible, *does* those things which a man is peculiarly fitted to do. In such a life there will be pleasure and satisfaction.

It is sometimes said of Aristotle that his view of morality is very low and unedifying; that his good man is simply a seeker after pleasure for himself; and that there is neither aspiration towards an ideal nor altruism in his system. It is alleged, too, that Aristotle merely collects together the views of ordinary people about morality, dressing up platitudes as philosophical profundities. Such criticisms are mistaken, though they contain a small element of the truth. Aristotle certainly starts from commonly held opinions about the good life for man. His aim is to analyse what the good life actually is, and he would have failed to do this if he had taken no account of what real people actually want. So he is bound to pay attention to what they say that they want. Thus, for example, since none would want to live a life quite devoid of pleasure, he is bound to include some element of pleasure in the total concept of the good life. But this does not entail that he is a hedonist. He does not believe that to seek the good life is the same as to seek pleasure but rather that if you lead a life which is good, pleasure will accompany it. Leading a good life means leading a life that is peculiarly suited to men placed as they are among other men. It is true that for those readers who have been brought up in an atmosphere of roughly-speaking Christian morality, the concept of the good life for man presented in Aristotle's moral philosophy may seem somewhat mundane; and it is also true that the ideas of self-denial and self-sacrifice are absent. Moreover, since man's peculiar function – what marks him off from other animals – is intellectual, the good life is in the last analysis largely the life of the intellect, though translated into action (exactly *how* it is translated is one of the problems which Aristotle has to solve). Such a concept goes against the egalitarian view of morality which we tend to assume. For Aristotle as for Plato it is not the case that everyone has an equal chance to be good. But one of the features of the good life in Aristotle's view is that a man should treat his fellowmen well, and be just and friendly to them. So that a man could not attain moral excellence who thought of nobody but himself. Neither could he attain it if he merely thought noble thoughts and did not put them into effect.

In general, the values implicit in Aristotle's ethical thought may be somewhat unfamiliar, but they are nevertheless intelligible to us. And the aim of his moral philosophy is certainly intelligible. Granted that we all aim to lead a good, satisfying and successful life, the question he asks is what we really mean when we say this. What counts as good in connexion with a man's life on earth? How is he to identify and explain the goals that he has? It is true that in reading Aristotle's moral philosophy we are seldom asked to lift our eyes to higher things, or to despise the world in which we live. But we are asked to think clearly about human beings, and to distinguish from one another things which are in fact different. These tasks are at least some of the proper tasks of philosophy.

MARY WARNOCK

CONTENTS

FOREWORD BY MARY WARNOCK	7
PREFACE	11

INTRODUCTION

1. General	13
2. Method	15
3. The Structure of the 'Nicomachean Ethics' (E.N.)	17
4. The good for man (E.N. I and X.6–8)	18
5. Moral virtue (E.N. II)	21
6. Action and responsibility (E.N. III.1–5)	24
7. Practical wisdom and the practical syllogism (E.N. VI)	28
8. 'Akrasia' (E.N. VII.1–10)	31
9. Pleasure (E.N. VII.11–14 and X.1–5)	33
NOTE ON TRANSLATION	35
NOTE ON ABBREVIATIONS AND REFERENCES	37

TEXT

NICOMACHEAN ETHICS

I	41
II	61
III	75
V. 1–2, 5 (end), 7–10	99
VI	113
VII	129
IX. 4, 8, 9	153
X	161

CONTENTS

EUDEMIAN ETHICS

I	185
II. 1, 6–11	197
VIII.3	215

DE ANIMA

III. 9–11	221

DE MOTU ANIMALIUM

6–11	229

NOTES

NICOMACHEAN ETHICS	241
EUDEMIAN ETHICS	266
DE ANIMA	270
DE MOTU ANIMALIUM	271
READING LIST	274
INDEX	281

PREFACE

THIS book is designed for the student of philosophy who wants to work on Aristotle's moral philosophy but does not read Greek. It includes most of the *Nicomachean Ethics*, but also a sizeable part of the *Eudemian Ethics*; a comparison between these two rather different treatments of much the same problems is instructive. Extended extracts from *De Anima* and *De Motu Animalium* are also printed, these being of particular interest and importance in connection with the psychology of action. The Introduction is introductory and fairly general. It aims at alerting the reader who is new to Aristotle to some of the questions that are raised in or by his ethical writings. The notes at the end, on the other hand, are sometimes on points of detail. They make free use of cross references and are intended for the student who is not just reading but is really working on the *Ethics*.

J.L.A.

INTRODUCTION

1. *General*

SOME of the questions that exercise moral philosophers today are not raised by Aristotle, but very many are. We have indeed inherited many problems from him, and often enough he has set the tone and terms of subsequent discussion. One should, however, study a philosopher like Aristotle not only to see what he has to say about problems we are familiar with, but also to see and understand why certain of our questions do not arise for him, and how some of our concerns look rather different – or seem to be of different importance – within a different, but not therefore necessarily wrong or defective, conceptual and ethical scheme. To study a great philosopher of another age helps us to recognise what is parochial not only in our contemporary answers to ethical questions but also in our contemporary questions.

Aristotle is in some ways and for some people a particularly attractive 'philosopher of another age'. Though his approach and presuppositions are strikingly different from ours, they are not bafflingly or repulsively so. Nor, of course, is this just a happy chance; the unique influence of Aristotle on the thought of Western civilisation has ensured that we should not find him alien. Again, Aristotle's method of philosophising and the whole temper of his mind are highly congenial to many modern students. He is cool, critical, and very acute. He knows the importance of drawing distinctions and clarifying issues. He realises that different kinds of question need different kinds of answer based on different types of argument or evidence. He aims at reaching conclusions by cogent argument from clear and agreed premisses. Lastly, several of the central themes of Aristotle's ethics happen to be central to contemporary debates on moral philosophy – the psychology of action, for instance, and the connection between morality and human nature and human wants.

Certain features of Aristotle's style are explained by the fact that most of his preserved works consist of or are derived from lecture-notes. This explains why his writing is often compressed or even elliptical, though in other places, where he has brought his material into a polished form, his style can be quite fluent. Again, lecture-notes often get added to and altered over a period of years. This must be remembered when one meets disjointed passages or unexpected juxtapositions in Aristotle. Finally, it must not be assumed that such a work as the *Nicomachean Ethics* (*E.N.*, i.e. *Ethica Nicomachea*) represents a single lecture course. Some parts are quite obviously separate, independent courses, though they have been given a reasonable place in the overall scheme of *E.N.* Thus, for example, books VIII and IX constitute a 'monograph' on different forms of human association. The most striking proof of the 'put together' character of *E.N.* as we have it is that it contains two long independent discussions of pleasure. The editor of the whole work has not made any serious attempt to conceal or explain this oddity, and we can of course be grateful that he did indeed preserve for us notes on two distinct courses – one of which presumably corrects or improves upon the other.

In the Aristotelian corpus there are three treatises on ethics, the *Nicomachean Ethics*, the *Eudemian Ethics* (*E.E.*), and the *Magna Moralia*. The last of these is almost certainly a later work containing post-Aristotelian material. The relation between the other two must be briefly explained. The authenticity of *E.E.* is now widely accepted, and it is usually supposed – though the point remains arguable – that it represents an *earlier* course (or set of courses) than *E.N.* There is one very curious problem. The books printed as *E.N.* V–VII are also *E.E.* IV–VI: the manuscripts of *E.E.* tell us at the end of book III that the next three books are the same as *E.N.* V–VII. How are we to understand this? Were these books originally part of one set of lectures, say *E.E.*, and later brought in by an editor to fill a gap, to replace lost books of a different course (*E.N.*)? The scholarly battle has ranged over many possibilities. For the philosopher the key question would be whether these books belong philosophically with the other *E.E.* books or with the other *E.N.* books, a question that still awaits a full and conclusive answer.

These 'common books' are traditionally printed, and normally

1. General

studied, as part of *E.N.* Indeed the study of the Eudemian lectures has almost been confined to specialist scholars. This is a pity. The differences between the two can be expected to throw light on the development of Aristotle's thought; and even if *E.E.* is earlier than *E.N.*, and also in general inferior to it, it is not therefore negligible. Moreover, just because *E.E.* has been far less studied and discussed there is more room for new ideas about it and for original interpretations. For these reasons I have printed in this book substantial extracts from *E.E.*, although this has involved omitting parts of *E.N.* These parts (most of IV, V, VIII-IX) are interesting, but not essential for the serious study of Aristotle's ethics. Instead of them the reader has before him an alternative version of Aristotle's thoughts on the good, on excellence of character, on the classification of actions, and on some other central themes. I have also added extracts from Aristotle's work on psychology and on animal movement (*De Anima* and *De Motu Animalium*). These concern the psychology and physiology of action, and will supplement material in *E.N.* and *E.E.* It would have been easy to find important extracts from other treatises to illuminate this or that aspect of the ethical works; political and metaphysical topics suggest themselves. But the passages printed here are perhaps as likely as any to interest the reader of this book.

2. Method

Aristotle's statements about philosophical method correspond pretty well to his actual practice. One basic statement is at *E.N.* VII.1145b2-7, where three stages are distinguished: first one should establish the *phainomena*, next one should formulate the difficulties and puzzles that arise, and finally one should solve or dissolve these problems without doing violence to the *phainomena*. It will be useful to say something about these stages and to illustrate them from actual discussions in *E.N.*

The word *phainomena* means 'things that appear'. In some contexts it is used of facts of perception, but in our context it refers to people's opinions. (So translations like 'observed facts' are liable to mislead: *E.N.* 1145b3, b28; *E.E.* 1216b27, 1217a13, 1228a19.) The philosopher's first step in a given inquiry is, then, to assemble the views held on the matter by all or most people or by any significant group or by any single serious thinker. Sometimes, as in *Metaphysics A* and *De Anima* I, this first step is a full-scale survey of the doctrines of earlier philosophers: 'we should call into council the views of our predecessors in order that we may profit by whatever is sound in their suggestions and avoid their errors' (*De Anima* 403 b 20). Sometimes, as often in *E.N.*, it is rather a round-up of ordinary opinions and ways of speaking: 'every man has some contribution to make to the truth' (*E.E.* 1216 b 31).

Puzzles arise, and apparent contradictions, when the various things thought and said are looked at together. Aristotle recommends a careful and forceful working out of these difficulties. 'For those who wish to get clear of difficulties it is advantageous to discuss the difficulties well; for the subsequent free play of thought implies the solution of the previous difficulties, and it is not possible to untie a knot of which one does not know ... People who inquire without first stating the difficulties are like those who do not know where they have to go.' The whole of *Metaphysics B* (from whose first chapter the foregoing quotation is taken) is devoted to a collection of *aporiai*, puzzles where different considerations seem to force us in opposite directions.

A philosophical solution is achieved (typically) by the drawing of distinctions and by the qualifying or clarifying of opinions put forward in an unqualified or unclear way. We free ourselves from 'knots' and intellectual cramps by understanding why each view was held and by seeing in what sense or within what limits each is acceptable. 'We must find a method that will best explain the views held on these topics, and also put an end to difficulties and contradictions. And this will happen if the contrary views are seen to be held with some show of reason; ... and both the contradictory statements will in the end stand, if what is said is true in one sense but untrue in another' (*E.E.* 1235 b 13). 'The solution of the difficulty is the discovery of the truth' (*E.N.* 1146 b 7).

The best example in *E.N.* of the above method is the discussion of *akrasia* in VII.1–3. The opinions or 'things said' are listed in chapter 1 (1145 b 8–20). *Aporiai* are worked out in chapter 2

2. Method

(see 1145b21 and 1146b6). The untying of a major knot is achieved in chapter 3 by the distinguishing of different sorts of knowledge or different senses of 'know' (1146b9, 1147b18). The discussion of self-love in *E.N.* IX.8 displays the same features. See also, on equity, *E.N.* V.10 ('they are all in a sense correct and not opposed to one another', 1137b7); on pleasure, *E.N.* VII.11-14 (where c.11 gives 'the things that are said', c.14 refers to the need to explain *why* a false view could have appeared true, 1154a22); and on the good for man, *E.N.* I.8 (where the conclusion of an argument about *eudaimonia* is tested for consistency with 'what is commonly said about it').

It will be clear that not all of Aristotle's investigations and arguments fall within the framework of the method just outlined. Sometimes he relies on premisses or operates with concepts that belong to his own philosophical position rather than to 'what everyone says' – though in such cases he is usually concerned to show that his results satisfy the demands of common sense. It is instructive to ask oneself how far Aristotle's explicit statements of method fall short of giving an adequate account of his actual procedures of inquiry and argument. It is also worth considering to what extent his positive ethical conclusions are rendered predictably unrevolutionary by his taking as his starting-point what people say.

3. *The structure of the 'Nicomachean Ethics'*

Book I seeks to establish what the best life for a man to lead is, and it concludes that the best life (*eudaimonia* or 'happiness') consists in 'activity of soul in accordance with virtue'. The relevant virtues or excellences of the soul comprise virtues of character and virtues of mind; and Aristotle proceeds in books II–V to an examination of the former, and in book VI to an examination of the latter. Book VII (chapters 1-10) discusses *akrasia* ('incontinence'), failure to do what one's own aims or principles demand, and then (chapters 11-14) examines various views about pleasure. Books VIII and IX treat of friendship and other types of human association. Book X (chapters 1-5) contains a second discussion of pleasure; and then (chapters 6-9) Aristotle returns to the theme of human happiness, arguing for the superiority of the theoretic or contemplative life over the practical life.

4. *The good for man* (E.N. I and X.6–8)

Before Aristotle comes (in I.7) to his answer to the question 'what is the best life for a man?' he seeks to elucidate the question itself. Two important points here are (a) his analysis of 'good', and (b) his distinction between what is wanted for its own sake and what is wanted for the sake of something else.

(a) Aristotle is very clear that goodness is not a single simple property; much of his attack on Plato's Form of Good in I.6 is in effect directed to this issue. He makes only tentative suggestions as to how various senses or uses of 'good' are inter-related. But he repeatedly insists on the necessary connection between the concepts *good* and *aiming at*: the good of a thing, activity, or agent is that at which it or he aims, the desired end.

Aristotle takes it to be a conceptual truth that men want to live a good life and indeed the best possible life; or, in other words, that men want *eudaimonia* – this being the word anyone uses for the life he thinks best, most worthwhile, most desirable. People differ however as to what sort of life *is* the best. This question is the central question of practical philosophy. Notice that it is a wider question than the question what sort of life is *morally* best; it may or may not prove to be the case that the most satisfying and desirable life for a man is always and necessarily the most morally good.

(b) Aristotle points out in I.1 that some things are sought for the sake of others, and that some arts and activities are naturally subordinate to others. His brief discussion leaves many distinctions undrawn; for example, while bridles just are – by definition – things for use in horse-riding, horse-riding itself is not by definition subordinate to the military art, although it is exploited by it. However, the most important point is the one made in the last sentence of the chapter: an activity A may be for the sake of B not only where A produces a product or outcome which subserves B but also where A is pursued as an activity and not for any out-

4. The good for man

come. The kind of case Aristotle must have in mind is a kind where our terminology of 'means' and 'ends' would not be appropriate, but where nevertheless the notion of one end being subordinate to another is appropriate. My objective is to have a good holiday. To that end I plan *inter alia* to go fishing. I shall not go fishing in order to do something afterwards (let alone in order to have a good holiday afterwards). Yet I can explain my intention to go fishing by saying that doing this is part of my idea of a good holiday. Compare and contrast: (i) I am playing this page of music because I want to play this sonata; playing this page is part of, not a means to, playing the sonata. (ii) I am writing the letter to keep a promise; writing the letter is not a means to, but a case of, promise-keeping.

So when Aristotle says that we want various things not only for their own sakes but also for the sake of *eudaimonia*, he means that we regard them not as means to subsequent felicity but as ingredients in the whole happy life we want. When he asks 'what is the good for man?' he is not assuming that there is just one single activity worth engaging in. If there are several such activities there can still be *the* good for man, namely the life that contains all these activities. Aristotle may wish in the end to identify the highest form of *eudaimonia* with one particular activity. But in working up to his question 'what is the best life for a man?' he is not assuming any such identification. The notion of *eudaimonia* or the best life is a comprehensive notion, and final: I can explain all my other aims by saying that I regard them as contributing – in one way or another – to *eudaimonia*, whereas I cannot say (or be sensibly asked) why I want *eudaimonia*.

Aristotle may be criticised for assuming that there is an answer to the question 'what is the best life for a man?' – as opposed to the question 'what is the best life for *this* man or *that* man?' He certainly does think that the nature of man – the powers and needs all men have – determines the character that any satisfying human life must have. But since his account of the nature of man is in general terms the corresponding specification of the best life for man is also general. So while his assumption puts some limits on the possible answers to the question 'how shall I live?' it leaves considerable scope for a discussion which takes account of my individual tastes, capacities, and circumstances.

In I.7 (from 1097b22) Aristotle seeks to discover what is the good for man by determining his specific function. His argument does not presuppose that men are made to serve a purpose, but only that men have certain distinctive powers. Excellence in the exercise of these will make a man a good man and his life a good life, just as excellence in cutting is what makes a knife a good knife. Aristotle holds that it is the ability to think that distinguishes men essentially from other animals, and that the good life is therefore one in which this activity is exercised well. This type of argument, first clearly formulated by Plato at the end of *Republic* I, has echoed down the centuries. I shall confine myself to three particular remarks about Aristotle's use of it.

First, if 'man' is a functional word in anything like the way that 'knife' is, criteria for being a good man may be derivable from consideration of man's distinctive powers. Aristotle, however, is not asking what it is to be a good man, but what is the good for man. It is not self-evident that the best thing for a man is to be the best possible man. This little slide is made easier for Plato and Aristotle by the fact that (as noted at 1095a19) 'living well' and 'doing well' are equivalent in Greek with *eudaimonia* ('happiness'). The danger of the slide is not of course apparent in the case of a knife or an eye, since we do not raise questions about the welfare of a knife or an eye, or regard them as deriving benefit from their performances.

Secondly, it is clear that at best the argument from function will give only a very general, almost formal, characterisation of the criteria for being a good so-and-so. What *is* excellence in the exercise of reason? Aristotle divides the excellences in question into two main kinds, intellectual virtues and virtues of character (for the latter depend upon the ability to think). But his list of these various virtues and his description of them do not flow straight from the formula reached by the function agreement. (Malice is as distinctive of man as charity is.)

Thirdly, after concluding that *eudaimonia* is a life of excellent activity, 'activity of soul in accordance with virtue', Aristotle adds:

4. The good for man

'and if there are more than one virtue, in accordance with the best and most complete' (1098a16). It is not immediately clear what he intends by this last phrase. One would suppose that full human excellence would require the display of *all* the distinctive virtues of a man. There is nothing in the function argument to imply that there is an order of importance among these, or that, if there is, excellence consists in the display of only the most important. Aristotle will in fact argue for the superiority of theoretic activity over practical, and he will distinguish the highest forms of happiness from a secondary form (X.7-8). But since he allows that man is capable only to a limited extent of pure theoretical activity – and 'not in so far as he is a man, but in so far as something divine is present in him' – his recipe for the best life must in the end presumably include a large dose of the 'secondary *eudaimonia*' to be found in action. It cannot be said that Aristotle resolves the tension between the line of thought that makes man's good something comprehensive, involving the display of all distinctive human virtues, and that which picks out one kind of activity and one virtue as constituting happiness *par excellence*.

5. Moral virtue (E.N. II)

Book II is concerned with moral virtues in general, these being virtues a man can possess in that his desires are subject to the influence of his reason (I.13); particular moral virtues are discussed at III.6–V. While it is convenient to use the term 'moral virtue' it must be remembered that 'excellence of character' would more closely represent the meaning of the Greek. Aristotle's list includes qualities we should certainly not call *moral*, just as his 'intellectual virtues' would not naturally be called *virtues* by us.

The first five chapters contain admirable remarks on states of character; how they differ from skills ('arts') or feelings ('passions') or natural faculties and powers; how they are developed and displayed; how they are connected with pleasure (or likes and dislikes); and how the appraisal of character differs from that of acts. In chapter 6 Aristotle establishes a definition of (moral) virtue, and it is this – his 'doctrine of the mean' – that will be briefly discussed here.

When Aristotle says that virtue is a state of character lying in a mean (a mean determined by reason or by rational principle), he is clearly not saying that the right thing to do on any occasion is something moderate – as if, when asked for money, I ought never to give nothing and ought never to give all I have. Nor is Aristotle purporting to give a criterion for virtue by saying that it lies in a mean: we await elucidation of the *logos*, the reason or rational principle of the man of practical wisdom which determines the mean. What then is conveyed by this abstract characterisation of a virtue as 'lying in a mean'? Aristotle is, I think, suggesting that no basic human tendency to feel or act in a certain way is *in itself* and *always* good, or bad. Any vice or bad trait can be seen as a perversion or exaggeration of some human feeling or tendency not in itself bad, or as a deficiency in some feeling or tendency not in itself good. Whether this contention is true – perhaps trivially true – will depend on the grounds on which tendencies etc. are picked out as basic. But it is at least clear that it is a very general view about the nature of certain moral concepts. It does not provide a detailed identification of moral virtues, nor a rule for fixing the relevant 'mean'. Insofar as Aristotle's accounts of particular virtues embody a particular moral outlook (and that is, perhaps, not far), this is due rather to his acquiescence in the vocabulary and outlook of his time than to his theoretical commitment to 'the doctrine of the mean'.

Aristotle often insists that there are many aspects of a given situation, many ways in which under given circumstances action may go wrong. One must, e.g., give the right amount at the right time, in the right way, to the right person, and so on. But he also of course takes it for granted that the virtuous man will do the right thing. How then can it be adequate to characterise a virtue as a 'mean'? Generosity is no doubt a mean in contrast with prodigality on the one hand and meanness on the other. But what of misplaced generosity? If I give away a reasonable amount of my income, but in foolish directions, am I generous – in which case the necessary connection between virtue and right action is broken – or am I both mean and prodigal, or what? No doubt

5. Moral virtue

control by practical wisdom would ensure that I behave rightly on all occasions. But does it make sense to speak of practical wisdom fixing my general tendency to give (be angry, etc.) in such a way that I always do the right thing?

One can perhaps meet this difficulty by bringing in another idea, that of the unity of the virtues. If *all* of a man's natural tendencies have been brought by training into a proper balance, there is no danger that a defect in one direction will impinge upon the operation of some other tendency; and provided that the agent knows the facts of the case he cannot fail to do the right thing. It is of course clear that the notion of a man practically wise and hence possessed of all virtues (1144b30–1145a2) is an ideal. In actual appraisals, as Aristotle recognises, we are prepared to call a man generous or brave though he is less than perfect: praise and blame are directed to those who are significantly above or below par. Moreover Aristotle discusses individual virtues and vices as though they were logically independent – so that a man could be brave but mean, or generous but cowardly. Nevertheless I suspect that the idea of a single virtue as lying in a mean is strictly unintelligible *if* it is a necessary truth that a virtue is displayed in doing acts right in all respects. Situations in which we act are always complicated, and the possession of a single virtue would be compatible with always acting wrongly. Successful handling of complex circumstances requires complex virtues (and skills), and no one of these will be good enough on its own. The virtues of a good man are not to be likened to a set of separately operating functions, each displayed in its own private set of actions, but to a set of nicely balanced inter-related functions all of which must be in order if good results in any direction are to be certainly achieved. Thus Aristotle's theory about the *unity* of virtue, connected with his account of *phronesis* (practical wisdom), is a natural and necessary adjunct to his characterisation of moral virtue as lying in a mean.

It is worth remarking that though Aristotle's general account of moral virtue is simplified and schematic, his discussions of individual virtues bring out the great variety of strengths and weaknesses of which human beings are capable and the great variety of contexts in which their characters are tested and revealed.

One final point. Aristotle insists that the virtuous man does what he does gladly, 'with pleasure'. But the pursuit of his own pleasure or satisfaction is not his motive. He does what he does 'for its own sake', or, as Aristotle repeatedly says, because it is *kalon* ('fine', 'noble', 'splendid'; 'right' misses the aesthetic note, and 'beautiful' forces it too hard). What then is the relation between this motive and man's pursuit of *eudaimonia*? For a utilitarian what makes an act or type of act right is that it promotes happiness. For Aristotle the doing of right acts for their own sake *constitutes* (a form of) happiness. What then is the ultimate criterion of right action? How might disputes as to what is *kalon* be settled? (If the good for man is – or includes – acting in a virtuous way, we cannot explain why a certain way of acting is virtuous by saying that it promotes the good for man.) On the one hand Aristotle clearly aligns himself with conventional values and takes them for granted; and when it comes to difficult cases he withdraws to the comment that decisions in indivual cases require a judgment or insight analogous to eye-sight (1109b23, 1142a27). On the other hand he recognises that he is under an obligation to give some account of the manner in which the man of practical wisdom determines virtue and right action (1107a1, 1138b18–34); but his answer remains obscure.

6. *Action and responsibility (E.N. III.1–5)*

The first five chapters of book III contain an analysis of such concepts as voluntary action, choice, and deliberation, and a discussion of responsibility. Though brief and necessarily oversimplified, Aristotle's treatment still provides an excellent starting-point for reflection on these topics.

The distinction in chapter 1 between actions for which the agent is held responsible and those for which he is not is firmly based on the ordinary practices of praise, blame, excuse, etc., and on familiar legal practice. Things done are 'involuntary' when the doer is forced by overwhelming physical constraint (1110a1–4, b1–3) or when he acts in ignorance of material facts (1110b18–1111a21); the voluntary is 'that of which the moving principle is in the agent himself, he being aware of the particular circum-

6. Action and responsibility

stances of the action' (1111a22-24). Aristotle has little to say of cases of physical constraint, where indeed the notion of an agent's performing an action is out of place; but he discusses the more interesting situation where threats or bribes or other pressure may excuse, mitigate, or even justify what is done.

Two points may be made about ignorance of fact. First, Aristotle tends to speak as if there is some single basic act, done in certain circumstances and having certain results, and that ignorance of any of these makes the act involuntary. In fact, however, acts cannot be identified for appraisal save by the use of some description, and various descriptions can be given of the same episode. When Oedipus struck his father he *struck his father* in ignorance, but he *struck a man* knowingly; and he perhaps *struck him* intentionally but *killed him* by accident. Secondly, Aristotle does not think that ignorance of fact always excuses: the agent may be to blame for what he does in ignorance if he can be held responsible for being ignorant, if, for example, he got drunk or negligently failed to find out the facts (1110b24-27, 1113b21-1114a3). There are questions here which Aristotle does not raise.

(a) That a man is blameworthy for the ignorance in which he committed an offence certainly prevents his denying all responsibility for what he did. But it is open to discussion exactly how he should be treated as regards moral appraisal and as regards legal penalties. Suppose his action caused terrible suffering. Perhaps he should be liable to pay damages to those who suffered; but should we wish to call him a cruel man, or only a negligent one?

(b) The notion of being responsible for one's ignorance requires investigation. A man may do something knowing that it is bound to put him in a state of dangerous ignorance. But culpable negligence is not like that. Indeed Aristotle's whole account of the voluntary and involuntary fails to cover *omissions*, though these are surely proper objects of blame and punishment.

(c) We may agree that a man can be to blame for killing his father even though he did not know it was his father, *if* he had culpably failed to find out. But we certainly cannot say that he killed his father voluntarily, nor could a Greek have said that this man did so *hekousios*. So the tie between the distinction *voluntary/ involuntary* and the distinction *liable to blame etc./not liable to blame etc.* is here cut or at least loosened.

In *E.N.* III.2–3 Aristotle distinguishes the concept of *prohairesis* ('choice') from neighbouring and related notions; it is a desire for something in one's power, the desire following from prior deliberation (1113a10–12). The word has, however, a much wider popular meaning – aim, purpose, intention – and it is often translated accordingly. There is clearly a connection between the technical and the popular senses, but it is a pity that Aristotle did not make use of two different words. For it is not always clear whether in speaking of an action as 'chosen' he means that it was done after deliberation or merely that it was done intentionally.

While the phenomenon of desire based on deliberation certainly occurs, it is not clear that this description is adequate for what Aristotle has in mind. For to say that a man desires something in his power seems to be compatible with adding that he makes no attempt to get it, while to say that a man 'chooses' to do something has a more decisive ring. Aristotle's description fails to capture the note of *decision* which his use of the term *prohairesis* ('choice') implies. (Moreover, if choice is desire of some kind, ought it not to fit into Aristotle's classification of types of desire? Yet it is neither wish – desire for the end; nor appetite – desire for the pleasant; nor 'anger' – desire for revenge.)

Deliberation is characterised as the working out of means to ends already adopted (1112b11–1113a2). (a) Surely practical deliberation is not always an investigation to find means to an end? One may, for example, ask what would be the kind thing to do; or one may weigh up the pros and cons of alternative courses of action. Insofar as this is a criticism of Aristotle for describing deliberation in terms of means and ends it is misdirected. The Greek words commonly rendered 'means to an end' mean literally 'things related to (or directed to) an end (or goal)', and *this* phrase *can* comfortably be used in contexts where the notion of instrumental means to an end is inappropriate. It remains true that Aristotle's examples in III.3 are in fact instrumental means. In

6. Action and responsibility

VI and VII examples of another type are used: I conclude that I should do a certain thing because it is a thing of a certain kind (say, kind, or healthy). It is clear that both these kinds of thinking are interlaced in life; and both are further complicated by the interplay and possible conflict between different goals and principles. Aristotle's only allusion to such complexity in III.3 is in the remark: 'and if it seems to be produced by several means they consider by which it is most easily and best produced' (1112b16). Must one suppose that III.3 was composed before those other books in which the other kind of deliberation – and the 'practical syllogism' associated with it – plays the leading role?

(b) Aristotle's statement that we do not deliberate about ends (1112b11) need not imply that some objectives are immune from being deliberated about (adopted or rejected), but only that any particular piece of deliberation must take some goals, aims, or principles for granted. I cannot simultaneously deliberate how to make a fortune and whether to adopt wealth as an objective; and I can think about the latter question only on the basis of *some* aims or wishes or preferences I already have and am not now scrutinising. It is of course true that nobody can debate with himself whether to aim at *eudaimonia*. What then is the status of Aristotle's own argument in I.7 to determine what *eudaimonia* consists in? Is *it* in fact practical deliberation to settle the final end?

In III.5 Aristotle argues that since it is by doing good or bad actions voluntarily that we come to have virtues or vices, the latter are themselves voluntary and we can be praised or blamed for them – even though we cannot now just decide to change our characters. Anyone but a fool knows that character traits are built up by corresponding behaviour; and we can certainly be blamed for the foreseen results of our voluntary actions. But suppose that a person claims to be by nature attracted to what is bad, or suppose that a child is brought up in evil ways. Might not every bad man claim that his present condition results from actions done before he was old enough to know better, actions for which his inherited temperament and environmental influence must be held responsible? Aristotle makes some suggestive remarks but gives no clear answer to these questions. He does rightly emphasise that a blanket rejection of culpability must carry with it an equal abandonment of praise. He also draws attention to the assumption, underlying our present practice, that blame is appropriate only where it can, by acting on a person's desires, effect changes in his conduct (1113 b 21-31).

It will be seen that though Aristotle raises a central question about responsibility he does not speak of 'free will' or ask 'could he have done otherwise?'. He thinks, with men in general, that people are commonly responsible for what they do: the 'moving principle' is in them, i.e. the agent's desire. But this is not some mysterious uncaused volition. It has its place in a natural causal sequence, desire being provoked by the thought, perception, or imagination of some attractive object. The physiological story corresponding to this psychological one is to be found in *De Motu Animalium* 7: pp. 230-32.

7. Practical wisdom and the practical syllogism (E.N. VI)

E.N. VI discusses a number of powers and dispositions of the mind, in particular the two main 'intellectual virtues' of *phronesis* ('practical wisdom') and *sophía* ('philosophic wisdom'). Many questions arise, some of which are touched on in the notes. Here I confine myself to some brief remarks about *phronesis* and about the practical syllogism.

The *phronimos* is good at deliberation: he can sum up a situation, weigh up various factors, and work out what to do to promote or achieve his objectives. Often enough, because of his experience and wisdom, he can see straight off the best thing to do, without having to go through a process of deliberation. Not only does the *phronimos* know what to do; he does it. For *phronesis* is 'epitactic'; it is not just the ability to give good advice from the sidelines. 'Practical wisdom issues commands, since its end is what ought to be done or not to be done; but understanding only judges' (1143 a 8-10). Moreover, the objectives or aims that the *phronimos* successfully pursues are the right ones. This distinguishes him from the merely 'clever' person (1144 a 23 - b 1). These last points imply that the man with *phronesis* has moral virtue as well, that his desires have been so trained that he now has a settled wish for

7. Practical wisdom and the practical syllogism

the right end and does not suffer from conflicting or rebellious desires that prevent his doing whatever he sees to be conducive to that end.

This rough outline of Aristotle's position suggests two comments:

(1) If *phronesis* and moral virtue are so related that it is logically impossible to have one without the other, is it possible to keep them apart conceptually? No doubt a given action can be described by reference to qualities of mind and qualities of character separately, even though it is the same action that displays both kinds of quality. But if 'he is *phronimos*' means 'he is clever etc. (and has good desires)', while 'he is virtuous' means 'he has good desires (and is clever etc.)' can one distinguish *phronesis* as an excellence of mind from moral virtue or excellence of character? Aristotle sometimes contrasts them by saying that the latter makes the *end* right while the former ensures that the right 'means' (things to attain or promote the end) are recognised. But since the pursuit of an objective involves thinking of it, while carrying out things necessary to be done depends on having a desire to do them, thought and desire seem to be involved with one another at each stage of effective deliberation and action. Both have to be faultless if a man is to be either *phronimos* or morally good; and if they are, he is both *phronimos* and good.

(2) What, according to Aristotle, *is* the right end at which the *phronimos* aims? To say '*eudaimonia*' is no help, insofar as virtuous action just is (a form of) *eudaimonia*. To settle what *is* in a given situation the right thing to do, Aristotle appeals to the judgment of the *phronimos*. With what aim in mind does he judge it right? Not the aim of doing what a *phronimos* would think right: that would be a futile circle. Does the *phronimos* aim at promoting theoretical thought? Though Aristotle gives this the highest value, he makes no attempt to show that the rules of conduct of ordinary life are to be justified (ultimately, if not immediately) by their tendency to promote that activity. (See notes on *E.E.* 1249a21 and b14.) In his actual discussions of excellences of character he seems to credit the good, wise man with the direct perception that this or that action is 'fine' (see note on 1142a25).

INTRODUCTION

Aristotle gives different examples of the practical syllogism in different contexts (see especially *E.N.* VI.7 and 8, VII.3, *De Anima* 434a16–21, *De Motu Animalium* 7). One characteristic form is:

> Such people ought to do such-and-such things
> I am such a person; this is such-and-such a thing
> Therefore I ought to do this.

Aristotle's remarks about such forms involve a great deal of oversimplification but constitute an important start in the task of analysing types of reasons for action and kinds of reasoning about action. Questions can be raised as to the status or character of the premisses Aristotle has in mind, and as to how we are supposed to acquire them. In particular, it is important (and not easy) to decide whether Aristotle envisages a minor premiss which states an ordinary fact – 'that child is drowning' – or rather one that itself involves a value-judgement – 'to save that child would be brave'. The latter is perhaps suggested by the claim (1143b4–5) that our grasp of major (general) premisses is acquired from particular minor premisses. One could not inculcate good principles by repeatedly telling one's pupil that 'this child is drowning' and the like; one could do so by saying in the right tone of voice 'it would be brave (kind, honourable, ...) to do this, that, and the other'.

Two very general questions. (1) Does a practical syllogism show us how men think (talk to themselves) when deliberating? Or does it show a logical structure which could be invoked to explain a man's having done something (e.g., 'because it was helpful') even if he had not deliberated at all before doing it? Does it give his reasoning or his reason? (2) Aristotle assumes that the agent adheres to the principle or objective formulated in the major premiss and (hence) feels effective desire to do the action specified in the conclusion. Thus to speak of a practical syllogism is not just to speak of an argument or inference; it is to speak of a situation in which action necessarily occurs. Is it a strength or a weakness in Aristotle that he thus blends together logical analysis and causal explanation? (See note on *De Motu Animalium* 701a12.)

8. 'Akrasia' (E.N. VII.1–10)

Holding as he does that there is a necessary connection between thinking something good and being disposed to choose it, Aristotle needs to explain the phenomenon of *akrasia* ('incontinence'), a man's failure to do what he knows (or firmly believes) to be best. This is the more necessary because of the well-known Socratic thesis that nobody ever does wrong willingly but always from ignorance, a severe paradox if taken to imply that there is no such thing as culpable wrong-doing.

Aristotle's central discussion is in VII.3 from 1146b31. He first makes some general points.

(a) Knowledge may be dispositional or actualised. There is nothing at all to be surprised at if a man acts against knowledge which he has but is not attending to.

(b) Nor will it be surprising that a man acts against his own principles if through ignorance of some relevant fact he fails to realise that the action is against his own principles. However keen I am not to touch liquor I shall of course break my rule if you lace my coffee with whisky and I don't know it.

(c) Two types of merely dispositional knowledge may be distinguished. The man who is asleep or drunk or in a fit is one stage further removed from actual knowledge than is a sober, sane, waking man.

(d) Saying something is not necessarily a display of knowledge. A parrot, a child, or a drunk may say something without understanding or 'really meaning' what he is saying.

Aristotle now (1147a24) comes closer to an actual akratic situation and seeks to explain how desire for the pleasant can impede recognition that some particular act or object is to be avoided. His account is not entirely clear, and two alternative interpretations suggest themselves. (1) The man is well aware that X-things are bad and that this is an X-thing. But he fails to draw – to see – the conclusion (that this is bad) because there is present in him a strong desire for pleasant things and the knowledge that X-things are pleasant. Thus:

    X-things are bad X-things are pleasant
               This is an X-thing
    (This is bad)   This is pleasant

That this is bad he fails to recognise. That this is pleasant he does realise, and consequently he does it or takes it. (2) Though well aware that X-things are bad, he fails to realise that this is an X-thing, and so fails to realise that it is bad. He does however realise that this is a Y-thing; and knowing Y-things to be pleasant he realises that this is pleasant, and so goes for it. Thus:

    X-things are bad Y-things are pleasant
    (this is an X-thing)   This is a Y-thing
    (this is bad)   This is pleasant

In either case the explanation for the brackets – for the man's *failure to realise* something – is that he is under the influence of strong desire for the pleasant. He is in a state like that of the drunken or sleeping man, and like him he may utter the words ('this is bad') but without really grasping their significance, without really knowing that this is bad.

Aristotle thus makes clear (a) that there can be cases of going against one's own principles which are not cases of doing what one realises at the moment of action to be wrong; (b) that the failure to see what is right and wrong now can be explained by the powerful effect of desire for the pleasant, which diverts our attention and suppresses other thoughts; (c) that when ignorance is so caused it does not exculpate, since we are held responsible for what we do in a condition (drunkenness or bad character) into which we ought not to have let ourselves get. Nevertheless Aristotle's detailed account of action which contravenes one's principles surely does not fit all cases of *akrasia*. Surely there is the case of the man who does wrong or does what is bad for him realising quite well at the time that he is doing so. Not everyone who says 'I know I oughtn't to be doing this' can plausibly be likened to a drunk or to a person in a frenzy. In his proper anxiety to maintain a necessary connection between thinking a certain

8. *Akrasia*

kind of thing good and being disposed to choose it Aristotle tries to show that thinking a particular thing good entails choosing it. But he could without damaging the former connection allow that desire sometimes breaks the latter.

It would be wrong to suppose that VII.3 contains all that Aristotle has to say about the nature of *akrasia*. In particular, he elsewhere quite often speaks in terms of a battle, a psychological conflict. And at 1150b19 he draws a distinction between two very different types of *akrasia*: weakness, where a man doesn't stick to the conclusion or decision he has reached, and impetuosity, where he doesn't stop to think at all. How are these types related to the situation outlined in VII.3?

9. *Pleasure (E.N. VII.11–14 and X.1–5)*

Aristotle's discussions of pleasure centre round various theses put forward in Plato's Academy and examined in Plato's *Philebus*. The main questions concern the *nature* of pleasure or enjoyment (the word *hedone* covers both) and its *value*. (1) Aristotle argues against the view that pleasure is a process of change or replenishment. Not all pleasures are due to, or involve, such processes, though concentration on 'bodily pleasures' might lead one to think so. Even pleasures that do involve such processes are not to be *identified* with the processes: enjoying a meal is not a process even though refilling the stomach is (1153a9–17, 1173a29–b20, 1174a13–b14). What then is enjoyment? In VII.12 Aristotle suggests that it is 'unimpeded activity of the natural state', in X.4 that it completes or perfects activity 'as a supervening end'. It looks as if the latter suggestion is a refinement on the former, and it may well be that the book X discussion is later than the book VII one. It will be clear that Aristotle is unlikely to find a fully adequate answer to the question What is *hedone*? if he does not stop to work out the many different ways in which the word and its cognates are used, and to distinguish radically different kinds of situation or experience that can be pleasures, or pleasant, or enjoyed.

(2) Some hold that pleasure is good or the good, yet it is usually thought that some pleasures are bad. Aristotle indicates

three possible ways of handling this problem (VII.12 and 1173 b 20–1174 a 12): (a) the so-called bad pleasures are not really pleasures – they only seem so to bad men; (b) the feeling of pleasure is always good in itself, but if it is derived from what is bad the total situation may be bad and to be avoided; (c) pleasures really are of different kinds, and they are good or bad according to whether the activities being enjoyed are good or bad. Aristotle's recognition that 'pleasure' is not the name of a single feeling capable of accompanying or being caused by diverse experiences etc. leads him decisively to reject the second and to adopt the third of these views. But he finds himself tempted back to the first: the good man is the only judge of what is really pleasant, just as he is the only judge of what is really good; so that instead of saying that the bad man's pleasures are bad we must say that they are not in fact pleasures. Plato too had made this desperate move, and the temptation to make it is certainly strong if one feels obliged to offer a proof that the good man's life is necessarily pleasanter than the bad man's.

NOTE ON TRANSLATION

The translations printed in this book are taken, by permission, from the Oxford University Press's 13-volume translation of Aristotle (*The Works of Aristotle translated into English*, edited by W. D. Ross). The translators are: W. D. Ross (*Nicomachean Ethics*), J. Solomon (*Eudemian Ethics*), J. A. Smith (*De Anima*) and A. S. L. Farquharson (*De Motu Animalium*). I have made a few minor changes where I thought the translation wrong or misleading; and I have made a number of verbal alterations in order to increase the consistency of translation of some key terms. What results is in no sense a new or even a revised translation; and the reader will easily see that the four different works here represented were translated by four different scholars with individual styles.

An English word used in a translation often corresponds only partly to the Greek word it renders. The following list shows some of the alternatives that are used or that might be used as renderings of certain important terms.

GREEK	NORMAL RENDERING(S)	ALTERNATIVES
aretē	virtue	excellence (and 'excellence of character' for 'moral virtue')
kakia	vice	fault, defect, flaw
lupē	pain	this term covers all adverse emotional reaction (grief, dislike, etc.)
lupēron	painful	unpleasant
hekousion	voluntary	intentional
akousion	involuntary	unintentional
enkrateia	continence	self-control
akrasia	incontinence	lack of self-control, weakness

NOTE ON TRANSLATION

GREEK	NORMAL RENDERING(S)	ALTERNATIVES
kalon	noble, fine, beautiful	sometimes simply 'good'
hexis	state of mind, state of character	really just 'state' (relatively permanent disposition)
teleion	final, complete, perfect	
ta pros to telos	the means to the end	literally 'things related to the end'
prāxis	action, conduct	this may refer to what is done or to the doing of it
aisthēsis	perception, sensation	
pathos	passion, emotion, feeling	
genesis	process, coming into being	literally 'becoming'
epistēmē	knowledge, science	branch of knowledge (covers arts and crafts)
eudaimonia	happiness	see note on 1095a18
logos	reason, reasoning, rule, rational principle, argument	the *E.N.* translator tends to prefer 'rule', *E.E.* 'reason'
dokei	it is thought that, it seems	often used to report what everyone thinks, without any suggestion that they may be wrong
prohairesis	choice, purpose, intention	
ergon	product, function, work	
biā, biaion	under compulsion, compulsory	better 'by force', 'forced'

NOTE ON ABBREVIATIONS AND REFERENCES

Abbreviations

The following list shows the abbreviations of titles of Aristotle's works that are used in this volume.

TITLE	ABBREVIATION
De Anima ('On the Soul')	*De An.*
Ethica Eudemia ('Eudemian Ethics')	*E.E.*
Ethica Nicomachea ('Nicomachean Ethics')	*E.N.*
De Generatione et Corruptione ('On Coming-to-be and Passing-away')	*G.C.*
De Motu Animalium ('On the Movement of Animals')	*M.A.*
Metaphysica ('Metaphysics')	*Met.*
De Partibus Animalium ('On the Parts of Animals')	*P.A.*

References

References to passages in Aristotle may be given by book and chapter, or use may be made of the page and line numbers (and the column letters) in the Berlin edition of the Greek text. Thus the first chapter of the *Nicomachean Ethics* could be referred to as '*E.N.* I.1' or as '1094 a 1–18'. It will be clear that the latter mode of reference is necessary when attention is to be drawn to a particular passage or line *within* a chapter.

Since the lines of the translation cannot correspond perfectly to the lines of the Greek text, small discrepancies arise. For example, more than five lines of English translation correspond to the Greek passage 1094 b 5–10; so that the reference '1094 b 8' (which refers to that line of *Greek*) does not point unambiguously to any single line of English. However, the reader should not have any difficulty in seeing what passage, sentence, or phrase his attention is being drawn to when a reference of this kind is used.

In the notes on the *Nicomachean Ethics* I have omitted '*E.N.*' in giving references to that work: 'see III.4' means 'see *E.N.* III.4'.

NICOMACHEAN ETHICS

NICOMACHEAN ETHICS

Book I

1 EVERY art and every inquiry, and similarly every action and 1094a
pursuit, is thought to aim at some good; and for this reason the
good has rightly been declared to be that at which all things aim.
But a certain difference is found among ends; some are activities,
others are products apart from the activities that produce them.
Where there are ends apart from the actions, it is the nature of the 5
products to be better than the activities. Now, as there are many
actions, arts, and sciences, their ends also are many; the end of the
medical art is health, that of shipbuilding a vessel, that of strategy
victory, that of economics wealth. But where such arts fall under a
single capacity – as bridle-making and the other arts concerned 10
with the equipment of horses fall under the art of riding, and this
and every military action under strategy, in the same way other
arts fall under yet others – in all of these the ends of the master
arts are to be preferred to all the subordinate ends; for it is for the
sake of the former that the latter are pursued. It makes no differ- 15
ence whether the activities themselves are the ends of the actions,
or something else apart from the activities, as in the case of the
sciences just mentioned.

2 If, then, there is some end of the things we do, which we desire for
its own sake (everything else being desired for the sake of this),
and if we do not choose everything for the sake of something else
(for at that rate the process would go on to infinity, so that our 20
desire would be empty and vain), clearly this must be the good and
the chief good. Will not the knowledge of it, then, have a great
influence on life? Shall we not, like archers who have a mark to
aim at, be more likely to hit upon what is right? If so, we must 25
try, in outline at least, to determine what it is, and of which of the
sciences or capacities it is the object. It would seem to belong to
the most authoritative art and that which is most truly the master

art. And politics appears to be of this nature; for it is this that ordains which of the sciences should be studied in a state, and which each class of citizens should learn and up to what point they should learn them; and we see even the most highly esteemed of capacities to fall under this, e.g. strategy, economics, rhetoric; now, since politics uses the rest of the sciences, and since, again, it legislates as to what we are to do and what we are to abstain from, the end of this science must include those of the others, so that this end must be the good for man. For even if the end is the same for a single man and for a state, that of the state seems at all events something greater and more complete whether to attain or to preserve; though it is worth while to attain the end merely for one man, it is finer and more godlike to attain it for a nation or for city-states. These, then, are the ends at which our inquiry aims, since it is political science, in one sense of that term.

Our discussion will be adequate if it has as much clearness as the subject-matter admits of, for precision is not to be sought for alike in all discussions, any more than in all the products of the crafts. Now fine and just actions, which political science investigates, exhibit much variety and fluctuation of opinion, so that they may be thought to exist only by convention, and not by nature. And goods also exhibit a similar fluctuation because they bring harm to many people; for before now men have been undone by reason of their wealth, and others by reason of their courage. We must be content, then, in speaking of such subjects and with such premisses to indicate the truth roughly and in outline, and in speaking about things which are only for the most part true and with premisses of the same kind to reach conclusions that are no better. In the same spirit, therefore, should each type of statement be *received*; for it is the mark of an educated man to look for precision in each class of things just so far as the nature of the subject admits; it is evidently equally foolish to accept probable reasoning from a mathematician and to demand from a rhetorician demonstrative proofs.

Now each man judges well the things he knows, and of these he is a good judge. And so the man who has been educated in a subject is a good judge of that subject, and the man who has received an all-round education is a good judge in general. Hence a young man is not a proper hearer of lectures on political science; for he is inexperienced in the actions that occur in life, but its discussions start from these and are about these; and, further, since he tends to follow his passions, his study will be vain and unprofitable, because the end aimed at is not knowledge but action. And it makes no difference whether he is young in years or youthful in character; the defect does not depend on time, but on his living, and pursuing each successive object, as passion directs. For to such persons, as to the incontinent, knowledge brings no profit; but to those who desire and act in accordance with a rational principle knowledge about such matters will be of great benefit.

These remarks about the student, the sort of treatment to be expected, and the purpose of the inquiry, may be taken as our preface.

4 Let us resume our inquiry and state, in view of the fact that all knowledge and every pursuit aims at some good, what it is that we say political science aims at and what is the highest of all goods achievable by action. Verbally there is very general agreement; for both the general run of men and people of superior refinement say that it is happiness, and identify living well and doing well with being happy; but with regard to what happiness is they differ, and the many do not give the same account as the wise. For the former think it is some plain and obvious thing, like pleasure, wealth, or honour; they differ, however, from one another – and often even the same man identifies it with different things, with health when he is ill, with wealth when he is poor; but, conscious of their ignorance, they admire those who proclaim some great thing that is above their comprehension. Now some thought that apart from these many goods there is another which is good in itself and causes the goodness of all these as well. To examine all the opinions that have been held were perhaps somewhat fruitless; enough to examine those that are most prevalent or that seem to be arguable.

Let us not fail to notice, however, that there is a difference between arguments from and those to the first principles. For Plato, too, was right in raising this question and asking, as he used to do, 'are we on the way from or to the first principles?' There is a difference, as there is in a race-course between the course from the judges to the turning-point and the way back. For, while we must begin with what is known, things are objects of knowledge in two senses — some to us, some without qualification. Presumably, then, *we* must begin with things known to *us*. Hence any one who is to listen intelligently to lectures about what is noble and just and, generally, about the subjects of political science must have been brought up in good habits. For the fact is a starting-point, and if this is sufficiently plain to him, he will not need the reason as well; and the man who has been well brought up has or can easily get starting-points. And as for him who neither has nor can get them, let him hear the words of Hesiod:

> Far best is he who knows all things himself;
> Good, he that hearkens when men counsel right;
> But he who neither knows, nor lays to heart
> Another's wisdom, is a useless wight.

Let us, however, resume our discussion from the point at which we digressed. To judge from the lives that men lead, most men, and men of the most vulgar type, seem (not without some ground) to identify the good, or happiness, with pleasure; which is the reason why they love the life of enjoyment. For there are, we may say, three prominent types of life — that just mentioned, the political, and thirdly the contemplative life. Now the mass of mankind are evidently quite slavish in their tastes, preferring a life suitable to beasts, but they get some ground for their view from the fact that many of those in high places share the tastes of Sardanapallus. A consideration of the prominent types of life shows that people of superior refinement and of active disposition identify happiness with honour; for this is, roughly speaking, the end of the political life. But it seems too superficial to be what we are looking for, since it is thought to depend on those who bestow honour rather than on him who receives it, but the good we divine to be something proper to a man and not easily taken from him. Further, men seem to pursue honour in order that they may be assured of their goodness; at least it is by men of practical wisdom that they seek to be honoured, and among those who know them, and on the ground of their virtue; clearly, then, according to them, at any rate, virtue is better. And perhaps one might even suppose this to be, rather than honour, the end of the political life. But even this appears somewhat incomplete; for possession of virtue seems actually compatible with being asleep, or with lifelong inactivity, and, further, with the greatest sufferings and misfortunes; but a man who was living so no one would call happy, unless he were maintaining a thesis at all costs. But enough of this; for the subject has been sufficiently treated even in the current discussions. Third comes the contemplative life, which we shall consider later.

The life of money-making is one undertaken under compulsion, and wealth is evidently not the good we are seeking; for it is merely useful and for the sake of something else. And so one might rather take the aforenamed objects to be ends; for they are loved for themselves. But it is evident that not even these are ends; yet many arguments have been thrown away in support of them. Let us leave this subject, then.

6 We had perhaps better consider the universal good and discuss thoroughly what is meant by it, although such an inquiry is made an uphill one by the fact that the Forms have been introduced by friends of our own. Yet it would perhaps be thought to be better, indeed to be our duty, for the sake of maintaining the truth even to destroy what touches us closely, especially as we are philosophers or lovers of wisdom; for, while both are dear, piety requires us to honour truth above our friends.

The men who introduced this doctrine did not posit Ideas of classes within which they recognized priority and posteriority (which is the reason why they did not maintain the existence of an Idea embracing all numbers); but the term 'good' is used both in the category of substance and in that of quality and in that of relation, and that which is *per se*, i.e. substance, is prior in nature to the relative (for the latter is like an offshoot and accident of being); so that there could not be a common Idea set over all these goods. Further, since 'good' has as many senses as 'being' (for it is predicated both in the category of substance, as of God and of reason, and in quality, i.e. of the virtues, and in quantity, i.e. of that which is moderate, and in relation, i.e. of the useful, and in time, i.e. of the right opportunity, and in place, i.e. of the right locality and the like), clearly it cannot be something universally present in all cases and single; for then it could not have been predicated in all the categories but in one only. Further, since of the things answering to one Idea there is one science, there would have been one science of all the goods; but as it is there are many sciences even of the things that fall under one category, e.g. of opportunity, for opportunity in war is studied by strategics and in disease by medicine, and the moderate in food is studied by medicine and in exercise by the science of gymnastics. And one might ask the question, what in the world they *mean* by 'a thing itself', if (as is the case) in 'man himself' and in a particular man the account of man is one and the same. For in so far as they are man, they will in no respect differ; and if this is so, neither will 'good itself' and particular goods, in so far as they are good. But again it will not be good any the more for being eternal, since that which lasts long is no whiter than that which perishes in a day. The Pythagoreans seem to give a more plausible account of the good, when they place the one in the column of goods; and it is they that Speusippus seems to have followed.

But let us discuss these matters elsewhere; an objection to what we have said, however, may be discerned in the fact that the Platonists have not been speaking about *all* goods, and that the goods that are pursued and loved for themselves are called good by reference to a single Form, while those which tend to produce or to preserve these somehow or to prevent their contraries are called so by reason of these, and in a different way. Clearly, then, goods must be spoken of in two ways, and some must be good in themselves, the others by reason of these. Let us separate, then, things good in themselves from things useful, and consider whether the former are called good by reference to a single Idea. What sort of goods would one call good in themselves? Is it those that are pursued even when isolated from others, such as intelligence, sight, and certain pleasures and honours? Certainly, if we pursue these also for the sake of something else, yet one would place them among things good in themselves. Or is nothing other than the Idea of good good in itself? In that case the Form will be empty. But if the things we have named are also things good in themselves, the account of the good will have to appear as something identical in them all, as that of whiteness is identical in snow and in white lead. But of honour, wisdom, and pleasure, just in respect of their goodness, the accounts are distinct and diverse. The good, therefore, is not something common answering to one Idea.

But what then do we mean by the good? It is surely not like the things that only chance to have the same name. Are goods one, then, by being derived from one good or by all contributing to one good, or are they rather one by analogy? Certainly as sight is in the body, so is reason in the soul, and so on in other cases. But perhaps these subjects had better be dismissed for the present; for perfect precision about them would be more appropriate to another branch of philosophy. And similarly with regard to the Idea; even if there is some one good which is universally predicable of goods or is capable of separate and independent existence, clearly it could not be achieved or attained by man; but we are now seeking something attainable. Perhaps, however, some one might think it worth while to recognize this with a view to the goods that *are* attainable and achievable; for having this as a sort of pattern we shall know better the goods that are good for us, and if we know them shall attain them. This argument has some plausibility, but seems to clash with the procedure of the sciences; for all of these, though they aim at some good and seek to supply the deficiency of it, leave on one side the knowledge of *the* good. Yet that all the exponents of the arts should be ignorant of, and should not even seek, so great an aid is not probable. It is hard, too, to see how a weaver or a carpenter will be benefited in regard to his own craft by knowing this 'good itself', or how the man who has viewed the Idea itself will be a better doctor or general thereby. For a doctor seems not even to study health in this way, but the health of man, or perhaps rather the health of a particular man; it is individuals that he is healing. But enough of these topics.

7 Let us again return to the good we are seeking, and ask what it can be. It seems different in different actions and arts; it is different

in medicine, in strategy, and in the other arts likewise. What then is the good of each? Surely that for whose sake everything else is done. In medicine this is health, in strategy victory, in architecture a house, in any other sphere something else, and in every action and pursuit the end; for it is for the sake of this that all men do whatever else they do. Therefore, if there is an end for all that we do, this will be the good achievable by action, and if there are more than one, these will be the goods achievable by action.

So the argument has by a different course reached the same point; but we must try to state this even more clearly. Since there are evidently more than one end, and we choose some of these (e.g. wealth, flutes, and in general instruments) for the sake of something else, clearly not all ends are final ends; but the chief good is evidently something final. Therefore, if there is only one final end, this will be what we are seeking, and if there are more than one, the most final of these will be what we are seeking. Now we call that which is in itself worthy of pursuit more final than that which is worthy of pursuit for the sake of something else, and that which is never desirable for the sake of something else more final than the things that are desirable both in themselves and for the sake of that other thing, and therefore we call final without qualification that which is always desirable in itself and never for the sake of something else.

Now such a thing happiness, above all else, is held to be; for this we choose always for itself and never for the sake of something else, but honour, pleasure, reason, and every virtue we choose indeed for themselves (for if nothing resulted from them we should still choose each of them), but we choose them also for the sake of happiness, judging that through them we shall be happy. Happiness, on the other hand, no one chooses for the sake of these, nor, in general, for anything other than itself.

From the point of view of self-sufficiency the same result seems to follow; for the final good is thought to be self-sufficient. Now by self-sufficient we do not mean that which is sufficient for a man by himself, for one who lives a solitary life, but also for parents, children, wife, and in general for his friends and fellow citizens, since man is born for citizenship. But some limit must be set to this; for if we extend our requirement to ancestors and

Book I.7

descendants and friends' friends we are in for an infinite series. Let us examine this question, however, on another occasion; the self-sufficient we now define as that which when isolated makes life desirable and lacking in nothing; and such we think happiness to be; and further we think it most desirable of all things, without being counted as one good thing among others – if it were so counted it would clearly be made more desirable by the addition of even the least of goods; for that which is added becomes an excess of goods, and of goods the greater is always more desirable. Happiness, then, is something final and self-sufficient, and is the end of action.

Presumably, however, to say that happiness is the chief good seems a platitude, and a clearer account of what it is is still desired. This might perhaps be given, if we could first ascertain the function of man. For just as for a flute-player, a sculptor, or any artist, and, in general, for all things that have a function or activity, the good and the 'well' is thought to reside in the function, so would it seem to be for man, if he has a function. Have the carpenter, then, and the tanner certain functions or activities, and has man none? Is he born without a function? Or as eye, hand, foot, and in general each of the parts evidently has a function, may one lay it down that man similarly has a function apart from all these? What then can this be? Life seems to be common even to plants, but we are seeking what is peculiar to man. Let us exclude, therefore, the life of nutrition and growth. Next there would be a life of perception, but *it* also seems to be common even to the horse, the ox, and every animal. There remains, then, an active life of the element that has a rational principle; of this, one part has such a principle in the sense of being obedient to one, the other in the sense of possessing one and exercising thought. And, as 'life of the rational element' also has two meanings, we must state that life in the sense of activity is what we mean; for this seems to be the more proper sense of the term. Now if the function of man is an activity of soul which follows or implies a rational principle, and if we say 'a so-and-so' and 'a good so-and-so' have a function which is the same in kind, e.g. a lyre-player and a good lyre-player, and so without qualification in all cases, eminence in respect of goodness being added to the name of the function (for the function of a lyre-player is to play the lyre, and that of a good lyre-player is to do so well): if this is the case, [and we state the function of man to be a certain kind of life, and this to be an activity or actions of the soul implying a rational principle, and the function of a good man to be the good and noble performance of these, and if any action is well performed when it is performed in accordance with the appropriate excellence: if this is the case,] human good turns out to be activity of soul in accordance with virtue, and if there are more than one virtue, in accordance with the best and most complete.

But we must add 'in a complete life'. For one swallow does not make a summer, nor does one day; and so too one day, or a short time, does not make a man blessed and happy.

Let this serve as an outline of the good; for we must presumably first sketch it roughly, and then later fill in the details. But it would seem that any one is capable of carrying on and articulating what has once been well outlined, and that time is a good discoverer or partner in such a work; to which facts the advances of the arts are due; for any one can add what is lacking. And we must also remember what has been said before, and not look for precision in all things alike, but in each class of things such precision as accords with the subject-matter, and so much as is appropriate to the inquiry. For a carpenter and a geometer investigate the right angle in different ways; the former does so in so far as the right angle is useful for his work, while the latter inquires what it is or what sort of thing it is; for he is a spectator of the truth. We must act in the same way, then, in all other matters as well, that our main task may not be subordinated to minor questions. Nor must we demand the cause in all matters alike; it is enough in some cases that the *fact* be well established, as in the case of the first principles; the fact is a primary thing or first principle. Now of first principles we see some by induction, some by perception, some by a certain habituation, and others too in other ways. But each set of principles we must try to investigate in the natural way, and we must take pains to determine them correctly, since they have a great influence on what follows. For the beginning is thought to be more than half of the whole, and many of the questions we ask are cleared up by it.

Book I.8

8 We must consider it, however, in the light not only of our conclusion and our premises, but also of what is commonly said about it; for with a true view all the data harmonize, but with a false one the facts soon clash. Now goods have been divided into three classes, and some are described as external, others as relating to soul or to body; we call those that relate to soul most properly and truly goods, and psychical actions and activities we class as relating to soul. Therefore our account must be sound, at least according to this view, which is an old one and agreed on by philosophers. It is correct also in that we identify the end with certain actions and activities; for thus it falls among goods of the soul and not among external goods. Another belief which harmonizes with our account is that the happy man lives well and does well; for we have practically defined happiness as a sort of good life and good action. The characteristics that are looked for in happiness seem also, all of them, to belong to what we have defined happiness as being. For some identify happiness with virtue, some with practical wisdom, others with a kind of philosophic wisdom, others with these, or one of these, accompanied by pleasure or not without pleasure; while others include also external prosperity. Now some of these views have been held by many men and men of old, others by a few eminent persons; and it is not probable that either of these should be entirely mistaken, but rather that they should be right in at least some one respect or even in most respects.

With those who identify happiness with virtue or some one virtue our account is in harmony; for to virtue belongs virtuous activity. But it makes, perhaps, no small difference whether we place the chief good in possession or in use, in state of mind or in activity. For the state of mind may exist without producing any good result, as in a man who is asleep or in some other way quite inactive, but the activity cannot; for one who has the activity will of necessity be acting, and acting well. And as in the Olympic Games it is not the most beautiful and the strongest that are crowned but those who compete (for it is some of these that are victorious), so those who act win, and rightly win, the noble and good things in life.

Their life is also in itself pleasant. For pleasure is a state of *soul*, and to each man that which he is said to be a lover of is pleasant; e.g. not only is a horse pleasant to the lover of horses, and a spectacle to the lover of sights, but also in the same way just acts are pleasant to the lover of justice and in general virtuous acts to the lover of virtue. Now for most men their pleasures are in conflict with one another because these are not by nature pleasant, but the lovers of what is noble find pleasant the things that are by nature pleasant; and virtuous actions are such, so that these are pleasant for such men as well as in their own nature. Their life, therefore, has no further need of pleasure as a sort of adventitious charm, but has its pleasure in itself. For, besides what we have said, the man who does not rejoice in noble actions is not even good; since no one would call a man just who did not enjoy acting justly, nor any man liberal who did not enjoy liberal actions; and similarly in all other cases. If this is so, virtuous actions must be in themselves pleasant. But they are also *good* and *noble*, and have each of these attributes in the highest degree, since the good man judges well about these attributes; his judgement is such as we have described. Happiness then is the best, noblest, and most pleasant thing in the world, and these attributes are not severed as in the inscription at Delos –

> Most noble is that which is justest, and best is health;
> But pleasantest is it to win what we love.

For all these properties belong to the best activities; and these, or one – the best – of these, we identify with happiness.

Yet evidently, as we said, it needs the external goods as well; for it is impossible, or not easy, to do noble acts without the proper equipment. In many actions we use friends and riches and political power as instruments; and there are some things the lack of which takes the lustre from happiness, as good birth, goodly children, beauty; for the man who is very ugly in appearance or ill-born or solitary and childless is not very likely to be happy, and perhaps a man would be still less likely if he had thoroughly bad children or friends or had lost good children or friends by death. As we said, then, happiness seems to need this sort of prosperity in addition; for which reason some identify happiness with good fortune, though others identify it with virtue.

9 For this reason also the question is asked, whether happiness is to be acquired by learning or by habituation or some other sort of training, or comes in virtue of some divine providence or again by chance. Now if there is *any* gift of the gods to men, it is reasonable that happiness should be god-given, and most surely god-given of all human things inasmuch as it is the best. But this question would perhaps be more appropriate to another inquiry; happiness seems, however, even if it is not god-sent but comes as a result of virtue and some process of learning or training, to be among the most godlike things; for that which is the prize and end of virtue seems to be the best thing in the world, and something godlike and blessed.

It will also on this view be very generally shared; for all who are not maimed as regards their potentiality for virtue may win it by a certain kind of study and care. But if it is better to be happy thus than by chance, it is reasonable that the facts should be so, since everything that depends on the action of nature is by nature as good as it can be, and similarly everything that depends on art or any rational cause, and especially if it depends on the best of all causes. To entrust to chance what is greatest and most noble would be a very defective arrangement.

The answer to the question we are asking is plain also from the definition of happiness; for it has been said to be a virtuous activity of soul, of a certain kind. Of the remaining goods, some must necessarily pre-exist as conditions of happiness, and others are naturally co-operative and useful as instruments. And this will be found to agree with what we said at the outset; for we stated the end of political science to be the best end, and political science spends most of its pains on making the citizens to be of a certain character, viz. good and capable of noble acts.

It is natural, then, that we call neither ox nor horse nor any other of the animals happy; for none of them is capable of sharing in such activity. For this reason also a boy is not happy; for he is not yet capable of such acts, owing to his age; and boys who are called happy are being congratulated by reason of the hopes we have for them. For there is required, as we said, not only complete virtue but also a complete life, since many changes occur in life, and all manner of chances, and the most prosperous may fall into great misfortunes in old age, as is told of Priam in the Trojan Cycle; and one who has experienced such chances and has ended wretchedly no one calls happy.

Must no one at all, then, be called happy while he lives; must we, as Solon says, see the end? Even if we are to lay down this doctrine, is it also the case that a man *is* happy when he is *dead*? Or is not this quite absurd, especially for us who say that happiness is an activity? But if we do not call the dead man happy, and if Solon does not mean this, but that one can then safely *call* a man blessed as being at last beyond evils and misfortunes, this also affords matter for discussion; for both evil and good are thought to exist for a dead man, as much as for one who is alive but not aware of them; e.g. honours and dishonours and the good or bad fortunes of children and in general of descendants. And this also presents a problem; for though a man has lived happily up to old age and has had a death worthy of his life, many reverses may befall his descendants – some of them may be good and attain the life they deserve, while with others the opposite may be the case; and clearly too the degrees of relationship between them and their ancestors may vary indefinitely. It would be odd, then, if the dead man were to share in these changes and become at one time happy, at another wretched; while it would also be odd if the fortunes of the descendants did not for *some* time have *some* effect on the happiness of their ancestors.

But we must return to our first difficulty; for perhaps by a consideration of it our present problem might be solved. Now if we must see the end and only then call a man happy, not as being happy but as having been so before, surely this is a paradox, that when he is happy the attribute that belongs to him is not to be truly predicated of him because we do not wish to call living men happy, on account of the changes that may befall them, and because we have assumed happiness to be something permanent and by no means easily changed, while a single man may suffer many turns of fortune's wheel. For clearly if we were to follow his fortunes, we should often call the same man happy and again wretched, making the happy man out to be a 'chameleon and insecurely based'. Or is this following his fortunes quite wrong?

Book I.10

Success or failure in life does not depend on these, but human life, as we said, needs these as well, while virtuous activities or their opposites are what determine happiness or the reverse.

The question we have now discussed confirms our definition. For no function of man has so much permanence as virtuous activities (these are thought to be more durable even than knowledge of the sciences), and of these themselves the most valuable are more durable because those who are happy spend their life most readily and most continuously in these; for this seems to be the reason why we do not forget them. The attribute in question, then, will belong to the happy man, and he will be happy throughout his life; for always, or by preference to everything else, he will be engaged in virtuous action and contemplation, and he will bear the chances of life most nobly and altogether decorously, if he is 'truly good' and 'foursquare beyond reproach'.

Now many events happen by chance, and events differing in importance; small pieces of good fortune or of its opposite clearly do not weigh down the scales of life one way or the other, but a multitude of great events if they turn out well will make life happier (for not only are they themselves such as to add beauty to life, but the way a man deals with them may be noble and good), while if they turn out ill they crush and maim happiness; for they both bring pain with them and hinder many activities. Yet even in these nobility shines through, when a man bears with resignation many great misfortunes, not through insensibility to pain but through nobility and greatness of soul.

If activities are, as we said, what determine the character of life, no happy man can become miserable; for he will never do the acts that are hateful and mean. For the man who is truly good and wise, we think, bears all the chances of life becomingly and always makes the best of circumstances, as a good general makes the best military use of the army at his command and a good shoemaker makes the best shoes out of the hides that are given him; and so with all other craftsmen. And if this is the case, the happy man can never become miserable – though he will not reach *blessedness*, if he meet with fortunes like those of Priam.

Nor, again, is he many-coloured and changeable; for neither will he be moved from his happy state easily or by any ordinary misadventures, but only by many great ones, nor, if he has had many great misadventures, will he recover his happiness in a short time, but if at all, only in a long and complete one in which he has attained many splendid successes.

Why then should we not say that he is happy who is active in accordance with complete virtue and is sufficiently equipped with external goods, not for some chance period but throughout a complete life? Or must we add 'and who is destined to live thus and die as befits his life'? Certainly the future is obscure to us, while happiness, we claim, is an end and something in every way final. If so, we shall call happy those among living men in whom these conditions are, and are to be, fulfilled – but happy *men*. So much for these questions.

That the fortunes of descendants and of all a man's friends should not affect his happiness at all seems a very unfriendly doctrine, and one opposed to the opinions men hold; but since the events that happen are numerous and admit of all sorts of difference, and some come more near to us and others less so, it seems a long – nay, an infinite – task to discuss each in detail; a general outline will perhaps suffice. If, then, as some of a man's own misadventures have a certain weight and influence on life while others are, as it were, lighter, so too there are differences among the misadventures of our friends taken as a whole, and it makes a difference whether the various sufferings befall the living or the dead (much more even than whether lawless and terrible deeds are presupposed in a tragedy or done on the stage), this difference also must be taken into account; or rather, perhaps, the fact that doubt is felt whether the dead share in any good or evil. For it seems, from these considerations, that even if anything whether good or evil penetrates to them, it must be something weak and negligible, either in itself or for them, or if not, at least it must be such in degree and kind as not to make happy those who are not happy nor to take away their blessedness from those who are. The good or bad fortunes of friends, then, seem to have some effects on the dead, but effects of such a kind and degree as neither to make the happy unhappy nor to produce any other change of the kind.

12 These questions having been definitely answered, let us consider whether happiness is among the things that are praised or rather among the things that are prized; for clearly it is not to be placed among *potentialities*. Everything that is praised seems to be praised because it is of a certain kind and is related somehow to something else; for we praise the just or brave man and in general both the good man and virtue itself because of the actions and functions involved, and we praise the strong man, the good runner, and so on, because he is of a certain kind and is related in a certain way to something good and important. This is clear also from the praises of the gods; for it seems absurd that the gods should be referred to our standard, but this *is* done because praise involves a reference, as we said, to something else. But if praise is for things such as we have described, clearly what applies to the best things is not praise, but something greater and better, as is indeed obvious; for what we do to the gods and the most godlike of men is to call them blessed and happy. And so too with good *things*; no one praises happiness as he does justice, but rather calls it blessed, as being something more divine and better.

Eudoxus also seems to have been right in his method of advocating the supremacy of pleasure; he thought that the fact that, though a good, it is not praised indicated it to be better than the things that are praised, and that this is what God and the good are; for by reference to these all other things are judged. *Praise* is appropriate to virtue, for as a result of virtue men tend to do noble deeds; but *encomia* are bestowed on acts, whether of the body or of the soul. But perhaps nicety in these matters is more proper to those who have made a study of encomia; to us it is clear from what has been said that happiness is among the things that are prized and perfect. It seems to be so also from the fact that it is a first principle; for it is for the sake of this that we all do everything else, and the first principle and cause of goods is, we claim, something prized and divine.

13 Since happiness is an activity of soul in accordance with perfect virtue, we must consider the nature of virtue; for perhaps we shall thus see better the nature of happiness. The true student of politics, too, is thought to have studied virtue above all things; for he wishes to make his fellow citizens good and obedient to the laws. As an example of this we have the lawgivers of the Cretans and the Spartans, and any others of the kind that there may have been. And if this inquiry belongs to political science, clearly the pursuit of it will be in accordance with our original plan. But clearly the virtue we must study is human virtue; for the good we were seeking was human good and the happiness human happiness. By human virtue we mean not that of the body but that of the soul; and happiness also we call an activity of soul. But if this is so, clearly the student of politics must know somehow the facts about soul, as the man who is to heal the eyes must know about the whole body also; and all the more since politics is more prized and better than medicine; but even among doctors the best educated spend much labour on acquiring knowledge of the body. The student of politics, then, must study the soul, and must study it with these objects in view, and do so just to the extent which is sufficient for the questions we are discussing; for further precision is perhaps something more laborious than our purposes require.

Some things are said about it, adequately enough, even in the discussions outside our school, and we must use these; e.g. that one element in the soul is irrational and one has a rational principle. Whether these are separated as the parts of the body or of anything divisible are, or are distinct by definition but by nature inseparable, like convex and concave in the circumference of a circle, does not affect the present question.

Of the irrational element one division seems to be widely distributed, and vegetative in its nature, I mean that which causes nutrition and growth; for it is this kind of power of the soul that one must assign to all nurslings and to embryos, and this same power to full-grown creatures; this is more reasonable than to assign some different power to them. Now the excellence of this seems to be common to all species and not specifically human; for this part or faculty seems to function most in sleep, while goodness and badness are least manifest in sleep (whence comes the saying that the happy are no better off than the wretched for half their lives; and this happens naturally enough, since sleep is an inactivity of the soul in that respect in which it is called good or bad), unless perhaps to a small extent some of the movements actually penetrate to the soul, and in this respect the dreams of good men are better than those of ordinary people. Enough of this subject, however; let us leave the nutritive faculty alone, since it has by its nature no share in human excellence.

There seems to be also another irrational element in the soul – one which in a sense, however, shares in a rational principle. For we praise the rational principle of the continent man and of the incontinent, and the part of their soul that has such a principle, since it urges them aright and towards the best objects; but there is naturally found in them also another element beside the rational principle, which fights against and resists that principle. For exactly as paralysed limbs when we intend to move them to the right turn on the contrary to the left, so is it with the soul; the impulses of incontinent people move in contrary directions. But while in the body we see that which moves astray, in the soul we do not. No doubt, however, we must none the less suppose that in the soul too there is something beside the rational principle, resisting and opposing it. In what sense it is distinct from the other elements does not concern us. Now even this seems to have a share in a rational principle, as we said; at any rate in the continent man it obeys the rational principle – and presumably in the temperate and brave man it is still more obedient; for in him it speaks, on all matters, with the same voice as the rational principle.

Therefore the irrational element also appears to be twofold. For the vegetative element in no way shares in a rational principle, but the appetitive and in general the desiring element in a sense shares in it, in so far as it listens to and obeys it; this is the sense in which we speak of 'taking account' of one's father or one's friends, not that in which we speak of 'accounting' for a mathematical property. That the irrational element is in some sense persuaded by a rational principle is indicated also by the giving of advice and by all reproof and exhortation. And if this element also must be said to have a rational principle, that which has a rational principle (as well as that which has not) will be twofold, one subdivision having it in the strict sense and in itself, and the other having a tendency to obey as one does one's father.

Virtue too is distinguished into kinds in accordance with this difference; for we say that some of the virtues are intellectual and others moral, philosophic wisdom and understanding and practical wisdom being intellectual, liberality and temperance moral. For in speaking about a man's character we do not say that he is wise or has understanding but that he is good-tempered or temperate; yet we praise the wise man also with respect to his state of mind; and of states of mind we call those which merit praise virtues.

Book II

1 Virtue, then, being of two kinds, intellectual and moral, intellectual virtue in the main owes both its birth and its growth to teaching (for which reason it requires experience and time), while moral virtue comes about as a result of habit, whence also its name (*ēthikē*) is one that is formed by a slight variation from the word *ethos* (habit). From this it is also plain that none of the moral virtues arises in us by nature; for nothing that exists by nature can form a habit contrary to its nature. For instance the stone which by nature moves downwards cannot be habituated to move upwards, not even if one tries to train it by throwing it up ten thousand times; nor can fire be habituated to move downwards, nor can anything else that by nature behaves in one way be trained to behave in another. Neither by nature, then, nor contrary to nature do the virtues arise in us; rather we are adapted by nature to receive them, and are made perfect by habit.

Again, of all the things that come to us by nature we first acquire the potentiality and later exhibit the activity (this is plain in the case of the senses; for it was not by often seeing or often hearing that we got these senses, but on the contrary we had them before we used them, and did not come to have them by using them); but the virtues we get by first exercising them, as also happens in the case of the arts as well. For the things we have to learn before we can do them, we learn by doing them, e.g. men become builders by building and lyre-players by playing the lyre; so too we become just by doing just acts, temperate by doing temperate acts, brave by doing brave acts.

This is confirmed by what happens in states; for legislators make the citizens good by forming habits in them, and this is the wish of every legislator, and those who do not effect it miss their mark, and it is in this that a good constitution differs from a bad one.

Again, it is from the same causes and by the same means that every virtue is both produced and destroyed, and similarly every art; for it is from playing the lyre that both good and bad lyre-players are produced. And the corresponding statement is true of builders and of all the rest; men will be good or bad builders as a result of building well or badly. For if this were not so, there would have been no need of a teacher, but all men would have been born good or bad at their craft. This, then, is the case with the virtues also; by doing the acts that we do in our transactions with other men we become just or unjust, and by doing the acts that we do in the presence of danger, and being habituated to feel fear or confidence, we become brave or cowardly. The same is true of appetites and feelings of anger; some men become temperate and good-tempered, others self-indulgent and irascible, by behaving in one way or the other in the appropriate circumstances. Thus, in one word, states of character arise out of like activities. This is why the activities we exhibit must be of a certain kind; it is because the states of character correspond to the differences between these. It makes no small difference, then, whether we form habits of one kind or of another from our very youth; it makes a very great difference, or rather *all* the difference.

Since, then, the present inquiry does not aim at theoretical 2 knowledge like the others (for we are inquiring not in order to know what virtue is, but in order to become good, since otherwise our inquiry would have been of no use), we must examine the nature of actions, namely how we ought to do them; for these determine also the nature of the states of character that are produced, as we have said. Now, that we must act according to the right rule is a common principle and must be assumed – it will be discussed later, i.e. both what the right rule is, and how it is related to the other virtues. But this must be agreed upon beforehand, that the whole account of matters of conduct must be given in outline and not precisely, as we said at the very beginning that the accounts we demand must be in accordance with the subject-matter; matters concerned with conduct and questions of what is good for us have no fixity, any more than matters of health. The general account being of this nature, the account of particular cases is yet more lacking in exactness; for they do not fall under any art or precept but the agents themselves must in each case consider what is appropriate to the occasion, as happens also in the art of medicine or of navigation.

But though our present account is of this nature we must give what help we can. First, then, let us consider this, that it is the nature of such things to be destroyed by defect and excess, as we see in the case of strength and of health (for to gain light on things imperceptible we must use the evidence of sensible things); both excessive and defective exercise destroys the strength, and similarly drink or food which is above or below a certain amount destroys the health, while that which is proportionate both produces and increases and preserves it. So too is it, then, in the case of temperance and courage and the other virtues. For the man who flies from and fears everything and does not stand his ground against anything becomes a coward, and the man who fears nothing at all but goes to meet every danger becomes rash; and similarly the man who indulges in every pleasure and abstains from none becomes self-indulgent, while the man who shuns every pleasure, as boors do, becomes in a way insensible; temperance and courage, then, are destroyed by excess and defect, and preserved by the mean.

But not only are the sources and causes of their origination and growth the same as those of their destruction, but also the sphere of their actualization will be the same; for this is also true of the things which are more evident to sense, e.g. of strength; it is produced by taking much food and undergoing much exertion, and it is the strong man that will be most able to do these things. So too is it with the virtues; by abstaining from pleasures we become temperate, and it is when we have become so that we are most able to abstain from them; and similarly too in the case of courage; for by being habituated to despise things that are fearful and to stand our ground against them we become brave, and it is when we have become so that we shall be most able to stand our ground against them.

3 We must take as a sign of states of character the pleasure or pain that supervenes upon acts; for the man who abstains from bodily pleasures and delights in this very fact is temperate, while the man who is annoyed at it is self-indulgent, and he who stands his ground against things that are terrible and delights in this or at

least is not pained is brave, while the man who is pained is a coward. For moral excellence is concerned with pleasures and pains; it is on account of the pleasure that we do bad things, and on account of the pain that we abstain from noble ones. Hence we ought to have been brought up in a particular way from our very youth, as Plato says, so as both to delight in and to be pained by the things that we ought; for this is the right education.

Again, if the virtues are concerned with actions and passions, and every passion and every action is accompanied by pleasure and pain, for this reason also virtue will be concerned with pleasures and pains. This is indicated also by the fact that punishment is inflicted by these means; for it is a kind of cure, and it is the nature of cures to be effected by contraries.

Again, as we said but lately, every state of soul has a nature relative to and concerned with the kind of things by which it tends to be made worse or better; but it is by reason of pleasures and pains that men become bad, by pursuing and avoiding these – either the pleasures and pains they ought not or when they ought not or as they ought not, or by going wrong in one of the other similar ways that may be distinguished. Hence men even define the virtues as certain states of impassivity and rest; not well, however, because they speak absolutely, and do not say 'as one ought' and 'as one ought not' and 'when one ought or ought not', and the other things that may be added. We assume, then, that this kind of excellence tends to do what is best with regard to pleasures and pains, and vice does the contrary.

The following facts also may show us that virtue and vice are concerned with these same things. There being three objects of choice and three of avoidance, the noble, the advantageous, the pleasant, and their contraries, the base, the injurious, the painful, about all of these the good man tends to go right and the bad man to go wrong, and especially about pleasure; for this is common to the animals, and also it accompanies all objects of choice; for even the noble and the advantageous appear pleasant.

Again, it has grown up with us all from our infancy; this is why it is difficult to rub off this passion, engrained as it is in our life. And we measure even our actions, some of us more and others less, by the rule of pleasure and pain. For this reason, then, our whole inquiry must be about these; for to feel delight and pain rightly or wrongly has no small effect on our actions.

Again, it is harder to fight with pleasure than with anger, to use Heraclitus' phrase, but both art and virtue are always concerned with what is harder; for even the good is better when it is harder. Therefore for this reason also the whole concern both of virtue and of political science is with pleasures and pains; for the man who uses these well will be good, he who uses them badly bad.

That virtue, then, is concerned with pleasures and pains, and that by the acts from which it arises it is both increased and, if they are done differently, destroyed, and that the acts from which it arose are those in which it actualizes itself — let this be taken as said.

4 The question might be asked, what we mean by saying that we must become just by doing just acts, and temperate by doing temperate acts; for if men do just and temperate acts, they are already just and temperate, exactly as, if they do what is in accordance with the laws of grammar and of music, they are grammarians and musicians.

Or is this not true even of the arts? It is possible to do something that is in accordance with the laws of grammar, either by chance or under the guidance of another. A man will be a grammarian, then, only when he has both done something grammatical and done it grammatically; and this means doing it in accordance with the grammatical knowledge in himself.

Again, the case of the arts and that of the virtues are not similar; for the products of the arts have their goodness in themselves, so that it is enough that they should have a certain character, but if the acts that are in accordance with the virtues have themselves a certain character it does not follow that they are done justly or temperately. The agent also must be in a certain condition when he does them; in the first place he must have knowledge, secondly he must choose the acts, and choose them for their own sakes, and thirdly his action must proceed from a firm and unchangeable character. These are not reckoned in as conditions of the possession of the arts, except the bare knowledge; but as a condition of the possession of the virtues knowledge has little or no weight, while the other conditions count not for a little but for everything, i.e.

the very conditions which result from often doing just and temperate acts.

Actions, then, are called just and temperate when they are such as the just or the temperate man would do; but it is not the man who does these that is just and temperate, but the man who also does them *as* just and temperate men do them. It is well said, then, that it is by doing just acts that the just man is produced, and by doing temperate acts the temperate man; without doing these no one would have even a prospect of becoming good.

But most people do not do these, but take refuge in theory and think they are being philosophers and will become good in this way, behaving somewhat like patients who listen attentively to their doctors, but do none of the things they are ordered to do. As the latter will not be made well in body by such a course of treatment, the former will not be made well in soul by such a course of philosophy.

Next we must consider what virtue is. Since things that are found in the soul are of three kinds – passions, faculties, state of character, virtue must be one of these. By passions I mean appetite, anger, fear, confidence, envy, joy, friendly feeling, hatred, longing, emulation, pity, and in general the feelings that are accompanied by pleasure or pain; by faculties the things in virtue of which we are said to be capable of feeling these, e.g. of becoming angry or being pained or feeling pity; by states of character the things in virtue of which we stand well or badly with reference to the passions, e.g. with reference to anger we stand badly if we feel it violently or too weakly, and well if we feel it moderately; and similarly with reference to the other passions.

Now neither the virtues nor the vices are *passions*, because we are not called good or bad on the ground of our passions, but are so called on the ground of our virtues and our vices, and because we are neither praised nor blamed for our passions (for the man who feels fear or anger is not praised, nor is the man who simply feels anger blamed, but the man who feels it in a certain way), but for our virtues and our vices we *are* praised or blamed.

Again, we feel anger and fear without choice, but the virtues are modes of choice or involve choice. Further, in respect of the passions we are said to be moved, but in respect of the virtues and the vices we are said not to be moved but to be disposed in a particular way.

For these reasons also they are not *faculties*; for we are neither called good nor bad, nor praised nor blamed, for the simple capacity of feeling the passions; again, we have the faculties by nature, but we are not made good or bad by nature; we have spoken of this before.

If, then, the virtues are neither passions nor faculties, all that remains is that they should be *states of character*.

Thus we have stated what virtue is in respect of its genus.

6 We must, however, not only describe virtue as a state of character, but also say what sort of state it is. We may remark, then, that every virtue or excellence both brings into good condition the thing of which it is the excellence and makes the work of that thing be done well; e.g. the excellence of the eye makes both the eye and its work good; for it is by the excellence of the eye that we see well. Similarly the excellence of the horse makes a horse both good in itself and good at running and at carrying its rider and at awaiting the attack of the enemy. Therefore, if this is true in every case, the virtue of man also will be the state of character which makes a man good and which makes him do his own work well.

How this is to happen we have stated already, but it will be made plain also by the following consideration of the specific nature of virtue. In everything that is continuous and divisible it is possible to take more, less, or an equal amount, and that either in terms of the thing itself or relatively to us; and the equal is an intermediate between excess and defect. By the intermediate in the object I mean that which is equidistant from each of the extremes, which is one and the same for all men; by the intermediate relatively to us that which is neither too much nor too little – and this is not one, nor the same for all. For instance, if ten is many and two is few, six is the intermediate, taken in terms of the object; for it exceeds and is exceeded by an equal amount; this is intermediate according to arithmetical proportion. But the intermediate relatively to us is not to be taken so; if ten pounds are too much for a particular person to eat and two too little, it does not follow that the trainer will order six pounds; for this also is perhaps too much for the person who is to take it, or too little – too little for Milo, too much for the beginner in athletic exercises. The same is true of running and wrestling. Thus a master of any art avoids excess and defect, but seeks the intermediate and chooses this – the intermediate not in the object but relatively to us.

If it is thus, then, that every art does its work well – by looking to the intermediate and judging its works by this standard (so that we often say of good works of art that it is not possible either to take away or to add anything, implying that excess and defect destroy the goodness of works of art, while the mean preserves it; and good artists, as we say, look to this in their work), and if, further, virtue is more exact and better than any art, as nature also is, then virtue must have the quality of aiming at the intermediate. I mean moral virtue; for it is this that is concerned with passions and actions, and in these there is excess, defect, and the intermediate. For instance, both fear and confidence and appetite and anger and pity and in general pleasure and pain may be felt both too much and too little, and in both cases not well; but to feel them at the right times, with reference to the right objects, towards the right people, with the right motive, and in the right way, is what is both intermediate and best, and this is characteristic of virtue. Similarly with regard to actions also there is excess, defect, and the intermediate. Now virtue is concerned with passions and actions, in which excess is a form of failure, and so is defect, while the intermediate is praised and is a form of success; and being praised and being successful are both characteristics of virtue. Therefore virtue is a kind of mean, since, as we have seen, it aims at what is intermediate.

Again, it is possible to fail in many ways (for evil belongs to the class of the unlimited, as the Pythagoreans conjectured, and good to that of the limited), while to succeed is possible only in one way (for which reason also one is easy and the other difficult – to miss the mark easy, to hit it difficult); for these reasons also, then, excess and defect are characteristic of vice, and the mean of virtue;

For men are good in but one way, but bad in many.

Book II.6

Virtue, then, is a state of character concerned with choice, lying in a mean, i.e. the mean relative to us, this being determined by a rational principle, and by that principle by which the man of practical wisdom would determine it. Now it is a mean between two vices, that which depends on excess and that which depends on defect; and again it is a mean because the vices respectively fall short of or exceed what is right in both passions and actions, while virtue both finds and chooses that which is intermediate. Hence in respect of its being, i.e. the definition which states its essence, virtue is a mean, with regard to what is best and right an extreme.

But not every action nor every passion admits of a mean; for some have names that already imply badness, e.g. spite, shamelessness, envy, and in the case of actions adultery, theft, murder; for all of these and suchlike things imply by their names that they are themselves bad, and not the excesses or deficiencies of them. It is not possible, then, ever to be right with regard to them; one must always be wrong. Nor does goodness or badness with regard to such things depend on committing adultery with the right woman, at the right time, and in the right way, but simply to do any of them is to go wrong. It would be equally absurd, then, to expect that in unjust, cowardly, and voluptuous action there should be a mean, an excess, and a deficiency; for at that rate there would be a mean of excess and of deficiency, an excess of excess, and a deficiency of deficiency. But as there is no excess and deficiency of temperance and courage because what is intermediate is in a sense an extreme, so too of the actions we have mentioned there is no mean nor any excess and deficiency, but however they are done they are wrong; for in general there is neither a mean of excess and deficiency, nor excess and deficiency of a mean.

7 We must, however, not only make this general statement, but also apply it to the individual facts. For among statements about conduct those which are general apply more widely, but those which are particular are more true, since conduct has to do with individual cases, and our statements must harmonize with the facts in these cases. We may take these cases from our table. With

regard to feelings of fear and confidence courage is the mean; of the people who exceed, he who exceeds in fearlessness has no name (many of the states have no name), while the man who exceeds in confidence is rash, and he who exceeds in fear and falls short in confidence is a coward. With regard to pleasures and pains – not all of them, and not so much with regard to the pains – the mean is temperance, the excess self-indulgence. Persons deficient with regard to the pleasures are not often found; hence such persons also have received no name. But let us call them 'insensible'.

With regard to giving and taking of money the mean is liberality, the excess and the defect prodigality and meanness. In these actions people exceed and fall short in contrary ways; the prodigal exceeds in spending and falls short in taking, while the mean man exceeds in taking and falls short in spending. (At present we are giving a mere outline or summary, and are satisfied with this; later these states will be more exactly determined.) With regard to money there are also other dispositions – a mean, magnificence (for the magnificent man differs from the liberal man; the former deals with large sums, the latter with small ones), an excess, tastelessness and vulgarity, and a deficiency, niggardliness; these differ from the states opposed to liberality, and the mode of their difference will be stated later.

With regard to honour and dishonour the mean is proper pride, the excess is known as a sort of 'empty vanity', and the deficiency is undue humility; and as we said liberality was related to magnificence, differing from it by dealing with small sums, so there is a state similarly related to proper pride, being concerned with small honours while that is concerned with great. For it is possible to desire honour as one ought, and more than one ought, and less, and the man who exceeds in his desires is called ambitious, the man who falls short unambitious, while the intermediate person has no name. The dispositions also are nameless, except that that of the ambitious man is called ambition. Hence the people who are at the extremes lay claim to the middle place; and we ourselves sometimes call the intermediate person ambitious and sometimes unambitious, and sometimes praise the ambitious man and sometimes the unambitious. The reason of our doing this will be stated in what follows; but now let us speak of the remaining states according to the method which has been indicated.

With regard to anger also there is an excess, a deficiency, and a mean. Although they can scarcely be said to have names, yet since we call the intermediate person good-tempered let us call the mean good temper; of the persons at the extremes let the one who exceeds be called irascible, and his vice irascibility, and the man who falls short an inirascible sort of person, and the deficiency inirascibility.

There are also three other means, which have a certain likeness to one another, but differ from one another: for they are all concerned with intercourse in words and actions, but differ in that one is concerned with truth in this sphere, the other two with pleasantness; and of this one kind is exhibited in giving amusement, the other in all the circumstances of life. We must therefore speak of these too, that we may the better see that in all things the mean is praiseworthy, and the extremes neither praiseworthy nor right, but worthy of blame. Now most of these states also have no names, but we must try, as in the other cases, to invent names ourselves so that we may be clear and easy to follow. With regard to truth, then, the intermediate is a truthful sort of person and the mean may be called truthfulness, while the pretence which exaggerates is boastfulness and the person characterized by it a boaster, and that which understates is mock modesty and the person characterized by it mock-modest. With regard to pleasantness in the giving of amusement the intermediate person is ready-witted and the disposition ready wit, the excess is buffoonery and the person characterized by it a buffoon, while the man who falls short is a sort of boor and his state is boorishness. With regard to the remaining kind of pleasantness, that which is exhibited in life in general, the man who is pleasant in the right way is friendly and the mean is friendliness, while the man who exceeds is an obsequious person if he has no end in view, a flatterer if he is aiming at his own advantage, and the man who falls short and is unpleasant in all circumstances is a quarrelsome and surly sort of person.

There are also means in the passions and concerned with the passions; since shame is not a virtue, and yet praise is extended to the modest man. For even in these matters one man is said to be intermediate, and another to exceed, as for instance the bashful man who is ashamed of everything; while he who falls short or is not ashamed of anything at all is shameless, and the intermediate person is modest. Righteous indignation is a mean between envy and spite, and these states are concerned with the pain and pleasure that are felt at the fortunes of our neighbours; the man who is characterized by righteous indignation is pained at undeserved good fortune, the envious man, going beyond him, is pained at all good fortune, and the spiteful man falls so far short of being pained that he even rejoices. But these states there will be an opportunity of describing elsewhere; with regard to justice, since it has not one simple meaning, we shall, after describing the other states, distinguish its two kinds and say how each of them is a mean; and similarly we shall treat also of the rational virtues.

There are three kinds of disposition, then, two of them vices, 8 involving excess and deficiency respectively, and one a virtue, viz. the mean, and all are in a sense opposed to all; for the extreme states are contrary both to the intermediate state and to each other, and the intermediate to the extremes; as the equal is greater relatively to the less, less relatively to the greater, so the middle states are excessive relatively to the deficiencies, deficient relatively to the excesses, both in passions and in actions. For the brave man appears rash relatively to the coward, and cowardly relatively to the rash man; and similarly the temperate man appears self-indulgent relatively to the insensible man, insensible relatively to the self-indulgent, and the liberal man prodigal relatively to the mean man, mean relatively to the prodigal. Hence also the people at the extremes push the intermediate man each over to the other, and the brave man is called rash by the coward, cowardly by the rash man, and correspondingly in the other cases.

These states being thus opposed to one another, the greatest contrariety is that of the extremes to each other, rather than to the intermediate; for these are further from each other than from the intermediate, as the great is further from the small and the small from the great than both are from the equal. Again, to the intermediate some extremes show a certain likeness, as that of rashness to courage and that of prodigality to liberality; but the extremes show the greatest unlikeness to each other; now contraries are defined as the things that are furthest from each other, so that things that are further apart are more contrary.

To the mean in some cases the deficiency, in some the excess is more opposed; e.g. it is not rashness, which is an excess, but cowardice, which is a deficiency, that is more opposed to courage, and not insensibility, which is a deficiency, but self-indulgence, which is an excess, that is more opposed to temperance. This happens from two reasons, one being drawn from the thing itself; for because one extreme is nearer and liker to the intermediate, we oppose not this but rather its contrary to the intermediate. E.g., since rashness is thought liker and nearer to courage, and cowardice more unlike, we oppose rather the latter to courage; for things that are further from the intermediate are thought more contrary to it. This, then, is one cause, drawn from the thing itself; another is drawn from ourselves; for the things to which we ourselves more naturally tend seem more contrary to the intermediate. For instance, we ourselves tend more naturally to pleasures, and hence are more easily carried away towards self-indulgence than towards propriety. We describe as contrary to the mean, then, rather the directions in which we more often go to great lengths; and therefore self-indulgence, which is an excess, is the more contrary to temperance.

9 That moral virtue is a mean, then, and in what sense it is so, and that it is a mean between two vices, the one involving excess, the other deficiency, and that it is such because its character is to aim at what is intermediate in passions and in actions, has been sufficiently stated. Hence also it is no easy task to be good. For in everything it is no easy task to find the middle, e.g. to find the middle of a circle is not for every one but for him who knows; so, too, any one can get angry – that is easy – or give or spend money; but to do this to the right person, to the right extent, at the right time, with the right motive, and in the right way, *that* is not for every one, nor is it easy; wherefore goodness is both rare and laudable and noble.

Hence he who aims at the intermediate must first depart from what is the more contrary to it, as Calypso advises –

> Hold the ship out beyond that surf and spray.

For of the extremes one is more erroneous, one less so; therefore, since to hit the mean is hard in the extreme, we must as a second best, as people say, take the least of the evils; and this will be done best in the way we describe.

But we must consider the things towards which we ourselves also are easily carried away; for some of us tend to one thing, some another; and this will be recognizable from the pleasure and the pain we feel. We must drag ourselves away to the contrary extreme; for we shall get into the intermediate state by drawing well away from error, as people do in straightening sticks that are bent.

Now in everything the pleasant or pleasure is most to be guarded against; for we do not judge it impartially. We ought, then, to feel towards pleasure as the elders of the people felt towards Helen, and in all circumstances repeat their saying; for if we dismiss pleasure thus we are less likely to go astray. It is by doing this, then, (to sum the matter up) that we shall best be able to hit the mean.

But this is no doubt difficult, and especially in individual cases; for it is not easy to determine both how and with whom and on what provocation and how long one should be angry; for we too sometimes praise those who fall short and call them good-tempered, but sometimes we praise those who get angry and call them manly. The man, however, who deviates little from goodness is not blamed, whether he do so in the direction of the more or of the less, but only the man who deviates more widely; for *he* does not fail to be noticed. But up to what point and to what extent a man must deviate before he becomes blameworthy it is not easy to determine by reasoning, any more than anything else that is perceived by the senses; such things depend on particular facts, and the decision rests with perception. So much, then, is plain, that the intermediate state is in all things to be praised, but that we must incline sometimes towards the excess, sometimes towards the deficiency; for so shall we most easily hit the mean and what is right.

Book III

1 Since virtue is concerned with passions and actions, and on those that are voluntary praise and blame are bestowed, but on those that are involuntary pardon, and sometimes also pity, to distinguish the voluntary and the involuntary is presumably necessary for those who are studying the nature of virtue, and useful also for legislators with a view to the assigning both of honours and of punishments.

Those things, then, are thought involuntary, which take place under compulsion or owing to ignorance; and that is compulsory of which the moving principle is outside, being a principle in which nothing is contributed by the person who acts – or, rather, is acted upon, e.g. if he were to be carried somewhere by a wind, or by men who had him in their power.

But with regard to the things that are done from fear of greater evils or for some noble object (e.g. if a tyrant were to order one to do something base, having one's parents and children in his power, and if one did the action they were to be saved, but otherwise would be put to death), it may be debated whether such actions are involuntary or voluntary. Something of the sort happens also with regard to the throwing of goods overboard in a storm; for in the abstract no one throws away voluntarily, but on condition of its securing the safety of himself and his crew any sensible man does so. Such actions, then, are mixed, but are more like voluntary actions; for they are worthy of choice at the time when they are done, and the end of an action is relative to the occasion. Both the terms, then, 'voluntary' and 'involuntary', must be used with reference to the moment of action. Now the man acts voluntarily; for the principle that moves the instrumental parts of the body in such actions is in him, and the things of which the moving principle is in a man himself are in his power to do or not to do. Such actions, therefore, are voluntary, but in the abstract perhaps involuntary; for no one would choose any such act in itself.

For such actions men are sometimes even praised, when they endure something base or painful in return for great and noble objects gained; in the opposite case they are blamed, since to endure the greatest indignities for no noble end or for a trifling end is the mark of an inferior person. On some actions praise indeed is not bestowed, but pardon is, when one does what he ought not under pressure which overstrains human nature and which no one could withstand. But some acts, perhaps, we cannot be forced to do, but ought rather to face death after the most fearful sufferings; for the things that 'forced' Euripides' Alcmaeon to slay his mother seem absurd. It is difficult sometimes to determine what should be chosen at what cost, and what should be endured in return for what gain, and yet more difficult to abide by our decisions; for as a rule what is expected is painful, and what we are forced to do is base, whence praise and blame are bestowed on those who have been compelled or have not.

What sort of acts, then, should be called compulsory? We answer that without qualification actions are so when the cause is in the external circumstances and the agent contributes nothing. But the things that in themselves are involuntary, but now and in return for these gains are worthy of choice, and whose moving principle is in the agent, are in themselves involuntary, but now and in return for these gains voluntary. They are more like voluntary acts; for actions are in the class of particulars, and the particular acts here are voluntary. What sort of things are to be chosen, and in return for what, it is not easy to state; for there are many differences in the particular cases.

But if some one were to say that pleasant and noble objects have a compelling power, forcing us from without, all acts would be for him compulsory; for it is for these objects that all men do everything they do. And those who act under compulsion and unwillingly act with pain, but those who do acts for their pleasantness and nobility do them with pleasure; it is absurd to make external circumstances responsible, and not oneself, as being easily caught by such attractions, and to make oneself responsible for noble acts but the pleasant objects responsible for base acts. The compulsory, then, seems to be that whose moving principle is outside, the person compelled contributing nothing.

Everything that is done by reason of ignorance is *not* voluntary; it is only what produces pain and repentance that is *in*voluntary.

For the man who has done something owing to ignorance, and feels not the least vexation at his action, has not acted voluntarily, since he did not know what he was doing, nor yet involuntarily, since he is not pained. Of people, then, who act by reason of ignorance he who repents is thought an involuntary agent, and the man who does not repent may, since he is different, be called a not voluntary agent; for, since he differs from the other, it is better that he should have a name of his own.

Acting by reason of ignorance seems also to be different from acting *in* ignorance; for the man who is drunk or in a rage is thought to act as a result not of ignorance but of one of the causes mentioned, yet not knowingly but in ignorance.

Now every wicked man is ignorant of what he ought to do and what he ought to abstain from, and error of this kind makes men unjust and in general bad; but the term 'involuntary' tends to be used not if a man is ignorant of what is to his advantage – for it is not mistaken purpose that makes an action involuntary (*it* makes men *wicked*), nor ignorance of the universal (for *that* men are *blamed*), but ignorance of particulars, i.e. of the circumstances of the action and the objects with which it is concerned. For it is on these that both pity and pardon depend, since the person who is ignorant of any of these acts involuntarily.

Perhaps it is just as well, therefore, to determine their nature and number. A man may be ignorant, then, of who he is, what he is doing, what or whom he is acting on, and sometimes also what (e.g. what instrument) he is doing it with, and to what end (e.g. he may think his act will conduce to some one's safety), and how he is doing it (e.g. whether gently or violently). Now of all of these no one could be ignorant unless he were mad, and evidently also he could not be ignorant of the agent; for how could he not know himself? But of what he is doing a man might be ignorant, as for instance people say 'it slipped out of their mouths as they were speaking', or 'they did not know it was a secret', as Aeschylus said of the mysteries, or a man might say he 'let it go off when he merely wanted to show its working', as the man did with the catapult. Again, one might think one's son was an enemy, as Merope did, or that a pointed spear had a button on it, or that a stone was pumice-stone; or one might give a man a draught to save him, and really kill him; or one might want to touch a man, as people do in sparring, and really wound him. The ignorance may relate, then, to any of these things, and the man who was ignorant of any of these is thought to have acted involuntarily, and especially if he was ignorant on the most important points; and these are thought to be the circumstances of the action and its end. Further, the doing of an act that is called involuntary in virtue of ignorance of this sort must be painful and involve repentance.

Since that which is done under compulsion or by reason of ignorance is involuntary, the voluntary would seem to be that of which the moving principle is in the agent himself, he being aware of the particular circumstances of the action. Presumably acts done by reason of anger or appetite are not rightly called involuntary. For in the first place, on that showing none of the other animals will act voluntarily, nor will children; and secondly, is it meant that we do not do voluntarily *any* of the acts that are due to appetite or anger, or that we do the noble acts voluntarily and the base acts involuntarily? Is not this absurd, when one and the same thing is the cause? But it would surely be odd to describe as involuntary the things one ought to desire; and we ought both to be angry at certain things and to have an appetite for certain things, e.g. for health and for learning. Also what is involuntary is thought to be painful, but what is in accordance with appetite is thought to be pleasant. Again, what is the difference in respect of involuntariness between errors committed upon calculation and those committed in anger? Both are to be avoided, but the irrational passions are thought not less human than reason is, and therefore also the actions which proceed from anger or appetite are the man's actions. It would be odd, then, to treat them as involuntary.

2 Both the voluntary and the involuntary having been delimited, we must next discuss choice; for it is thought to be most closely bound up with virtue and to discriminate characters better than actions do.

Choice, then, seems to be voluntary, but not the same thing as the voluntary; the latter extends more widely. For both children and the lower animals share in voluntary action, but not in choice, and acts done on the spur of the moment we describe as voluntary, but not as chosen.

Those who say it is appetite or anger or wish or a kind of opinion do not seem to be right. For choice is not common to irrational creatures as well, but appetite and anger are. Again, the incontinent man acts with appetite, but not with choice; while the continent man on the contrary acts with choice, but not with appetite. Again, appetite is contrary to choice, but not appetite to appetite. Again, appetite relates to the pleasant and the painful, choice neither to the painful nor to the pleasant.

Still less is it anger; for acts due to anger are thought to be less than any others objects of choice.

But neither is it wish, though it seems near to it; for choice cannot relate to impossibles, and if any one said he chose them he would be thought silly; but there may be a wish even for impossibles, e.g. for immortality. And wish may relate to things that could in no way be brought about by one's own efforts, e.g. that a particular actor or athlete should win in a competition; but no one chooses such things, but only the things that he thinks could be brought about by his own efforts. Again, wish relates rather to the end, choice to the means; for instance, we wish to be healthy, but we choose the acts which will make us healthy, and we wish to be happy and say we do, but we cannot well say we choose to be so; for, in general, choice seems to relate to the things that are in our own power.

For this reason, too, it cannot be opinion; for opinion is thought to relate to all kinds of things, no less to eternal things and impossible things than to things in our own power; and it is distinguished by its falsity or truth, not by its badness or goodness, while choice is distinguished rather by these.

Now with opinion in general perhaps no one even says it is identical. But it is not identical even with any kind of opinion; for by choosing what is good or bad we are men of a certain character, which we are not by holding certain opinions. And we choose to get or avoid something good or bad, but we have opinions about what a thing is or whom it is good for or how it is good for him; we can hardly be said to opine to get or avoid anything. And choice is praised for being related to the right object or for being right, opinion for being true. And we choose what we best know to be good, but we opine what we do not in the least know to be good; and it is not the same people that are thought to make the best choices and to have the best opinions, but some are thought to have fairly good opinions, but by reason of vice to choose what they should not. If opinion precedes choice or accompanies it, that makes no difference; for it is not this that we are considering, but whether it is *identical* with some kind of opinion.

What, then, or what kind of thing is it, since it is none of the things we have mentioned? It seems to be voluntary, but not all that is voluntary to be an object of choice. Is it, then, what has been deliberated about before? At any rate choice involves a rational principle and thought. Even the name seems to suggest that it is what is chosen before other things.

Do we deliberate about everything, and is everything a possible subject of deliberation, or is deliberation impossible about some things? We ought presumably to call not what a fool or a madman would deliberate about, but what a sensible man would deliberate about, a subject of deliberation. Now about eternal things no one deliberates, e.g. about the material universe or the incommensurability of the diagonal and the side of a square. But no more do we deliberate about the things that involve movement but always happen in the same way, whether of necessity or by nature or from any other cause, e.g. the solstices and the risings of the stars; nor about things that happen now in one way, now in another, e.g. droughts and rains; nor about chance events, like the finding of treasure. But we do not deliberate even about all human affairs; for instance, no Spartan deliberates about the best constitution for the Scythians. For none of these things can be brought about by our own efforts.

We deliberate about things that are in our power and can be done; and these are in fact what is left. For nature, necessity, and chance are thought to be causes, and also reason and everything that depends on man. Now every class of men deliberates about the things that can be done by their own efforts. And in the case of exact and self-contained sciences there is no deliberation, e.g.

about the letters of the alphabet (for we have no doubt how they should be written); but the things that are brought about by our own efforts, but not always in the same way, are the things about which we deliberate, e.g. questions of medical treatment or of money-making. And we do so more in the case of the art of navigation than in that of gymnastics, inasmuch as it has been less exactly worked out, and again about other things in the same ratio, and more also in the case of the arts than in that of the sciences; for we have more doubt about the former. Deliberation is concerned with things that happen in a certain way for the most part, but in which the event is obscure, and with things in which it is indeterminate. We call in others to aid us in deliberation on important questions, distrusting ourselves as not being equal to deciding.

We deliberate not about ends but about means. For a doctor does not deliberate whether he shall heal, nor an orator whether he shall persuade, nor a statesman whether he shall produce law and order, nor does any one else deliberate about his end. They assume the end and consider how and by what means it is to be attained; and if it seems to be produced by several means they consider by which it is most easily and best produced, while if it is achieved by one only they consider how it will be achieved by this and by what means *this* will be achieved, till they come to the first cause, which in the order of discovery is last. For the person who deliberates seems to inquire and analyse in the way described as though he were analysing a geometrical construction (not all inquiry appears to be deliberation – for instance mathematical inquiries – but all deliberation is inquiry), and what is last in the order of analysis seems to be first in the order of becoming. And if we come on an impossibility, we give up the search, e.g. if we need money and this cannot be got; but if a thing appears possible we try to do it. By 'possible' things I mean things that might be brought about by our own efforts; and these in a sense include things that can be brought about by the efforts of our friends, since the moving principle is in ourselves. The subject of investigation is sometimes the instruments, sometimes the use of them; and similarly in the other cases – sometimes the means, sometimes the mode of using it or the means of bringing it about. It seems, then, as has been said, that man is a moving principle of actions; now deliberation is about the things to be done by the agent himself, and actions are for the sake of things other than themselves. For the end cannot be a subject of deliberation, but only the means; nor indeed can the particular facts be a subject of it, as whether this is bread or has been baked as it should; for these are matters of perception. If we are to be always deliberating, we shall have to go on to infinity.

The same thing is deliberated upon and is chosen, except that the object of choice is already determinate, since it is that which has been decided upon as a result of deliberation that is the object of choice. For every one ceases to inquire how he is to act when he has brought the moving principle back to himself and to the ruling part of himself; for this is what chooses. This is plain also from the ancient constitutions, which Homer represented; for the kings announced their choices to the people. The object of choice being one of the things in our own power which is desired after deliberation, choice will be deliberate desire of things in our own power; for when we have reached a judgment as a result of deliberation, we desire in accordance with our deliberation.

We may take it, then, that we have described choice in outline, and stated the nature of its objects and the fact that it is concerned with means.

That *wish* is for the end has already been stated; some think it is for the good, others for the apparent good. Now those who say that the good is the object of wish must admit in consequence that that which the man who does not choose aright wishes for is not an object of wish (for if it is to be so, it must also be good; but it was, if it so happened, bad); while those who say the apparent good is the object of wish must admit that there is no natural object of wish, but only what seems good to each man. Now different things appear good to different people, and, if it so happens, even contrary things.

If these consequences are unpleasing, are we to say that absolutely and in truth the good is the object of wish, but for each person the apparent good; that that which is in truth an object of wish is an object of wish to the good man, while any chance thing

Book III.4

may be so to the bad man, as in the case of bodies also the things that are in truth wholesome are wholesome for bodies which are in good condition, while for those that are diseased other things are wholesome – or bitter or sweet or hot or heavy, and so on; since the good man judges each class of things rightly, and in each the truth appears to him? For each state of character has its own ideas of the noble and the pleasant, and perhaps the good man differs from others most by seeing the truth in each class of things, being as it were the norm and measure of them. In most things the error seems to be due to pleasure; for it appears a good when it is not. We therefore choose the pleasant as a good, and avoid pain as an evil.

The end, then, being what we wish for, the means what we deliberate about and choose, actions concerning means must be according to choice and voluntary. Now the exercise of the virtues is concerned with means. Therefore virtue also is in our own power, and so too vice. For where it is in our power to act it is also in our power not to act, and *vice versa*; so that, if to act, where this is noble, is in our power, not to act, which will be base, will also be in our power, and if not to act, where this is noble, is in our power, to act, which will be base, will also be in our power. Now if it is in our power to do noble or base acts, and likewise in our power not to do them, and this was what being good or bad meant, then it is in our power to be virtuous or vicious.

The saying that 'no one is voluntarily wicked nor involuntarily happy' seems to be partly false and partly true; for no one is involuntarily happy, but wickedness *is* voluntary. Or else we shall have to dispute what has just been said, at any rate, and deny that man is a moving principle or begetter of his actions as of children. But if these facts are evident and we cannot refer actions to moving principles other than those in ourselves, the acts whose moving principles are in us must themselves also be in our power and voluntary.

Witness seems to be borne to this both by individuals in their private capacity and by legislators themselves; for these punish and take vengeance on those who do wicked acts (unless they have acted under compulsion or as a result of ignorance for which they are not themselves responsible), while they honour those who do noble acts, as though they meant to encourage the latter and deter the former. But no one is encouraged to do the things that are neither in our power nor voluntary: it is assumed that there is no gain in being persuaded not to be hot or in pain or hungry or the like, since we shall experience these feelings none the less. Indeed, we punish a man for his very ignorance, if he is thought responsible for the ignorance, as when penalites are doubled in the case of drunkenness; for the moving principle is in the man himself, since he had the power of not getting drunk and his getting drunk was the cause of his ignorance. And we punish those who are ignorant of anything in the laws that they ought to know and that is not difficult, and so too in the case of anything else that they are thought to be ignorant of through carelessness; we assume that it is in their power not to be ignorant, since they have the power of taking care.

But perhaps a man is the kind of man not to take care. Still they are themselves by their slack lives responsible for becoming men of that kind, and men are themselves responsible for being unjust or self-indulgent, in that they cheat or spend their time in drinking bouts and the like; for it is activities exercised on particular objects that make the corresponding character. This is plain from the case of people training for any contest or action; they practise the activity the whole time. Now not to know that it is from the exercise of activities on particular objects that states of character are produced is the mark of a thoroughly senseless person. Again, it is irrational to suppose that a man who acts unjustly does not wish to be unjust or a man who acts self-indulgently to be self-indulgent. But if *without* being ignorant a man does the things which will make him unjust, he will be unjust voluntarily. Yet it does not follow that if he wishes he will cease to be unjust and will be just. For neither does the man who is ill become well on those terms. We may suppose a case in which he is ill voluntarily, through living incontinently and disobeying his doctors. In that case it was *then* open to him not to be ill, but not now, when he has thrown away his chance, just as when you have let a stone go it is too late to recover it; but yet it was in your power to throw it, since the moving principle was in you. So, too, to the unjust and to

Book III.5

the self-indulgent man it was open at the beginning not to become men of this kind, and so they are unjust and self-indulgent voluntarily; but now that they have become so it is not possible for them not to be so.

But not only are the vices of the soul voluntary, but those of the body also for some men, whom we accordingly blame; while no one blames those who are ugly by nature, we blame those who are so owing to want of exercise and care. So it is, too, with respect to weakness and infirmity; no one would reproach a man blind from birth or by disease or from a blow, but rather pity him, while every one would blame a man who was blind from drunkenness or some other form of self-indulgence. Of vices of the body, then, those in our own power are blamed, those not in our power are not. And if this be so, in the other cases also the vices that are blamed must be in our own power.

Now some one may say that all men aim at the apparent good, but have no control over the appearance, but the end appears to each man in a form answering to his character. We reply that if each man is somehow responsible for his state of character, he will also be himself somehow responsible for the appearance; but if not, no one is responsible for his own evildoing, but every one does evil acts through ignorance of the end, thinking that by these he will get what is best, and the aiming at the end is not self-chosen but one must be born with an eye, as it were, by which to judge rightly and choose what is truly good, and he is well endowed by nature who is well endowed with this. For it is what is greatest and most noble, and what we cannot get or learn from another, but must have just such as it was when given us at birth, and to be well and nobly endowed with this will be perfect and true excellence of natural endowment. If this is true, then, how will virtue be more voluntary than vice? To both men alike, the good and the bad, the end appears and is fixed by nature or however it may be, and it is by referring everything else to this that men do whatever they do.

Whether, then, it is not by nature that the end appears to each man such as it does appear, but something also depends on him, or the end is natural but because the good man adopts the means voluntarily virtue is voluntary, vice also will be none the less voluntary; for in the case of the bad man there is equally present that which depends on himself in his actions even if not in his end. If, then, as is asserted, the virtues are voluntary (for we are ourselves somehow partly responsible for our states of character, and it is by being persons of a certain kind that we assume the end to be so and so), the vices also will be voluntary; for the same is true of them.

With regard to the virtues in *general* we have stated their genus in outline, viz. that they are means and that they are states of character, and that they tend, and by their own nature, to the doing of the acts by which they are produced, and that they are in our power and voluntary, and act as the right rule prescribes. But actions and states of character are not voluntary in the same way; for we are masters of our actions from the beginning right to the end, if we know the particular facts, but though we control the beginning of our states of character the gradual progress is not obvious, any more than it is in illnesses; because it was in our power, however, to act in this way or not in this way, therefore the states are voluntary.

Let us take up the several virtues, however, and say which they are and what sort of things they are concerned with and how they are concerned with them; at the same time it will become plain how many they are. And first let us speak of courage.

That it is a mean with regard to feelings of fear and confidence 6 has already been made evident; and plainly the things we fear are fearful things, and these are, to speak without qualification, evils; for which reason people even define fear as expectation of evil. Now we fear all evils, e.g. disgrace, poverty, disease, friendlessness, death, but the brave man is not thought to be concerned with all; for to fear some things is even right and noble, and it is base not to fear them – e.g. disgrace; he who fears this is good and modest, and he who does not is shameless. He is, however, by some people called brave, by a transference of the word to a new meaning; for he has in him something which is like the brave man, since the brave man also is a fearless person. Poverty and disease we perhaps ought not to fear, nor in general the things that do not proceed from vice and are not due to a man himself. But not even the man who is fearless of these is brave. Yet we apply the word to him also in virtue of a similarity; for some who in the dangers of war are cowards are liberal and are confident in face of the loss of money. Nor is a man a coward if he fears insult to his wife and children or envy or anything of the kind; nor brave if he is confident when he is about to be flogged. With what sort of fearful things, then, is the brave man concerned? Surely with the greatest; for no one is more likely than he to stand his ground against what is awe-inspiring. Now death is the most fearful of all things; for it is the end, and nothing is thought to be any longer either good or bad for the dead. But the brave man would not seem to be concerned even with death in *all* circumstances, e.g. at sea or in disease. In what circumstances, then? Surely in the noblest. Now such deaths are those in battle; for these take place in the greatest and noblest danger. And these are correspondingly honoured in city-states and at the courts of monarchs. Properly, then, he will be called brave who is fearless in face of a noble death, and of all emergencies that involve death; and the emergencies of war are in the highest degree of this kind. Yet at sea also, and in disease, the brave man is fearless, but not in the same way as the seamen; for he has given up hope of safety, and is disliking the thought of death in this shape, while they are hopeful because of their experience. At the same time, we show courage in situations where there is the opportunity of showing prowess or where death is noble; but in these forms of death neither of these conditions is fulfilled.

7 What is fearful is not the same for all men; but we say there are things fearful even beyond human strength. These, then, are fearful to every one – at least to every sensible man; but the fearful things that are *not* beyond human strength differ in magnitude and degree, and so too do the things that inspire confidence. Now the brave man is as dauntless as man may be. Therefore, while he will fear even the things that are not beyond human strength, he will face them as he ought and as the rule directs, for honour's sake; for this is the end of virtue. But it is possible to fear these more, or less, and again to fear things that are not fearful as if they were. Of the faults that are committed one consists in fearing what one should not, another in fearing as we should not, another in fearing when we should not, and so on; and so too with respect

to the things that inspire confidence. The man, then, who faces and who fears the right things and from the right motive, in the right way and at the right time, and who feels confidence under the corresponding conditions, is brave; for the brave man feels and acts according to the merits of the case and in whatever way the rule directs. Now the end of every activity is conformity to the corresponding state of character. This is true, therefore, of the brave man as well as of others. But courage is noble. Therefore the end also is noble; for each thing is defined by its end. Therefore it is for a noble end that the brave man endures and acts as courage directs.

Of those who go to excess he who exceeds in fearlessness has no name (we have said previously that many states of character have no names), but he would be a sort of madman or insensitive to pain if he feared nothing, neither earthquakes nor the waves, as they say the Celts do not; while the man who exceeds in confidence about what really is fearful is rash. The rash man, however, is also thought to be boastful and only a pretender to courage; at all events, as the brave man *is* with regard to what is fearful, so the rash man wishes to *appear*; and so he imitates him in situations where he can. Hence also most of them are a mixture of rashness and cowardice; for, while in these situations they display confidence, they do not hold their ground against what is really fearful. The man who exceeds in fear is a coward; for he fears both what he ought not and as he ought not, and all the similar characterizations attach to him. He is lacking also in confidence; but he is more conspicuous for his excess of fear in painful situations. The coward, then, is a despairing sort of person; for he fears everything. The brave man, on the other hand, has the opposite disposition; for confidence is the mark of a hopeful disposition. The coward, the rash man, and the brave man, then, are concerned with the same objects but are differently disposed towards them; for the first two exceed and fall short, while the third holds the middle, which is the right, position; and rash men are precipitate, and wish for dangers beforehand but draw back when they are in them, while brave men are keen in the moment of action, but quiet beforehand.

As we have said, then, courage is a mean with respect to things that inspire confidence or fear, in the circumstances that have been stated; and it chooses or endures things because it is noble to do so, or because it is base not to do so. But to die to escape from poverty or love or anything painful is not the mark of a brave man, but rather of a coward; for it is softness to fly from what is troublesome, and such a man endures death not because it is noble but to fly from evil.

8 Courage, then, is something of this sort, but the name is also applied to five other kinds. (1) First comes the courage of the citizen-soldier; for this is most like true courage. Citizen-soldiers seem to face dangers because of the penalties imposed by the laws and the reproaches they would otherwise incur, and because of the honours they win by such action; and therefore those peoples seem to be bravest among whom cowards are held in dishonour and brave men in honour. This is the kind of courage that Homer depicts, e.g. in Diomede and in Hector:

> First will Polydamas be to heap reproach on me then;

and

> For Hector one day 'mid the Trojans shall utter
>   his vaulting harangue:
> 'Afraid was Tydeides, and fled from my face.'

This kind of courage is most like to that which we described earlier, because it is due to virtue; for it is due to shame and to desire of a noble object (i.e. honour) and avoidance of disgrace, which is ignoble. One might rank in the same class even those who are compelled by their rulers; but they are inferior, inasmuch as they do what they do not from shame but from fear, and to avoid not what is disgraceful but what is painful; for their masters compel them, as Hector does:

> But if I shall spy any dastard that cowers far from the fight,
> Vainly will such an one hope to escape from the dogs.

And those who give them their posts, and beat them if they retreat, do the same, and so do those who draw them up with trenches or something of the sort behind them; all of these apply compulsion. But one ought to be brave not under compulsion but because it is noble to be so.

(2) Experience with regard to particular facts is also thought to be courage; this is indeed the reason why Socrates thought courage was knowledge. Other people exhibit this quality in other dangers, and professional soldiers exhibit it in the dangers of war; for there seem to be many empty alarms in war, of which these have had the most comprehensive experience; therefore they seem brave, because the others do not know the nature of the facts. Again, their experience makes them most capable in attack and in defence, since they can use their arms and have the kind that are likely to be best both for attack and for defence; therefore they fight like armed men against unarmed or like trained athletes against amateurs; for in such contests too it is not the bravest men that fight best, but those who are strongest and have their bodies in the best condition. Professional soldiers turn cowards, however, when the danger puts too great a strain on them and they are inferior in numbers and equipment; for they are the first to fly, while citizen-forces die at their posts, as in fact happened at the temple of Hermes. For to the latter flight is disgraceful and death is preferable to safety on those terms; while the former from the very beginning faced the danger on the assumption that they were stronger, and when they know the facts they fly, fearing death more than disgrace; but the brave man is not that sort of person.

(3) Passion also is sometimes reckoned as courage; those who act from passion, like wild beasts rushing at those who have wounded them, are thought to be brave, because brave men also are passionate; for passion above all things is eager to rush on danger, and hence Homer's 'put strength into his passion' and 'aroused their spirit and passion' and 'hard he breathed panting' and 'his blood boiled'. For all such expressions seem to indicate the stirring and onset of passion. Now brave men act for honour's sake, but passion aids them; while wild beasts act under the influence of pain; for they attack because they have been wounded or because they are afraid, since if they are in a forest they do not come near one. Thus they are not brave because, driven by pain and passion, they rush on danger without foreseeing any of the perils, since at that rate even asses would be brave when they are

hungry; for blows will not drive them from their food; and lust also makes adulterers do many daring things. [Those creatures are not brave, then, which are driven on to danger by pain or passion.] The 'courage' that is due to passion seems to be the most natural, and to be courage if choice and motive be added.

Men, then, as well as beasts, suffer pain when they are angry, and are pleased when they exact their revenge; those who fight for these reasons, however, are pugnacious but not brave; for they do not act for honour's sake nor as the rule directs, but from strength of feeling; they have, however, something akin to courage.

(4) Nor are sanguine people brave; for they are confident in danger only because they have conquered often and against many foes. Yet they closely resemble brave men, because both are confident; but brave men are confident for the reasons stated earlier, while these are so because they think they are the strongest and can suffer nothing. (Drunken men also behave in this way; they become sanguine). When their adventures do not succeed, however, they run away; but it was the mark of a brave man to face things that are, and seem, fearful for a man, because it is noble to do so and disgraceful not to do so. Hence also it is thought the mark of a braver man to be fearless and undisturbed in sudden alarms than to be so in those that are foreseen; for it must have proceeded more from a state of character, because less from preparation; acts that are foreseen may be chosen by calculation and rule, but sudden actions must be in accordance with one's state of character.

(5) People who are ignorant of the danger also appear brave, and they are not far removed from those of a sanguine temper, but are inferior inasmuch as they have no self-reliance while these have. Hence also the sanguine hold their ground for a time; but those who have been deceived about the facts fly if they know or suspect that these are different from what they supposed, as happened to the Argives when they fell in with the Spartans and took them for Sicyonians.

9 We have, then, described the character both of brave men and of those who are thought to be brave.

Though courage is concerned with feelings of confidence and of fear, it is not concerned with both alike, but more with the things that inspire fear; for he who is undisturbed in face of these and bears himself as he should towards these is more truly brave than the man who does so towards the things that inspire confidence. It is for facing what is painful, then, as has been said, that men are called brave. Hence also courage involves pain, and is justly praised; for it is harder to face what is painful than to abstain from what is pleasant. Yet the end which courage sets before it would seem to be pleasant, but to be concealed by the attending circumstances, as happens also in athletic contests; for the end at which boxers aim is pleasant – the crown and the honours – but the blows they take are distressing to flesh and blood, and painful, and so is their whole exertion; and because the blows and the exertions are many the end, which is but small, appears to have nothing pleasant in it. And so, if the case of courage is similar, death and wounds will be painful to the brave man and against his will, but he will face them because it is noble to do so or because it is base not to do so. And the more he is possessed of virtue in its entirety and the happier he is, the more he will be pained at the thought of death; for life is best worth living for such a man, and he is knowingly losing the greatest goods, and this is painful. But he is none the less brave, and perhaps all the more so, because he chooses noble deeds of war at that cost. It is not the case, then, with all the virtues that the exercise of them is pleasant, except in so far as it attains its end. But it is quite possible that the best soldiers may be not men of this sort but those who are less brave but have no other good; for these are ready to face danger, and they sell their life for trifling gains.

So much, then, for courage; it is not difficult to grasp its nature in outline, at any rate, from what has been said.

After courage let us speak of temperance; for these seem to be the virtues of the irrational parts. We have said that temperance is a mean with regard to pleasures (for it is less, and not in the same way, concerned with pains); self-indulgence also is manifested in the same sphere. Now, therefore, let us determine with what sort of pleasures they are concerned. We may assume the distinction between bodily pleasures and those of the soul, such as love of honour and love of learning; for the lover of each of these delights in that of which he is a lover, the body being in no way affected, but rather the mind; but men who are concerned with such pleasures are called neither temperate nor self-indulgent. Nor, again, are those who are concerned with the other pleasures that are not bodily; for those who are fond of hearing and telling stories and who spend their days on anything that turns up are called gossips, but not self-indulgent, nor are those who are pained at the loss of money or of friends.

Temperance must be concerned with bodily pleasures, but not all even of these; for those who delight in objects of vision, such as colours and shapes and painting, are called neither temperate nor self-indulgent; yet it would seem possible to delight even in these either as one should or to excess or to a deficient degree.

And so too is it with objects of hearing; no one calls those who delight extravagantly in music or acting self-indulgent, nor those who do so as they ought temperate.

Nor do we apply these names to those who delight in odour, unless it be incidentally; we do not call those self-indulgent who delight in the odour of apples or roses or incense, but rather those who delight in the odour of unguents or of dainty dishes; for self-indulgent people delight in these because these remind them of the objects of their appetite. And one may see even other people, when they are hungry, delighting in the smell of food; but to delight in this kind of thing is the mark of the self-indulgent man; for these are objects of appetite to him.

Nor is there in animals other than man any pleasure connected with these senses, except incidentally. For dogs do not delight in the scent of hares, but in the eating of them, but the scent told them the hares were there; nor does the lion delight in the lowing of the ox, but in eating it; but he perceived by the lowing that it was near, and therefore appears to delight in the lowing; and similarly he does not delight because he sees 'a stag or a wild goat', but because he is going to make a meal of it. Temperance and self-indulgence, however, are concerned with the kind of pleasures that the other animals share in, which therefore appear slavish and brutish; these are touch and taste. But even of taste they appear to make little or no use; for the business of taste is the discriminating of flavours, which is done by wine-tasters and people who season dishes; but they hardly take pleasure in making these discriminations, or at least self-indulgent people do not, but in the actual enjoyment, which in all cases comes through touch, both in the case of food and in that of drink and in that of sexual intercourse. This is why a certain gourmand prayed that his throat might become longer than a crane's, implying that it was the contact that he took pleasure in. Thus the sense with which self-indulgence is connected is the most widely shared of the senses; and self-indulgence would seem to be justly a matter of reproach, because it attaches to us not as men but as animals. To delight in such things, then, and to love them above all others, is brutish. For even of the pleasures of touch the most liberal have been eliminated, e.g. those produced in the gymnasium by rubbing and by the consequent heat; for the contact characteristic of the self-indulgent man does not affect the whole body but only certain parts.

Of the appetites some seem to be common, others to be peculiar to individuals and acquired; e.g. the appetite for food is natural, since every one who is without it craves for food or drink, and sometimes for both, and for love also (as Homer says) if he is young and lusty; but not every one craves for this or that kind of nourishment or love, nor for the same things. Hence such craving appears to be our very own. Yet it has of course something natural about it; for different things are pleasant to different kinds of people, and some things are more pleasant to every one than chance objects. Now in the natural appetites few go wrong, and only in one direction, that of excess; for to eat or drink whatever offers itself till one is surfeited is to exceed the natural amount, since natural appetite is the replenishment of one's deficiency. Hence these people are called belly-gods, this implying that they fill their belly beyond what is right. It is people of entirely slavish character that become like this. But with regard to the pleasures peculiar to individuals many people go wrong and in many ways. For while the people who are 'fond of so and so' are so called because they delight either in the wrong things, or more than most people do, or in the wrong way, the self-indulgent exceed in all three ways; they both delight in some things that they ought not to delight in (since they are hateful), and if one ought to delight in some of the things they delight in, they do so more than one ought and than most men do.

Plainly, then, excess with regard to pleasures is self-indulgence and is culpable; with regard to pains one is not, as in the case of courage, called temperate for facing them or self-indulgent for not doing so, but the self-indulgent man is so called because he is pained more than he ought at not getting pleasant things (even his pain being caused by pleasure), and the temperate man is so called because he is not pained at the absence of what is pleasant and at his abstinence from it.

The self-indulgent man, then, craves for all pleasant things or those that are most pleasant, and is led by his appetite to choose these at the cost of everything else; hence he is pained both when he fails to get them and when he is merely craving for them (for appetite involves pain); but it seems absurd to be pained for the sake of pleasure. People who fall short with regard to pleasures and delight in them less than they should are hardly found; for such insensibility is not human. Even the other animals distinguish different kinds of food and enjoy some and not others; and if there is any one who finds nothing pleasant and nothing more attractive than anything else, he must be something quite different from a man; this sort of person has not received a name because he hardly occurs. The temperate man occupies a middle position with regard to these objects. For he neither enjoys the things that the self-indulgent man enjoys most – but rather dislikes them – nor in general the things that he should not, nor anything of this sort to excess, nor does he feel pain or craving when they are absent, or does so only to a moderate degree, and not more than he should, nor when he should not, and so on; but the things that, being pleasant, make for health or for good condition, he will desire moderately and as he should, and also other pleasant things if they are not hindrances to these ends, or contrary to what is noble, or beyond his means. For he who neglects these conditions loves such pleasures more than they are worth, but the temperate man is not that sort of person, but the sort of person that the right rule prescribes.

Self-indulgence is more like a voluntary state than cowardice. For the former is actuated by pleasure, the latter by pain, of which the one is to be chosen and the other to be avoided; and pain upsets and destroys the nature of the person who feels it, while pleasure does nothing of the sort. Therefore self-indulgence is more voluntary. Hence also it is more a matter of reproach; for it is easier to become accustomed to its objects, since there are many things of this sort in life, and the process of habituation to them is free from danger, while with fearful things the reverse is the case. But cowardice would seem to be voluntary in a different degree from its particular manifestations; for it is itself painless, but in these we are upset by pain, so that we even throw down our arms and disgrace ourselves in other ways; hence our acts are even thought to be done under compulsion. For the self-indulgent man, on the other hand, the particular acts are voluntary (for he does them with craving and desire), but the whole state is less so; for no one craves to be self-indulgent.

The name self-indulgence is applied also to childish faults; for they bear a certain resemblance to what we have been considering. Which is called after which, makes no difference to our present purpose; plainly, however, the later is called after the earlier. The transference of the name seems not a bad one; for that which desires what is base and which develops quickly ought to be kept in a chastened condition, and these characteristics belong above all to appetite and to the child, since children in fact live at the beck and call of appetite, and it is in them that the desire for what is pleasant is strongest. If, then, it is not going to be obedient and subject to the ruling principle, it will go to great lengths; for in an irrational being the desire for pleasure is insatiable even if it tries every source of gratification, and the exercise of appetite increases its innate force, and if appetites are strong and violent they even expel the power of calculation. Hence they should be moderate and few, and should in no way oppose the rational principle – and this is what we call an obedient and chastened state – and as the child should live according to the direction of his tutor, so the appetitive element should live according to rational principle. Hence the appetitive element in a temperate man should harmonize with the rational principle; for the noble is the mark at which both aim, and the temperate man craves for the things he ought, as he ought, and when he ought; and this is what rational principle directs.

Here we conclude our account of temperance.

Book V

chapters 1-2

end of chapter 5

chapters 7-10

1 WITH regard to justice and injustice we must consider (1) what kind of actions they are concerned with, (2) what sort of mean justice is, and (3) between what extremes the just act is intermediate. Our investigation shall follow the same course as the preceding discussions.

We see that all men mean by justice that kind of state of character which makes people disposed to do what is just and makes them act justly and wish for what is just; and similarly by injustice that state which makes them act unjustly and wish for what is unjust. Let us too, then, lay this down as a general basis. For the same is not true of the sciences and the faculties as of states of character. A faculty or a science which is one and the same is held to relate to contrary objects, but a state of character which is one of two contraries does *not* produce the contrary results; e.g. as a result of health we do not do what is the opposite of healthy, but only what is healthy; for we say a man walks healthily, when he walks as a healthy man would.

Now often one contrary state is recognized from its contrary, and often states are recognized from the subjects that exhibit them; for (A) if good condition is known, bad condition also becomes known, and (B) good condition is known from the things that are in good condition, and they from it. If good condition is firmness of flesh, it is necessary both that bad condition should be flabbiness of flesh and that the wholesome should be that which causes firmness in flesh. And it follows for the most part that if one contrary is ambiguous the other also will be ambiguous; e.g. if 'just' is so, that 'unjust' will be so too.

Now 'justice' and 'injustice' seem to be ambiguous, but because their different meanings approach near to one another the ambiguity escapes notice and is not obvious as it is, comparatively, when the meanings are far apart, e.g. (for here the difference in outward form is great) as the ambiguity in the use of *kleis* for the collar-bone of an animal and for that with which we lock a door. Let us take as a starting-point, then, the various meanings of 'an unjust man'. Both the lawless man and the grasping and unfair man are thought to be unjust, so that evidently both the law-abiding and the fair man will be just. The just, then, is the lawful and the fair, the unjust the unlawful and the unfair.

Since the unjust man is grasping, he must be concerned with goods – not all goods, but those with which prosperity and adversity have to do, which taken absolutely are always good, but for a particular person are not always good. Men pray for and pursue these things, but they should not. They should *pray* that the things that are good absolutely may also be good for them, but should *choose* the things that *are* good for them. The unjust man does not always choose the greater, but also the less – in the case of things bad absolutely; but because the lesser evil is itself thought to be in a sense good, and graspingness is directed at the good, therefore he is thought to be grasping. And he is unfair; for this contains and is common to both.

Since the lawless man was seen to be unjust and the law-abiding man just, evidently all lawful acts are in a sense just acts; for the acts laid down by the legislative art are lawful, and each of these, we say, is just. Now the laws in their enactments on all subjects aim at the common advantage either of all or of the best or of those who hold power, or something of the sort; so that in one sense we call those acts just that tend to produce and preserve happiness and its components for the political society. And the law bids us do both the acts of a brave man (e.g. not to desert our post nor take to flight nor throw away our arms), and those of a temperate man (e.g. not to commit adultery nor to gratify one's lust), and those of a good-tempered man (e.g. not to strike another nor to speak evil), and similarly with regard to the other virtues and forms of wickedness, commanding some acts and forbidding others; and the rightly-framed law does this rightly, and the hastily conceived one less well.

This form of justice, then, is complete virtue, although not

Book V.1

without qualification but in relation to our neighbour. And therefore justice is often thought to be the greatest of virtues, and 'neither evening nor morning star' is so wonderful; and proverbially 'in justice is every virtue comprehended'. And it is complete virtue in its fullest sense, because it is the actual exercise of complete virtue. It is complete because he who possesses it can exercise his virtue not only in himself but towards his neighbour also; for many men can exercise virtue in their own affairs, but not in their relations to their neighbour. This is why the saying of Bias is thought to be true, that 'rule will show the man'; for a ruler is necessarily in relation to other men and a member of a society. For this same reason justice, alone of the virtues, is thought to be 'another's good', because it is related to our neighbour; for it does what is advantageous to another, either a ruler or a copartner. Now the worst man is he who exercises his wickedness both towards himself and towards his friends, and the best man is not he who exercises his virtue towards himself but he who exercises it towards another; for this is a difficult task. Justice in this sense, then, is nor part of virtue but virtue entire, nor is the contrary injustice a part of vice but vice entire. What the difference is between virtue and justice in this sense is plain from what we have said; they are the same but their essence is not the same; what, as a relation to one's neighbour, is justice is, as a certain kind of state without qualification, virtue.

2 But at all events what we are investigating is the justice which is a *part* of virtue; for there is a justice of this kind, as we maintain. Similarly it is with injustice in the particular sense that we are concerned.

That there is such a thing is indicated by the fact that while the man who exhibits in action the other forms of wickedness acts wrongly indeed, but not graspingly (e.g. the man who throws away his shield through cowardice or speaks harshly through bad temper or fails to help a friend with money through meanness), when a man acts graspingly he often exhibits none of these vices, – no, nor all together, but certainly wickedness of some kind (for we blame him) and injustice. There is, then, another kind of injustice which is a part of injustice in the wide sense, and a use of the word 'unjust' which answers to a part of what is unjust in the wide sense of 'contrary to the law'. Again, if one man commits adultery for the sake of gain and makes money by it, while another does so at the bidding of appetite though he loses money and is penalized for it, the latter would be held to be self-indulgent rather than grasping, but the former is unjust, but not self-indulgent; evidently, therefore, he is unjust by reason of his making gain by his act. Again, all other unjust acts are ascribed invariably to some particular kind of wickedness, e.g. adultery to self-indulgence, the desertion of a comrade in battle to cowardice, physical violence to anger; but if a man makes gain, his action is ascribed to no form of wickedness but injustice. Evidently, therefore, there is apart from injustice in the wide sense another, 'particular', injustice which shares the name and nature of the first, because its definition falls within the same genus; for the significance of both consists in a relation to one's neighbour, but the one is concerned with honour or money or safety — or that which includes all these, if we had a single name for it — and its motive is the pleasure that arises from gain; while the other is concerned with all the objects with which the good man is concerned.

It is clear, then, that there is more than one kind of justice, and that there is one which is distinct from virtue entire; we must try to grasp its genus and differentia.

The unjust has been divided into the unlawful and the unfair, and the just into the lawful and the fair. To the unlawful answers the afore-mentioned sense of injustice. But since the unfair and the unlawful are not the same, but are different as a part is from its whole (for all that is unfair is unlawful, but not all that is unlawful is unfair), the unjust and injustice in the sense of the unfair are not the same as but different from the former kind, as part from whole; for injustice in this sense is a part of injustice in the wide sense, and similarly justice in the one sense of justice in the other. Therefore we must speak also about particular justice and particular injustice, and similarly about the just and the unjust. The justice, then, which answers to the whole of virtue, and the corresponding injustice, one being the exercise of virtue as a whole, and the other that of vice as a whole, towards one's neighbour, we may leave on one side. And how the meanings of 'just' and 'unjust'

Book V.2   1130b

which answer to these are to be distinguished is evident; for practically the majority of the acts commanded by the law are those which are prescribed from the point of view of virtue taken as a whole; for the law bids us practise every virtue and forbids us to practise any vice. And the things that tend to produce virtue taken as a whole are those of the acts prescribed by the law which have been prescribed with a view to education for the common good. But with regard to the education of the individual as such, which makes him without qualification a good *man*, we must determine later whether this is the function of the political art or of another; for perhaps it is not the same to be a good man and a good citizen of any state taken at random.

Of particular justice and that which is just in the corresponding sense, (A) one kind is that which is manifested in distributions of honour or money or the other things that fall to be divided among those who have a share in the constitution (for in these it is possible for one man to have a share either unequal or equal to that of another), and (B) one is that which plays a rectifying part in transaction between man and man. Of this there are two divisions; of transactions (1) some are voluntary and (2) others involuntary – voluntary such transactions as sale, purchase, loan for consumption, pledging, loan for use, depositing, letting (they are called voluntary because the origin of these transactions is voluntary), while of the involuntary (a) some are clandestine, such as theft, adultery, poisoning, procuring, enticement of slaves, assassination, false witness, and (b) others are violent, such as assault, imprisonment, murder, robbery with violence, mutilation, abuse, insult.

We have now defined the unjust and the just. These having been marked off from each other, it is plain that just action is intermediate between acting unjustly and being unjustly treated; for the one is to have too much and the other to have too little. Justice is a kind of mean, but not in the same way as the other virtues, but because it relates to an intermediate amount, while injustice relates to the extremes. And justice is that in virtue of which the just man is said to be a doer, by choice, of that which is just, and one who will distribute either between himself and another or between two others not so as to give more of what is desirable to himself and less to his neighbour (and conversely with what is harmful), but so as to give what is equal in accordance with proportion; and similarly in distributing between two other persons. Injustice on the other hand is similarly related to the unjust, which is excess and defect, contrary to proportion, of the useful or hurtful. For which reason injustice is excess and defect, viz. because it is productive of excess and defect – in one's own case excess of what is in its own nature useful and defect of what is hurtful, while in the case of others it is as a whole like what it is in one's own case, but proportion may be violated in either direction. In the unjust act to have too little is to be unjustly treated; to have too much is to act unjustly.

Let this be taken as our account of the nature of justice and injustice, and similarly of the just and the unjust in general.

Of political justice part is natural, part legal, – natural, that which everywhere has the same force and does not exist by people's thinking this or that; legal, that which is originally indifferent, but when it has been laid down is not indifferent, e.g. that a prisoner's ransom shall be a mina, or that a goat and not two sheep shall be sacrificed, and again all the laws that are passed for particular cases, e.g. that sacrifice shall be made in honour of Brasidas, and the provisions of decrees. Now some think that all justice is of this sort, because that which is by nature is unchangeable and has everywhere the same force (as fire burns both here and in Persia), while they see change in the things recognized as just. This, however, is not true in this unqualified way, but is true in a sense; or rather, with the gods it is perhaps not true at all, while with us there is something that is just even by nature, yet all of it is changeable; but still some is by nature, some not by nature. It is evident which sort of thing, among things capable of being otherwise, is by nature, and which is not but is legal and conventional, assuming that both are equally changeable. And in all other things the same distinction will apply; by nature the right hand is stronger, yet it is possible that all men should come to be ambidextrous. The things which are just by virtue of convention and expediency are like measures; for wine and corn measures are not everywhere equal, but larger in wholesale and smaller in retail

Book V.7

markets. Similarly, the things which are just not by nature but by human enactment are not everywhere the same, since constitutions also are not the same, though there is but one which is everywhere by nature the best.

Of things just and lawful each is related as the universal to its particulars; for the things that are done are many, but of *them* each is one, since it is universal.

There is a difference between the act of injustice and what is unjust, and between the act of justice and what is just; for a thing is unjust by nature or by enactment; and this very thing, when it has been done, is an act of injustice, but before it is done is not yet that but is unjust. So, too, with an act of justice (though the general term is rather 'just action', and 'act of justice' is applied to the correction of the act of injustice).

Each of these must later be examined separately with regard to the nature and number of its species and the nature of the things with which it is concerned.

8 Acts just and unjust being as we have described them, a man acts unjustly or justly whenever he does such acts voluntarily; when involuntarily, he acts neither unjustly nor justly except in an incidental way; for he does things which happen to be just or unjust. Whether an act is or is not one of injustice (or of justice) is determined by its voluntariness or involuntariness; for when it is voluntary it is blamed, and at the same time is then an act of injustice; so that there will be things that are unjust but not yet acts of injustice, if voluntariness be not present as well. By the voluntary I mean, as has been said before, any of the things in a man's own power which he does with knowledge, i.e. not in ignorance either of the person acted on or of the instrument used or of the end that will be attained (e.g. whom he is striking, with what, and to what end), each such act being done not incidentally nor under compulsion (e.g. if A takes B's hand and therewith strikes C, B does not act voluntarily; for the act was not in his own power). The person struck may be the striker's father, and the striker may know that it is a man or one of the persons present, but not know that it is his father; a similar distinction may be made in the case of the end, and with regard to the whole action. Therefore that

which is done in ignorance, or though not done in ignorance is not in the agent's power, or is done under compulsion, is involuntary (for many natural processes too we knowingly perform or undergo, none of which is either voluntary or involuntary; e.g. growing old or dying). But in the case of unjust and just acts alike the injustice or justice may be only incidental; for a man might return a deposit unwillingly and from fear, and then he must not be said either to do what is just or to act justly, except in an incidental way. Similarly the man who under compulsion and unwillingly fails to return the deposit must be said to act unjustly, and to do what is unjust, only incidentally. Of voluntary acts we do some by choice, others not by choice; by choice those which we do after deliberation, not by choice those which we do without previous deliberation. Thus there are three kinds of injury in transactions between man and man; those done in ignorance are *mistakes* when the person acted on, the act, the instrument, or the end that will be attained is other than the agent supposed; the agent thought either that he was not hitting any one or that he was not hitting with this missile or not hitting this person or to this end, but a result followed other than that which he thought likely (e.g. he threw not with intent to wound but only to prick), or the person hit or the missile was other than he supposed. Now when (1) the injury takes place contrary to reasonable expectation, it is a *misadventure*. When (2) it is not contrary to reasonable expectation, but does not imply vice, it is a *mistake* (for a man makes a mistake when the fault originates in him, but is the victim of accident when the origin lies outside him). When (3) he acts with knowledge but not after deliberation, it is an *act of injustice* – e.g. the acts due to anger or to other passions necessary or natural to man; for when men do such harmful and mistaken acts they act unjustly, and the acts are acts of injustice, but this does not imply that the doers are unjust or wicked; for the injury is not due to vice. But when (4) a man acts from choice, he is an *unjust man* and a vicious man.

Hence acts proceeding from anger are rightly judged not to be done of malice aforethought; for it is not the man who acts in anger but he who enraged him that starts the mischief. Again, the matter in dispute is not whether the thing happened or not, but its justice; for it is apparent injustice that occasions rage. For they do not dispute about the occurrence of the act – as in commercial transactions where one of the two parties *must* be vicious – unless they do so owing to forgetfulness; but, agreeing about the fact, they dispute on which side justice lies (whereas a man who has deliberately injured another cannot help knowing that he has done so), so that the one thinks he is being treated unjustly and the other disagrees.

But if a man harms another by choice, he acts unjustly; and *these* are the acts of injustice which imply that the doer is an unjust man, provided that the act violates proportion or equality. Similarly, a man *is just* when he acts justly be choice; but he *acts justly* if he merely acts voluntarily.

Of involuntary acts some are excusable, others not. For the mistakes which men make not only in ignorance but also from ignorance are excusable, while those which men do not from ignorance but (though they do them *in* ignorance) owing to a passion which is neither natural nor such as man is liable to, are not excusable.

9 Assuming that we have sufficiently defined the suffering and doing of injustice, it may be asked (1) whether the truth is expressed in Euripides' paradoxical words:

> 'I slew my mother, that's my tale in brief.'
> 'Were you both willing, or unwilling both?'

Is it truly possible to be willingly treated unjustly, or is all suffering of injustice on the contrary involuntary, as all unjust action is voluntary? And is all suffering of injustice of the latter kind or else all of the former, or is it sometimes voluntary, sometimes involuntary? So, too, with the case of being justly treated; all just action is voluntary, so that it is reasonable that there should be a similar opposition in either case – that both being unjustly and being justly treated should be either alike voluntary or alike involuntary. But it would be thought paradoxical even in the case of being justly treated, if it were always voluntary; for some are unwillingly treated justly. (2) One might raise this question also, whether every one who has suffered what is unjust is being unjustly treated, or on the other hand it is with suffering as with acting. In action and in passivity alike it is possible to partake of justice incidentally, and similarly (it is plain) of injustice; for to do what is unjust is not the same as to act unjustly, nor to suffer what is unjust as to be treated unjustly, and similarly in the case of acting justly and being treated justly; for it is impossible to be unjustly treated if the other does not act unjustly, or justly treated unless he acts justly. Now if to act unjustly is simply to harm some one voluntarily, and 'voluntarily' means 'knowing the person acted on, the instrument, and the manner of one's acting', and the incontinent man voluntarily harms himself, not only will he voluntarily be unjustly treated but it will be possible to treat oneself unjustly. (This also is one of the questions in doubt, whether a man can treat himself unjustly.) Again, a man may voluntarily, owing to incontinence, be harmed by another who acts voluntarily, so that it would be possible to be voluntarily treated unjustly. Or is our definition incorrect; must we to 'harming another, with knowledge both of the person acted on, of the instrument, and of the manner' add 'contrary to the wish of the person acted on'? Then a man may be voluntarily harmed and voluntarily suffer what is unjust, but no one is voluntarily treated unjustly; for no one wishes to be unjustly treated, not even the incontinent man. He acts contrary to his wish; for no one *wishes* for what he does not think to be good, but the incontinent man does *do* things that he does not think he ought to do. Again, one who gives what is his own, as Homer says Glaucus gave Diomede

> Armour of gold for brazen, the price of a hundred beeves for nine,

is not unjustly treated; for though to give is in his power, to be unjustly treated is not, but there must be some one to treat him unjustly. It is plain, then, that being unjustly treated is not voluntary.

Of the questions we intended to discuss two still remain for discussion; (3) whether it is the man who has assigned to another more than his share that acts unjustly, or he who has the excessive share, and (4) whether it is possible to treat oneself unjustly. The questions are connected; for if the former alternative is possible and the distributor acts unjustly and not the man who has the excessive share; then if a man assigns more to another than to himself, knowingly and voluntarily, he treats himself unjustly; which is what modest people seem to do, since the virtuous man tends to take less than his share. Or does this statement too need qualification? For (*a*) he perhaps gets more than his share of some other good, e.g. of honour or of intrinsic nobility. (*b*) The question is solved by applying the distinction we applied to unjust action; for he suffers nothing contrary to his own wish, so that he is not unjustly treated as far as this goes, but at most only suffers harm.

It is plain too that the distributor acts unjustly, but not always the man who has the excessive share; for it is not he to whom what is unjust appertains that acts unjustly, but he to whom it appertains to do the unjust act voluntarily, i.e. the person in whom lies the origin of the action, and this lies in the distributor, not in the receiver. Again, since the word 'do' is ambiguous, and there is a sense in which lifeless things, or a hand, or a servant who obeys an order, may be said to slay, he who gets an excessive share does not act unjustly, though he 'does' what is unjust.

Again, if the distributor gave his judgement in ignorance, he does not act unjustly in respect of legal justice, and his judgement is not unjust in this sense, but in a sense it *is* unjust (for legal justice and primordial justice are different); but if with knowledge he judged unjustly, he is himself aiming at an excessive share either of gratitude or of revenge. As much, then, as if he were to share in the plunder, the man who has judged unjustly for these reasons has got too much; the fact that what he gets is different from what he distributes makes no difference, for even if he awards land with a view to sharing in the plunder he gets not land but money.

Men think that acting unjustly is in their power, and therefore that being just is easy. But it is not; to lie with one's neighbour's wife, to wound another, to deliver a bribe, is easy and in our power, but to do these things as a result of a certain state of character is neither easy nor in our power. Similarly to know what is just and what is unjust requires, men think, no great wisdom, because it is not hard to understand the matters dealt with by the laws (though these are not the things that are just, except incidentally); but how actions must be done and distributions effected in order to be just, to know *this* is a greater achievement than knowing what is good for the health; though even there, while it is easy to know that honey, wine, hellebore, cautery, and the use of the knife are so, to know how, to whom, and when these should be applied with a view to producing health, is no less an achievement than that of being a physician. Again, for this very reason men think that acting unjustly is characteristic of the just man no less than of the unjust, because he would be not less but even more capable of doing each of these unjust acts; for he could lie with a woman or wound a neighbour; and the brave man could throw away his shield and turn to flight in this direction or in that. But to play the coward or to act unjustly consists not in doing these things, except incidentally, but in doing them as the result of a certain state of character, just as to practise medicine and healing consists not in applying or not applying the knife, in using or not using medicines, but in doing so in a certain way.

Just acts occur between people who participate in things good in themselves and can have too much or too little of them; for some beings (e.g. presumably the gods) cannot have too much of them, and to others, those who are incurably bad, not even the smallest share in them is beneficial but all such goods are harmful, while to others they are beneficial up to a point; therefore justice is essentially something human.

Our next subject is equity and the equitable and their respective relations to justice and the just. For on examination they appear to be neither absolutely the same nor generically different; and while we sometimes praise what is equitable and the equitable man (so that we apply the name by way of praise even to instances of the other virtues, instead of 'good', meaning by 'more equitable' that a thing is better), at other times, when we reason it out, it seems strange if the equitable, being something different from the just, is yet praiseworthy; for either the just or the equitable is not good, if they are different; or, if both are good, they are the same.

These, then, are pretty much the considerations that give rise to the problem about the equitable; they are all in a sense correct and not opposed to one another; for the equitable, though it is better than one kind of justice, yet is just, and it is not as being a different class of thing that it is better than the just. The same thing, then, is just and equitable, and while both are good the equitable is superior. What creates the problem is that the equitable is just, but not the legally just but a correction of legal justice. The reason is that all law is universal but about some things it is not possible to make a universal statement which shall be correct. In those cases, then, in which it is necessary to speak universally, but not possible to do so correctly, the law takes the usual case, though it is not ignorant of the possibility of error. And it is none the less correct; for the error is not in the law nor in the legislator but in the nature of the thing, since the matter of practical affairs is of this kind from the start. When the law speaks universally, then, and a case arises on it which is not covered by the universal statement, then it is right, where the legislator fails us and has erred by over-simplicity, to correct the omission — to say what the legislator himself would have said had he been present, and would have put into this law if he had known. Hence the equitable is just, and better than one kind of justice — not better than absolute justice but better than the error that arises from the absoluteness of the statement. And this is the nature of the equitable, a correction of law where it is defective owing to its universality. In fact this is the reason why all things are not determined by law, viz. that about some things it is impossible to lay down a law, so that a decree is needed. For when the thing is indefinite the rule also is indefinite, like the leaden rule used in making the Lesbian moulding; the rule adapts itself to the shape of the stone and is not rigid, and so too the decree is adapted to the facts.

It is plain, then, what the equitable is, and that it is just and is better than one kind of justice. It is evident also from this who the equitable man is; the man who chooses and does such acts, and is no stickler for his rights in a bad sense but tends to take less than his share though he has the law on his side, is equitable, and this state of character is equity, which is a sort of justice and not a different state of character.

Book VI

1 SINCE we have previously said that one ought to choose that which is intermediate, not the excess nor the defect, and that the intermediate is determined by the dictates of the right rule, let us discuss the nature of these dictates. In all the states of character we have mentioned, as in all other matters, there is a mark to which the man who has the rule looks, and heightens or relaxes his activity accordingly, and there is a standard which determines the mean states which we say are intermediate between excess and defect, being in accordance with the right rule. But such a statement, though true, is by no means clear; for not only here but in all other pursuits which are objects of knowledge it is indeed true to say that we must not exert ourselves nor relax our efforts too much nor too little, but to an intermediate extent and as the right rule dictates; but if a man had only this knowledge he would be none the wiser – e.g. we should not know what sort of medicines to apply to our body if some one were to say 'all those which the medical art prescribes, and which agree with the practice of one who possesses the art'. Hence it is necessary with regard to the states of the soul also not only that this true statement should be made, but also that it should be determined what is the right rule and what is the standard that fixes it.

We divided the virtues of the soul and said that some are virtues of character and others of intellect. Now we have discussed in detail the moral virtues; with regard to the others let us express our view as follows, beginning with some remarks about the soul. We said before that there are two parts of the soul – that which grasps a rule or rational principle, and the irrational; let us now draw a similar distinction within the part which grasps a rational principle. And let it be assumed that there are two parts which grasp a rational principle – one by which we contemplate the kind of things whose originative causes are invariable, and one by which we contemplate variable things; for where objects differ in kind the part of the soul answering to each of the two is different in kind, since it is in virtue of a certain likeness and kinship with their objects that they have the knowledge they have. Let one of these parts be called the scientific and the other the calculative; for to deliberate and to calculate are the same thing, but no one deliberates about the invariable. Therefore the calculative is one part of the faculty which grasps a rational principle. We must, then, learn what is the best state of each of these two parts; for this is the virtue of each.

The virtue of a thing is relative to its proper work. Now there are three things in the soul which control action and truth — sensation, reason, desire.

Of these sensation originates no action; this is plain from the fact that the lower animals have sensation but no share in action.

What affirmation and negation are in thinking, pursuit and avoidance are in desire; so that since moral virtue is a state of character concerned with choice, and choice is deliberate desire, therefore both the reasoning must be true and the desire right, if the choice is to be good, and the latter must pursue just what the former asserts. Now this kind of intellect and of truth is practical; of the intellect which is contemplative, not practical nor productive, the good and the bad state are truth and falsity respectively (for this is the work of everything intellectual); while of the part which is practical and intellectual the good state is truth in agreement with right desire.

The origin of action — its efficient, not its final cause — is choice, and that of choice is desire and reasoning with a view to an end. This is why choice cannot exist either without reason and intellect or without a moral state; for good action and its opposite cannot exist without a combination of intellect and character. Intellect itself, however, moves nothing, but only the intellect which aims at an end and is practical; for this rules the productive intellect as well, since every one who makes makes for an end, and that which is made is not an end in the unqualified sense (but only an end in a particular relation, and the end of a particular operation) — only that which is *done* is that; for good action is an end, and desire aims at this. Hence choice is either desiderative reason or ratiocinative desire, and such an origin of action is a man. (It is to be noted that nothing that is past is an object of choice, e.g. no one chooses to have sacked Troy; for no one *deliberates* about the past, but about what is future and capable of being otherwise, while what is past is not capable of not having taken place; hence Agathon is right in saying

> For this alone is lacking even to God,
> To make undone things that have once been done.)

The work of both the intellectual parts, then, is truth. Therefore the states that are most strictly those in respect of which each of these parts will reach truth are the virtues of the two parts.

3 Let us begin, then, from the beginning, and discuss these states once more. Let it be assumed that the states by virtue of which the soul possesses truth by way of affirmation or denial are five in number, i.e. art, scientific knowledge, practical wisdom, philosophic wisdom, intuitive reason; we do not include judgement and opinion because in these we may be mistaken.

Now what *scientific knowledge* is, if we are to speak exactly and not follow mere similarities, is plain from what follows. We all suppose that what we know is not even capable of being otherwise; of things capable of being otherwise we do not know, when they have passed outside our observation, whether they exist or not. Therefore the object of scientific knowledge is of necessity. Therefore it is eternal; for things that are of necessity in the unqualified sense are all eternal; and things that are eternal are ungenerated and imperishable. Again, every science is thought to be capable of being taught, and its object of being learned. And all teaching starts from what is already known, as we maintain in the *Analytics* also; for it proceeds sometimes through induction and sometimes syllogism. Now induction is the starting-point which knowledge even of the universal presupposes, while syllogism proceeds *from* universals. There are therefore starting-points from which syllogism proceeds, which are not reached by syllogism; it is therefore by induction that they are acquired. Scientific knowledge is, then, a state of capacity to demonstrate, and has the other limiting characteristics which we specify in the *Analytics*; for it is when a man believes in a certain way and the starting-points are known to him that he has scientific knowledge, since if they are not better known to him than the conclusion he will have his knowledge only incidentally.

Let this, then, be taken as our account of scientific knowledge.

In the variable are included both things made and things done; making and acting are different (for their nature we treat even the discussions outside our school as reliable); so that the reasoned state of capacity to act is different from the reasoned state of capacity to make. Hence too they are not included one in the other; for neither is acting making nor is making acting. Now since architecture is an art and is essentially a reasoned state of capacity to make, and there is neither any art that is not such a state nor any such state that is not an art, *art* is identical with a state of capacity to make, involving a true course of reasoning. All art is concerned with coming into being, i.e. with contriving and considering how something may come into being which is capable of either being or not being, and whose origin is in the maker and not in the thing made; for art is concerned neither with things that are, or come into being, by necessity, nor with things that do so in accordance with nature (since these have their origin in themselves). Making and acting being different, art must be a matter of making, not of acting. And in a sense chance and art are concerned with the same objects; as Agathon says, 'art loves chance and chance loves art'. Art, then, as has been said, is a state concerned with making, involving a true course of reasoning, and lack of art on the contrary is a state concerned with making, involving a false course of reasoning; both are concerned with the variable.

Regarding *practical wisdom* we shall get at the truth by considering who are the persons we credit with it. Now it is thought to be a mark of a man of practical wisdom to be able to deliberate well about what is good and expedient for himself, not in some particular respect, e.g. about what sorts of thing conduce to health or to strength, but about what sorts of thing conduce to the good life in general. This is shown by the fact that we credit men with practical wisdom in some particular respect when they have calculated well with a view to some good end which is one of those that are not the object of any art. It follows that in the general sense also the man who is capable of deliberating has practical wisdom. Now no one deliberates about things that are invariable, nor about things that it is impossible for him to do. Therefore, since scientific knowledge involves demonstration, but there is no demonstration of things whose first principles are variable (for all such things might actually be otherwise), and since it is impossible to deliberate about things that are of necessity, practical wisdom cannot be scientific knowledge nor art; not science because that which can be done is capable of being otherwise, not art because action and making are different kinds of thing. The remaining alternative, then, is that it is a true and reasoned state of capacity to act with regard to the things that are good or bad for man. For while making has an end other than itself, action cannot; for good action itself is its end. It is for this reason that we think Pericles and men like him have practical wisdom, viz. because they can see what is good for themselves and what is good for men in general; we consider that those can do this who are good at managing households or states. (This is why we call temperance, *sōphrosunē*, by this name; we imply that it preserves one's practical wisdom, *sōzousa tēn phronēsin*. Now what it preserves is a judgement of the kind we have described. For it is not any and every judgement that pleasant and painful objects destroy and pervert, e.g. the judgement that the triangle has or has not its angles equal to two right angles, but only judgements about what is to be done. For the originating causes of the things that are done consist in the end at which they are aimed; but the man who has been ruined by pleasure or pain forthwith fails to see any such originating cause – to see that for the sake of this or because of this he ought to choose and do whatever he chooses and does; for vice is destructive of the originating cause of action.)

Practical wisdom, then, must be a reasoned and true state of capacity to act with regard to human goods. But further, while there is such a thing as excellence in art, there is no such thing as excellence in practical wisdom; and in art he who errs willingly is preferable, but in practical wisdom, as in the virtues, he is the reverse. Plainly, then, practical wisdom is a virtue and not an art.

There being two parts of the soul that can follow a course of reasoning, it must be the virtue of one of the two, i.e. of that part which forms opinions; for opinion is about the variable and so is practical wisdom. But yet it is not only a reasoned state; this is shown by the fact that a state of that sort may be forgotten but practical wisdom cannot.

Scientific knowledge is judgement about things that are universal and necessary, and the conclusions of demonstration, and all scientific knowledge, follow from first principles (for scientific knowledge involves proof). This being so, the first principle from which what is scientifically known follows cannot be an object of scientific knowledge, of art, or of practical wisdom; for that which can be scientifically known can be demonstrated, and art and practical wisdom deal with things that are variable. Nor are these first principles the objects of philosophic wisdom, for it is a mark of the philosopher to have *demonstration* about some things. If, then, the states of mind by which we have truth and are never deceived about things invariable or even variable are scientific knowledge, practical wisdom, philosophic wisdom, and intuitive reason, and it cannot be any of the three (i.e. practical wisdom, scientific knowledge, or philosophic wisdom), the remaining alternative is that it is *intuitive reason* that grasps the first principles.

6

Wisdom (1) in the arts we ascribe to their most finished exponents, e.g. to Phidias as a sculptor and to Polyclitus as a maker of portrait-statues, and here we mean nothing by wisdom except excellence in art; but (2) we think that some people are wise in general, not in some particular field or in any other limited respect, as Homer says in the *Margites*,

7

Him did the gods make neither a digger nor yet a ploughman
Nor wise in anything else.

Therefore wisdom must plainly be the most finished of the forms of knowledge. It follows that the wise man must not only know what follows from the first principles, but must also possess truth about the first principles. Therefore wisdom must be intuitive reason combined with scientific knowledge – scientific knowledge of the highest objects which has received as it were its proper completion.

Of the highest objects, we say; for it would be strange to think that the art of politics, or practical wisdom, is the best knowledge, since man is not the best thing in the world. Now if what is healthy or good is different for men and for fishes, but what is white or straight is always the same, any one would say that what is wise is the same but what is practically wise is different; for it is to that which observes well the various matters concerning itself that one ascribes practical wisdom, and it is to this that one will entrust such matters. This is why we say that some even of the lower animals have practical wisdom, viz. those which are found to have a power of foresight with regard to their own life. It is evident also that philosophic wisdom and the art of politics cannot be the same; for if the state of mind concerned with a man's own interests is to be called philosophic wisdom, there will be many philosophic wisdoms; there will not be one concerned with the good of all animals (any more than there is one art of medicine for all existing things), but a different philosophic wisdom about the good of each species.

But if the argument be that man is the best of the animals, this makes no difference; for there are other things much more divine in their nature even than man, e.g., most conspicuously, the bodies of which the heavens are framed. From what has been said it is plain, then, that philosophic wisdom is scientific knowledge, combined with intuitive reason, of the things that are highest by nature. This is why we say Anaxagoras, Thales, and men like them have philosophic but not practical wisdom, when we see them ignorant of what is to their own advantage, and why we say that they know things that are remarkable, admirable, difficult, and divine, but useless; viz. because it is not human goods that they seek.

Practical wisdom on the other hand is concerned with things human and things about which it is possible to deliberate; for we say this is above all the work of the man of practical wisdom, to deliberate well, but no one deliberates about things invariable, nor about things which have not an end, and that a good that can be brought about by action. The man who is without qualification good at deliberating is the man who is capable of aiming in accordance with calculation at the best for man of things attainable by action. Nor is practical wisdom concerned with universals only – it must also recognize the particulars; for it is practical, and practice is concerned with particulars. This is why in other fields too some who do not *know* are more practical than others who do – they are *experienced*. For if a man knew that light meats are digestible and wholesome, but did not know which sorts of meat are light, he would not produce health, but the man who knows that chicken is wholesome is more likely to produce health.

Now practical wisdom is concerned with action; therefore one should have both forms of it, or the latter in preference to the former. But here too there must be a controlling kind.

Political wisdom and practical wisdom are the same state of mind, but their essence is not the same. Of the wisdom concerned with the city, the practical wisdom which plays a controlling part is legislative wisdom, while that which is related to this as particulars to their universal is known by the general name 'political wisdom'; this has to do with action and deliberation, for a decree is a thing to be carried out in the form of an individual act. This is why the exponents of this art are alone said to 'take part in politics'; for these alone 'do things' as manual labourers 'do things'.

Practical wisdom also is identified especially with that form of it which is concerned with a man himself – with the individual; and this is known by the general name 'practical wisdom'; of the other kinds one is called household management, another legislation, the third politics, and of the latter one part is called deliberative and the other judicial. Now knowing what is good for oneself will be one kind of knowledge, but it is very different from the other kinds; and the man who knows and concerns himself with his own interests is thought to have practical wisdom, while politicians are thought to be busybodies; hence the words of Euripides,

> But how could I be wise, who might at ease,
> Numbered among the army's multitude,
> Have had an equal share? . . .
> For those who aim too high and do too much . . . .

Those who think thus seek their own good, and consider that one ought to do so. From this opinion, then, has come the view that such men have practical wisdom; yet perhaps one's own good cannot exist without household management, nor without a form of government. Further, how one should order one's own affairs is not clear and needs inquiry.

What has been said is confirmed by the fact that while young men become geometricians and mathematicians and wise in matters like these, it is thought that a young man of practical wisdom cannot be found. The cause is that such wisdom is concerned not only with universals but with particulars, which become familiar from experience, but a young man has no experience, for it is length of time that gives experience; indeed one might ask this question too, why a boy may become a mathematician, but not a philosopher or a physicist. Is it because the objects of mathematics exist by abstraction, while the first principles of these other subjects come from experience, and because young men have no conviction about the latter but merely use the proper language, while the essence of mathematical objects is plain enough to them?

Further, error in deliberation may be either about the universal or about the particular; we may fail to know either that all water that weighs heavy is bad, or that this particular water weighs heavy.

That practical wisdom is not scientific knowledge is evident; for it is, as has been said, concerned with the ultimate particular fact, since the thing to be done is of this nature. It is opposed, then, to intuitive reason; for intuitive reason is of the terms of which no account can be given, while practical wisdom is concerned with the ultimate particular, which is the object not of scientific knowledge but of perception – not the perception of qualities peculiar to one sense but a perception akin to that by which we perceive that the particular figure before us is a triangle; for in that direction as well there will be a limit. But this is rather perception than practical wisdom, though it is another kind of perception than that of the qualities peculiar to each sense.

9 There is a difference between inquiry and deliberation; for deliberation is a particular kind of inquiry. We must grasp the nature of excellence in deliberation as well – whether it is a form of scientific knowledge, or opinion, or skill in conjecture, or some other kind of thing. *Scientific knowledge* it is not; for men do not inquire about the things they know about, but good deliberation is a kind of deliberation, and he who deliberates inquires and calculates. Nor is it *skill in conjecture*; for this both involves no reasoning and is something that is quick in its operation, while men deliberate a long time, and they say that one should carry out quickly the conclusions of one's deliberation, but should deliberate slowly. Again, *readiness of mind* is different from excellence in deliberation; it is a sort of skill in conjecture. Nor again is excellence in deliberation *opinion* of any sort. But since the man who deliberates badly makes a mistake, while he who deliberates well does so correctly, excellence in deliberation is clearly a kind of correctness, but neither of knowledge nor of opinion; for there is no such thing as correctness of knowledge (since there is no such thing as error of knowledge), and correctness of opinion is truth; and at the same time everything that is an object of opinion is already determined. But again excellence in deliberation involves reasoning. The remaining alternative, then, is that it is *correctness of thinking*; for this is not yet assertion, since, while even opinion is not inquiry but has reached the stage of assertion, the man who is deliberating, whether he does so well or ill, is searching for something and calculating.

But excellence in deliberation is a certain correctness of deliberation; hence we must first inquire what deliberation is and what it is about. And, there being more than one kind of correctness, plainly excellence in deliberation is not any and every kind; for (1) the incontinent man and the bad man, if he is clever, will reach as a result of his calculation what he sets before himself, so that he will have deliberated correctly, but he will have got for himself a great evil. Now to have deliberated well is thought to be a good thing; for it is this kind of correctness of deliberation that is excellence in deliberation, viz. that which tends to attain what is good. But (2) it is possible to attain even good by a false syllogism, and to attain what one ought to do but not by the right means, the middle term being false; so that this too is not yet excellence in deliberation – this state in virtue of which one attains what one ought but not by the right means. Again (3) it is possible to attain it by long deliberation while another man attains it quickly. Therefore in the former case we have not yet got excellence in deliberation, which is rightness with regard to the expedient – rightness in respect both of the end, the manner, and the time. (4) Further it is possible to have deliberated well either in the unqualified sense or with reference to a particular end. Excellence in deliberation in the unqualified sense, then, is that which succeeds, with reference to what is the end in the unqualified sense, and excellence in deliberation in a particular sense is that which succeeds relatively to a particular end. If, then, it is characteristic of men of practical wisdom to have deliberated well, excellence in deliberation will be correctness with regard to what conduces to the end of which practical wisdom is the true apprehension.

10 Understanding, also, and goodness of understanding, in virtue of which men are said to be men of understanding or of good understanding, are neither entirely the same as opinion or scientific knowledge (for at that rate all men would have been men of understanding), nor are they one of the particular sciences, such as medicine, the science of things connected with health, or geometry, the science of spatial magnitudes. For understanding is neither about things that are always and are unchangeable, nor about any and every one of the things that come into being, but about things which may become subjects of questioning and deliberation. Hence it is about the same objects as practical wisdom; but understanding and practical wisdom are not the same. For practical wisdom issues commands, since its end is what ought to be done or not to be done; but understanding only judges. (Understanding is identical with goodness of understanding, men of understanding with men of good understanding.) Now understanding is neither the having nor the acquiring of practical wisdom; but as learning is called understanding when it means the exercise of the faculty of knowledge, so 'understanding' is applicable to the exercise of the faculty of opinion for the purpose of judging of what some one else says about matters with which practical wisdom is concerned – and of judging

soundly; for 'well' and 'soundly' are the same thing. And from this has come the use of the name 'understanding' in virtue of which men are said to be 'of good understanding', viz. from the application of the word to the grasping of scientific truth; for we often call such grasping understanding.

What is called judgement, in virtue of which men are said to 'be sympathetic judges' and to 'have judgement', is the right discrimination of the equitable. This is shown by the fact that we say the equitable man is above all others a man of sympathetic judgement, and identify equity with sympathetic judgement about certain facts. And sympathetic judgement is judgement which discriminates what is equitable and does so correctly; and correct judgement is that which judges what is true.

Now all the states we have considered converge, as might be expected, to the same point; for when we speak of judgement and understanding and practical wisdom and intuitive reason we credit the same people with possessing judgement and having reached years of reason and with having practical wisdom and understanding. For all these faculties deal with ultimates, i.e. with particulars; and being a man of understanding and of good or sympathetic judgement consists in being able to judge about the things with which practical wisdom is concerned; for the equities are common to all good men in relation to other men. Now all things which have to be done are included among particulars or ultimates; for not only must the man of practical wisdom know particular facts, but understanding and judgement are also concerned with things to be done, and these are ultimates. And intuitive reason is concerned with the ultimates in both directions; for both the first terms and the last are objects of intuitive reason and not of argument, and the intuitive reason which is presupposed by demonstrations grasps the unchangeable and first terms, while the intuitive reason involved in practical reasonings grasps the last and variable fact, i.e. the minor premiss. For these variable facts are the starting-points for the apprehension of the end, since the universals are reached from the particulars; of these therefore we must have perception, and this perception is intuitive reason.

This is why these states are thought to be natural endowments – why, while no one is thought to be a philosopher by nature, people are thought to have by nature judgement, understanding, and intuitive reason. This is shown by the fact that we think our powers correspond to our time of life, and that a particular age brings with it intuitive reason and judgement; this implies that nature is the cause. [Hence intuitive reason is both beginning and end; for demonstrations are from these and about these.] Therefore we ought to attend to the undemonstrated sayings and opinions of experienced and older people or of people of practical wisdom not less than to demonstrations; for because experience has given them an eye they see aright.

We have stated, then, what practical and philosophic wisdom are, and with what each of them is concerned, and we have said that each is the virtue of a different part of the soul.

12 Difficulties might be raised as to the utility of these qualities of mind. For (1) philosophic wisdom will contemplate none of the things that will make a man happy (for it is not concerned with any coming into being), and though practical wisdom has *this* merit, for what purpose do we need it? Practical wisdom is the quality of mind concerned with things just and noble and good for man, but these are the things which it is the mark of a *good* man to do, and we are none the more able to act for *knowing* them if the virtues are states of *character*, just as we are none the better able to act for knowing the things that are healthy and sound, in the sense not of producing but of issuing from the state of health; for we are none the more able to act for having the art of medicine or of gymnastics. But (2) if we are to say that a man should have practical wisdom not for the sake of knowing moral truths but for the sake of becoming good, practical wisdom will be of no use to those who *are* good; but again it is of no use to those who have *not* virtue; for it will make no difference whether they have practical wisdom themselves or obey others who have it, and it would be enough for us to do what we do in the case of health; though we wish to become healthy, yet we do not learn the art of medicine. (3) Besides this, it would be thought strange if practical wisdom, being inferior to philosophic wisdom, is to be put in authority

over it, as seems to be implied by the fact that the art which produces anything rules and issues commands about that thing.

These, then, are the questions we must discuss; so far we have only stated the difficulties.

(1) Now first let us say that in themselves these states must be worthy of choice because they are the virtues of the two parts of the soul respectively, even if neither of them produce anything.

(2) Secondly, they do produce something, not as the art of medicine produces health, however, but as health produces health; so does philosophic wisdom produce happiness; for, being a part of virtue entire, by being possessed and by actualizing itself it makes a man happy.

(3) Again, the work of man is achieved only in accordance with practical wisdom as well as with moral virtue; for virtue makes us aim at the right mark, and practical wisdom makes us take the right means. (Of the fourth part of the soul – the nutritive – there is no such virtue; for there is nothing which it is in its power to do or not to do.)

(4) With regard to our being none the more able to do because of our practical wisdom what is noble and just, let us begin a little further back, starting with the following principle. As we say that some people who do just acts are not necessarily just, i.e. those who do the acts ordained by the laws either unwillingly or owing to ignorance or for some other reason and not for the sake of the acts themselves (though, to be sure, they do what they should and all the things that the good man ought), so is it, it seems, that in order to be good one must be in a certain state when one does the several acts, i.e. one must do them as a result of choice and for the sake of the acts themselves. Now virtue makes the choice right, but the question of the things which should naturally be done to carry out our choice belongs not to virtue but to another faculty. We must devote our attention to these matters and give a clearer statement about them. There is a faculty which is called cleverness; and this is such as to be able to do the things that tend towards the mark we have set before ourselves, and to hit it. Now if the mark be noble, the cleverness is laudable, but if the mark be bad, the cleverness is mere smartness (which is why the clever get called

both 'wise' and 'smart'). Practical wisdom is not the faculty, but it does not exist without this faculty. And this eye of the soul acquires its formed state not without the aid of virtue, as has been said and is plain; for the syllogisms which deal with acts to be done are things which involve a starting-point, viz. 'since the end, i.e. what is best, is of such and such a nature', whatever it may be (let it for the sake of argument be what we please); and this is not evident except to the good man; for wickedness perverts us and causes us to be deceived about the starting-points of action. Therefore it is evident that it is impossible to be practically wise without being good.

13 We must therefore consider virtue also once more; for virtue too is similarly related; as practical wisdom is to cleverness – not the same, but like it – so is natural virtue to virtue in the strict sense. For all men think that each type of character belongs to its possessors in some sense by nature; for from the very moment of birth we are just or fitted for self-control or brave or have the other moral qualities; but yet we seek something else as that which is good in the strict sense – we seek for the presence of such qualities in another way. For both children and brutes have the natural dispositions to these qualities, but without reason these are evidently hurtful. Only we seem to see this much, that, while one may be led astray by them, as a strong body which moves without sight may stumble badly because of its lack of sight, still, if a man once acquires reason, that makes a difference in action; and his state, while still like what it was, will then be virtue in the strict sense. Therefore, as in the part of us which forms opinions there are two types, cleverness and practical wisdom, so too in the moral part there are two types, natural virtue and virtue in the strict sense, and of these the latter involves practical wisdom. This is why some say that all the virtues are forms of practical wisdom, and why Socrates in one respect was on the right track while in another he went astray; in thinking that all the virtues were forms of practical wisdom he was wrong, but in saying they implied practical wisdom he was right. This is confirmed by the fact that even now all men, when they define virtue, after naming the state of character and its objects add 'that (state) which is in accordance

with the right rule'; now the right rule is that which is in accordance with practical wisdom. All men, then, seem somehow to divine that this kind of state is virtue, viz. that which is in accordance with practical wisdom. But we must go a little further. For it is not merely the state in accordance with the right rule, but the state that implies the *presence* of the right rule, that is virtue; and practical wisdom is a right rule about such matters. Socrates, then, thought the virtues were rules or rational principles (for he thought they were, all of them, forms of scientific knowledge), while we think they *involve* a rational principle.

It is clear, then, from what has been said, that it is not possible to be good in the strict sense without practical wisdom, nor practically wise without moral virtue. But in this way we may also refute the dialectical argument whereby it might be contended that the virtues exist in separation from each other; the same man, it might be said, is not best equipped by nature for all the virtues, so that he will have already acquired one when he has not yet acquired another. This is possible in respect of the natural virtues, but not in respect of those in respect of which a man is called without qualification good; for with the presence of the one quality, practical wisdom, will be given all the virtues. And it is plain that, even if it were of no practical value, we should have needed it because it is the virtue of the part of us in question; plain too that the choice will not be right without practical wisdom any more than without virtue; for the one determines the end and the other makes us do the things that lead to the end.

But again it is not *supreme* over philosophic wisdom, i.e. over the superior part of us, any more than the art of medicine is over health; for it does not use it but provides for its coming into being; it issues orders, then, for its sake, but not to it. Further, to maintain its supremacy would be like saying that the art of politics rules the gods because it issues orders about all the affairs of the state.

Book VII

1 Let us now make a fresh beginning and point out that of moral states to be avoided there are three kinds – vice, incontinence, brutishness. The contraries of two of these are evident – one we call virtue, the other continence; to brutishness it would be most fitting to oppose superhuman virtue, a heroic and divine kind of virtue, as Homer has represented Priam saying of Hector that he was very good,

> For he seemed not, he,
> The child of a mortal man, but as one that of God's seed came.

Therefore if, as they say, men become gods by excess of virtue, of this kind must evidently be the state opposed to the brutish state; for as a brute has no vice or virtue, so neither has a god; his state is higher than virtue, and that of a brute is a different kind of state from vice.

Now, since it is rarely that a godlike man is found – to use the epithet of the Spartans, who when they admire any one highly call him a 'godlike man' – so too the brutish type is rarely found among men; it is found chiefly among barbarians, but some brutish qualities are also produced by disease or deformity; and we also call by this evil name those who surpass ordinary men in vice. Of this kind of disposition, however, we must later make some mention, while we have discussed vice before; we must now discuss incontinence and softness (or effeminacy), and continence and endurance; for we must treat each of the two neither as identical with virtue or wickedness, nor as a different genus. We must, as in all other cases, set the observed facts before us and, after first discussing the difficulties, go on to prove, if possible, the truth of all the common opinions about these affections of the mind, or, failing this, of the greater number and the most authoritative; for if we both resolve the difficulties and leave the common opinions undisturbed, we shall have proved the case sufficiently.

Now (1) both continence and endurance are thought to be

included among things good and praiseworthy, and both incontinence and softness among things bad and blameworthy; and the same man is thought to be continent and ready to abide by the result of his calculations, or incontinent and ready to abandon them. And (2) the incontinent man, knowing that what he does is bad, does it as a result of passion, while the continent man, knowing that his appetites are bad, refuses on account of his rational principle to follow them. (3) The temperate man all men call continent and disposed to endurance, while the continent man some maintain to be always temperate but others do not; and some call the self-indulgent man incontinent and the incontinent man self-indulgent indiscriminately, while others distinguish them. (4) The man of practical wisdom, they sometimes say, cannot be incontinent, while sometimes they say that some who are practically wise and clever *are* incontinent. Again (5) men are said to be incontinent even with respect to anger, honour, and gain. – These, then, are the things that are said.

Now we may ask (1) how a man who judges rightly can behave incontinently. That he should behave so when he has knowledge, some say is impossible; for it would be strange – so Socrates thought – if when knowledge was in a man something else could master it and drag it about like a slave. For *Socrates* was entirely opposed to the view in question, holding that there is no such thing as incontinence; no one, he said, when he judges acts against what he judges best – people act so only by reason of ignorance. Now this view plainly contradicts the observed facts, and we must inquire about what happens to such a man; if he acts by reason of ignorance, what is the manner of his ignorance? For that the man who behaves incontinently does not, before he gets into this state, *think* he ought to act so, is evident. But there are *some* who concede certain of Socrates' contentions but not others; that nothing is stronger than knowledge they admit, but not that no one acts contrary to what has seemed to him the better course, and therefore they say that the incontinent man has not knowledge when he is mastered by his pleasures, but opinion. But *if* it is opinion and not knowledge, if it is not a strong conviction that resists but a weak one, as in men who hesitate, we sympathize with

Book VII.2

their failure to stand by such convictions against strong appetites; but we do not sympathize with wickedness, nor with any of the other blameworthy states. Is it then *practical wisdom* whose resistance is mastered? That is the strongest of all states. But this is absurd; the same man will be at once practically wise and incontinent, but *no one* would say that it is the part of a practically wise man to do willingly the basest acts. Besides, it has been shown before that the man of practical wisdom is one who will *act* (for he is a man concerned with the individual facts) and who has the other virtues.

(2) Further, if continence involves having strong and bad appetites, the temperate man will not be continent nor the continent man temperate; for a temperate man will have neither excessive nor bad appetites. But the continent man *must*; for if the appetites are good, the state of character that restrains us from following them is bad, so that not all continence will be good; while if they are weak and not bad, there is nothing admirable in resisting them, and if they are weak and bad, there is nothing great in resisting these either.

(3) Further, if continence makes a man ready to stand by any and every opinion, it is bad, i.e. if it makes him stand even by a false opinion; and if incontinence makes a man apt to abandon any and every opinion, there will be a good incontinence, of which Sophocles' Neoptolemus in the *Philoctetes* will be an instance; for he is to be praised for not standing by what Odysseus persuaded him to do, because he is pained at telling a lie.

(4) Further, the sophistic argument presents a difficulty; the syllogism arising from men's wish to expose paradoxical results arising from an opponent's view, in order that they may be admired when they succeed, is one that puts us in a difficulty (for thought is bound fast when it will not rest because the conclusion does not satisfy it, and cannot advance because it cannot refute the argument). There is an argument from which it follows that folly coupled with incontinence is virtue; for a man does the opposite of what he judges, owing to incontinence, but judges what is good to be evil and something that he should not do, and in consequence he will do what is good and not what is evil.

(5) Further, he who on conviction does and pursues and chooses

what is pleasant would be thought to be better than one who does so as a result not of calculation but of incontinence; for he is easier to cure since he may be persuaded to change his mind. But to the incontinent man may be applied the proverb 'when water chokes, what is one to wash it down with?' If he had been persuaded of the rightness of what he does, he would have desisted when he was persuaded to change his mind; but now he acts in spite of his being persuaded of something quite different.

(6) Further, if incontinence and continence are concerned with any and every kind of object, who is it that is incontinent in the unqualified sense? No one has all the forms of incontinence, but we say some people are incontinent without qualification.

Of some such kind are the difficulties that arise; some of these points must be refuted and the others left in possession of the field; for the solution of the difficulty is the discovery of the truth. (1) We must consider first, then, whether incontinent people act knowingly or not, and in what sense knowingly; then (2) with what sorts of object the incontinent and the continent man may be said to be concerned (i.e. whether with any and every pleasure and pain or with certain determinate kinds), and whether the continent man and the man of endurance are the same or different; and similarly with regard to the other matters germane to this inquiry. The starting-point of our investigation is (*a*) the question whether the continent man and the incontinent are differentiated by their objects or by their attitude, i.e. whether the incontinent man is incontinent simply by being concerned with such and such objects, or, instead, by his attitude, or, instead of that, by both these things; (*b*) the second question is whether incontinence and continence are concerned with any and every object or not. The man who is incontinent in the unqualified sense is neither concerned with any and every object, but with precisely those with which the self-indulgent man is concerned, nor is he characterized by being simply related to these (for then his state would be the same as self-indulgence), but by being related to them in a certain way. For the one is led on in accordance with his own choice, thinking that he ought always to pursue the present pleasure; while the other does not think so, but yet pursues it.

Book VII.3

(1) As for the suggestion that it is true opinion and not knowledge against which we act incontinently, that makes no difference to the argument; for some people when in a state of opinion do not hesitate, but think they know exactly. If, then, the notion is that owing to their weak conviction those who have opinion are more likely to act against their judgement than those who know, we answer that there need be no difference between knowledge and opinion in this respect; for some men are no less convinced of what they think than others of what they know; as is shown by the case of Heraclitus. But (a), since we use the word 'know' in two senses (for both the man who has knowledge but is not using it and he who is using it are said to know), it *will* make a difference whether, when a man does what he should not, he has the knowledge but is not exercising it, or *is* exercising it; for the latter seems strange, but not the former.

(b) Further, since there are two kinds of premisses, there is nothing to prevent a man's having both premisses and acting against his knowledge, provided that he is using only the universal premiss and not the particular; for it is particular acts that have to be done. And there are also two kinds of universal term; one is predicable of the agent, the other of the object; e.g. 'dry food is good for every man', and 'I am a man', or 'such and such food is dry'; but whether 'this food is such and such', of this the incontinent man either has not or is not exercising the knowledge. There will, then, be, firstly, an enormous difference between these manners of knowing, so that to know in one way when we act incontinently would not seem anything strange, while to know in the other way would be extraordinary.

And further (c) the possession of knowledge in another sense than those just named is something that happens to men; for within the case of having knowledge but not using it we see a difference of state, admitting of the possibility of having knowledge in a sense and yet not having it, as in the instance of a man asleep, mad, or drunk. But now this is just the condition of men under the influence of passions; for outbursts of anger and sexual appetites and some other such passions, it is evident, actually alter our bodily condition, and in some men even produce fits of madness. It is plain, then, that incontinent people must be said to be in a similar condition to men asleep, mad, or drunk. The fact that men use the language that flows from knowledge proves nothing; for even men under the influence of these passions utter scientific proofs and verses of Empedocles, and those who have just begun to learn a science can string together its phrases, but do not yet know it; for it has to become part of themselves, and that takes time; so that we must suppose that the use of language by men in an incontinent state means no more than its utterance by actors on the stage.

(*d*) Again, we may also view the cause as follows in the way a natural scientist would. The one opinion is universal, the other is concerned with the particular facts, and here we come to something within the sphere of perception; when a single opinion results from the two, the soul must in one type of case affirm the conclusion, while in the case of opinions concerned with production it must immediately act (e.g. if 'everything sweet ought to be tasted', and 'this is sweet', in the sense of being one of the particular sweet things, the man who can act and is not prevented must at the same time actually act accordingly). When, then, the universal opinion is present in us forbidding us to taste, and there is also the opinion that 'everything sweet is pleasant', and that 'this is sweet' (now this is the opinion that is active), and when appetite happens to be present in us, the one opinion bids us avoid the object, but appetite leads us towards it (for it can move each of our bodily parts); so that it turns out that a man behaves incontinently under the influence (in a sense) of a rule and an opinion, and of one not contrary in itself, but only incidentally – for the appetite is contrary, not the opinion – to the right rule. It also follows that this is the reason why the lower animals are not incontinent, viz. because they have no universal judgement but only imagination and memory of particulars.

The explanation of how the ignorance is dissolved and the incontinent man regains his knowledge, is the same as in the case of the man drunk or asleep and is not peculiar to this condition; we must go to the students of natural science for it. Now, the last premiss both being an opinion about a perceptible object, and being what determines our actions, this a man either has not when he is in the state of passion, or has it in the sense in which having knowledge did not mean knowing but only talking, as a drunken man may mutter the verses of Empedocles. And because the last term is not universal nor equally an object of scientific knowledge with the universal term, the position that Socrates sought to establish actually seems to result; for it is not in the presence of what is thought to be knowledge proper that the affection of incontinence arises (nor is it this that is 'dragged about' as a result of the state of passion), but in that of perceptual knowledge.

This must suffice as our answer to the question whether an incontinent man acts knowingly or not, and in what sense he may act knowingly.

4 (2) We must next discuss whether there is any one who is incontinent without qualification, or all men who are incontinent are so in a particular sense, and if there is, with what sort of objects he is concerned. That both continent persons and persons of endurance, and incontinent and soft persons, are concerned with pleasures and pains, is evident.

Now of the things that produce pleasure some are necessary, while others are worthy of choice in themselves but admit of excess, the bodily causes of pleasure being necessary (by such I mean both those concerned with food and those concerned with sexual intercourse, i.e. the bodily matters with which we defined self-indulgence and temperance as being concerned), while the others are not necessary but worthy of choice in themselves (e.g. victory, honour, wealth, and good and pleasant things of this sort). This being so, (*a*) those who go to excess with reference to the latter, contrary to the right rule which is in themselves, are not called incontinent simply, but incontinent with the qualification 'in respect of money, gain, honour, or anger', – not simply incontinent, on the ground that they are different from incontinent people and are called incontinent by reason of a resemblance. (Compare the case of Anthropos (Man), who won a contest at the Olympic games; in his case the general definition of man differed little from the definition peculiar to *him*, but yet it *was* different.) This is shown by the fact that incontinence either without qualification or in respect of some particular bodily pleasure is blamed not only as a fault but as a kind of vice, while none of the people who are incontinent in these other respects is so blamed.

But (b) of the people who are incontinent with respect to bodily enjoyments, with which we say the temperate and the self-indulgent man are concerned, he who pursues the excesses of things pleasant – and shuns those of things painful, of hunger and thirst and heat and cold and all the objects of touch and taste – not by choice but contrary to his choice and his judgement, is called incontinent, not with the qualification 'in respect of this or that', e.g. of anger, but just simply. This is confirmed by the fact that men are called 'soft' with regard to these pleasures, but not with regard to any of the others. And for this reason we group together the incontinent and the self-indulgent, the continent and the temperate man – but not any of these other types – because they are concerned somehow with the same pleasures and pains; but though these are concerned with the same objects, they are not simply related to them, but some of them make a deliberate choice while the others do not.

This is why we should describe as self-indulgent rather the man who without appetite or with but a slight appetite pursues the excesses of pleasure and avoids moderate pains, than the man who does so because of his strong appetites; for what would the former do, if he had in addition a vigorous appetite, and a violent pain at the lack of the 'necessary' objects?

Now of appetites and pleasures some belong to the class of things generically noble and good – for some pleasant things are by nature worthy of choice, while others are contrary to these, and others are intermediate, to adopt our previous distinction – e.g. wealth, gain, victory, honour. And with reference to all objects whether of this or of the intermediate kind men are not blamed for being affected by them, for desiring and loving them, but for doing so in a certain way, i.e. for going to excess. (This is why all those who contrary to the rule either are mastered by or pursue one of the objects which are naturally noble and good, e.g. those who busy themselves more than they ought about honour or about children and parents, ⟨are not wicked⟩; for these too are goods, and those who busy themselves about them are praised; but yet there is an excess even in them – if like Niobe one were to fight even against the gods, or were to be as much devoted to one's father as Satyrus nicknamed 'the filial', who was thought to be very silly on this point.) There is no wickedness, then, with regard to these objects, for the reason named, viz. because each of them is by nature a thing worthy of choice for its own sake; yet excesses in respect of them are bad and to be avoided. Similarly there is no incontinence with regard to them; for incontinence is not only to be avoided but is also a thing worthy of blame; but owing to a similarity in the state of feeling people apply the name incontinence, adding in each case what it is in respect of, as we may describe as a bad doctor or a bad actor one whom we should not call bad, simply. As, then, in this case we do not apply the term without qualification because each of these conditions is not badness but only analogous to it, so it is clear that in the other case also that alone must be taken to be incontinence and continence which is concerned with the same objects as temperance and self-indulgence, but we apply the term to anger by virtue of a resemblance; and this is why we say with a qualification 'incontinent in respect of anger' as we say 'incontinent in respect of honour, or of gain'.

5 (1) Some things are pleasant by nature, and of these (*a*) some are so without qualification, and (*b*) others are so with reference to particular classes either of animals or of men; while (2) others are not pleasant by nature, but (*a*) some of them become so by reason of injuries to the system, and (*b*) others by reason of acquired habits, and (*c*) others by reason of originally bad natures. This being so, it is possible with regard to each of the latter kinds to discover similar states of character to those recognized with regard to the former; I mean (A) the brutish states, as in the case of the female who, they say, rips open pregnant women and devours the infants, or of the things in which some of the tribes about the Black Sea that have gone savage are said to delight – in raw meat or in human flesh, or in lending their children to one another to feast upon – or of the story told of Phalaris.

These states are brutish, but (B) others arise as a result of disease (or, in some cases, of madness, as with the man who sacrificed and ate his mother, or with the slave who ate the liver of his fellow), and others are morbid states (C) resulting from custom, e.g. the habit of plucking out the hair or of gnawing the nails, or even coals or earth, and in addition to these paederasty; for these arise in some by nature and in others, as in those who have been the victims of lust from childhood, from habit.

Now those in whom nature is the cause of such a state no one would call incontinent, any more than one would apply the epithet to women because of the passive part they play in copulation; nor would one apply it to those who are in a morbid condition as a result of habit. To have these various types of habit is beyond the limits of vice, as brutishness is too; for a man who has them to master or be mastered by them is not simple ⟨continence or⟩ incontinence but that which is so by analogy, as the man who is in this condition in respect of fits of anger is to be called incontinent in respect of that feeling, but not incontinent simply.

For every excessive state whether of folly, of cowardice, of self-indulgence, or of bad temper, is either brutish or morbid; the man who is by nature apt to fear everything, even the squeak of a mouse, is cowardly with a brutish cowardice, while the man who feared a weasel did so in consequence of disease; and of foolish people those who by nature are thoughtless and live by their senses alone are brutish, like some races of the distant barbarians, while those who are so as a result of disease (e.g. of epilepsy) or of madness are morbid. Of these characteristics it is possible to have some only at times, and not to be mastered by them, e.g. Phalaris may have restrained a desire to eat the flesh of a child or an appetite for unnatural sexual pleasure; but it is also possible to be mastered, not merely to have the feelings. Thus, as the wickedness which is on the human level is called wickedness simply, while that which is not is called wickedness not simply but with the qualification 'brutish' or 'morbid', in the same way it is plain that some incontinence is brutish and some morbid, while only that which corresponds to *human* self-indulgence is incontinence simply.

That incontinence and continence, then, are concerned only with the same objects as self-indulgence and temperance and that what is concerned with other objects is a type distinct from incontinence, and called incontinence by a metaphor and not simply, is plain.

6 That incontinence in respect of anger is less disgraceful than that in respect of the appetites is what we will now proceed to see. (1) Anger seems to listen to argument to some extent, but to mishear it, as do hasty servants who run out before they have heard the whole of what one says, and then muddle the order, or as dogs bark if there is but a knock at the door, before looking to see if it is a friend. So anger, by reason of the warmth and hastiness of its nature, when it hears, though not hearing an order, springs to take revenge. For argument or imagination informs us that we have been insulted or slighted, and anger, reasoning as it were that anything like this must be fought against, boils up straightway; while appetite, if argument or perception merely says that an object is pleasant, springs to the enjoyment of it. Therefore anger obeys the argument in a sense, but appetite does not. It is therefore more disgraceful; for the man who is incontinent in respect of anger is in a sense conquered by argument, while the other is conquered by appetite and not by argument.

(2) Further, we pardon people more easily for following natural desires, since we pardon them more easily for following such appetites as are common to all men, and in so far as they are common; now anger and bad temper are more natural than the appetites for excess, i.e. for unnecessary objects. Take for instance the man who defended himself on the charge of striking his father by saying 'yes, but *he* struck *his* father, and *he* struck *his*, and' (pointing to his child) 'this boy will strike *me* when he is a man; it runs in the family'; or the man who when he was being dragged along by his son bade him stop at the doorway, since he himself had dragged his father only as far as that.

(3) Further, those who are more given to plotting against others are more criminal. Now a passionate man is not given to plotting, nor is anger itself – it is open; but the nature of appetite is illustrated by what the poets call Aphrodite, 'guile-weaving daughter of Cyprus', and by Homer's words about her 'embroidered girdle':

    And the whisper of wooing is there,
Whose subtlety stealeth the wits of the wise, how prudent soe'er.

Therefore if this form of incontinence is more criminal and

disgraceful than that in respect of anger, it is both incontinence without qualification and in a sense vice.

(4) Further, no one commits wanton outrage with a feeling of pain, but every one who acts in anger acts with pain, while the man who commits outrage acts with pleasure. If, then, those acts at which it is most just to be angry are more criminal than others, the incontinence which is due to appetite is the more criminal; for there is no wanton outrage involved in anger.

Plainly, then, the incontinence concerned with appetite is more disgraceful than that concerned with anger, and continence and incontinence are concerned with bodily appetites and pleasures; but we must grasp the differences among the latter themselves. For, as has been said at the beginning, some are human and natural both in kind and in magnitude, others are brutish, and others are due to organic injuries and diseases. Only with the first of these are temperance and self-indulgence concerned; this is why we call the lower animals neither temperate nor self-indulgent except by a metaphor, and only if some one race of animals exceeds another as a whole in wantonness, destructiveness, and omnivorous greed; these have no power of choice or calculation, but they *are* departures from the natural norm, as, among men, madmen are. Now brutishness is a less evil than vice, though more alarming; for it is not that the better part has been perverted, as in man, – they *have* no better part. Thus it is like comparing a lifeless thing with a living in respect of badness; for the badness of that which has no originative source of movement is always less hurtful, and reason is an originative source. Thus it is like comparing injustice in the abstract with an unjust man. Each is in some sense worse; for a bad man will do ten thousand times as much evil as a brute.

7 With regard to the pleasures and pains and appetites and aversions arising through touch and taste, to which both self-indulgence and temperance were formerly narrowed down, it is possible to be in such a state as to be defeated even by those of them which most people master, or to master even those by which most people are defeated; among these possibilities, those relating to pleasures are incontinence and continence, those relating to pains softness and

endurance. The state of most people is intermediate, even if they lean more towards the worse states.

Now, since some pleasures are necessary while others are not, and are necessary up to a point while the excesses of them are not, nor the deficiencies, and this is equally true of appetites and pains, the man who pursues the excesses of things pleasant, or pursues to excess necessary objects, and does so by choice, for their own sake and not at all for the sake of any result distinct from them, is self-indulgent; for such a man is of necessity unlikely to repent, and therefore incurable, since a man who cannot repent cannot be cured. The man who is deficient in his pursuit of them is the opposite of self-indulgent; the man who is intermediate is temperate. Similarly, there is the man who avoids bodily pains not because he is defeated by them but by choice. (Of those who do not *choose* such acts, one kind of man is led to them as a result of the pleasure involved, another because he avoids the pain arising from the appetite, so that these types differ from one another. Now any one would think worse of a man if with no appetite or with weak appetite he were to do something disgraceful, than if he did it under the influence of powerful appetite, and worse of him if he struck a blow not in anger than if he did it in anger; for what would he have done if he *had* been strongly affected? This is why the self-indulgent man is worse than the incontinent.) Of the states named, then, the latter is rather a kind of softness; the former is self-indulgence. While to the incontinent man is opposed the continent, to the soft is opposed the man of endurance; for endurance consists in resisting, while continence consists in conquering, and resisting and conquering are different, as not being beaten is different from winning; this is why continence is also more worthy of choice than endurance. Now the man who is defective in respect of resistance to the things which most men both resist and resist successfully is soft and effeminate; for effeminacy too is a kind of softness; such a man trails his cloak to avoid the pain of lifting it, and plays the invalid without thinking himself wretched, though the man he imitates is a wretched man.

The case is similar with regard to continence and incontinence. For if a man is defeated by violent and excessive pleasures or pains, there is nothing wonderful in that; indeed we are ready to pardon him if he has resisted, as Theodectes' Philoctetes does when bitten by the snake, or Carcinus' Cercyon in the *Alope*, and as people who try to restrain their laughter burst out in a guffaw, as happened to Xenophantus. But it is surprising if a man is defeated by and cannot resist pleasures or pains which most men can hold out against, when this is not due to heredity or disease, like the softness that is hereditary with the kings of the Scythians, or that which distinguishes the female sex from the male.

The lover of amusement, too, is thought to be self-indulgent, but is really soft. For amusement is a relaxation, since it is a rest from work; and the lover of amusement is one of the people who go to excess in this.

Of incontinence one kind is impetuosity, another weakness. For some men after deliberating fail, owing to their emotion, to stand by the conclusions of their deliberation, others because they have not deliberated are led by their emotion; since some men (just as people who first tickle others are not tickled themselves), if they have first perceived and seen what is coming and have first roused themselves and their calculative faculty, are not defeated by their emotion, whether it be pleasant or painful. It is keen and excitable people that suffer especially from the impetuous form of incontinence; for the former by reason of their quickness and the latter by reason of the violence of their passions do not await the argument, because they are apt to follow their imagination.

8 The self-indulgent man, as was said, is not apt to repent; for he stands by his choice; but any incontinent man is likely to repent. This is why the position is not as it was expressed in the formulation of the problem, but the self-indulgent man is incurable and the incontinent man curable; for wickedness is like a disease such as dropsy or consumption, while incontinence is like epilepsy; the former is a permanent, the latter an intermittent badness. And generally incontinence and vice are different in kind; vice is unconscious of itself, incontinence is not (of incontinent men themselves, those who become temporarily beside themselves are better than those who have the rational principle but do not abide by it, since the latter are defeated by a weaker passion, and do not act without previous deliberation like the others); for the incon-

tinent man is like the people who get drunk quickly and on little wine, i.e. on less than most people.

Evidently, then, incontinence is not vice (though perhaps it is so in a qualified sense); for incontinence is contrary to choice while vice is in accordance with choice; not but what they are similar in respect of the actions they lead to; as in the saying of Demodocus about the Milesians, 'the Milesians are not without sense, but they do the things that senseless people do', so too incontinent people are not criminal, but they will do criminal acts.

Now, since the incontinent man is apt to pursue, not on conviction, bodily pleasures that are excessive and contrary to the right rule, while the self-indulgent man is convinced because he is the sort of man to pursue them, it is on the contrary the former that is easily persuaded to change his mind, while the latter is not. For virtue and vice respectively preserve and destroy the first principle, and in actions the final cause is the first principle, as the hypotheses are in mathematics; neither in that case is it argument that teaches the first principles, nor is it so here – virtue either natural or produced by habituation is what teaches right opinion about the first principle. Such a man as this, then, is temperate; his contrary is the self-indulgent.

But there is a sort of man who is carried away as a result of passion and contrary to the right rule – a man whom passion masters so that he does not act according to the right rule, but does not master to the extent of making him ready to believe that he ought to pursue such pleasures without reserve; this is the incontinent man, who is better than the self-indulgent man, and not bad without qualification; for the best thing in him, the first principle, is preserved. And contrary to him is another kind of man, he who abides by his convictions and is not carried away, at least as a result of passion. It is evident from these considerations that the latter is a good state and the former a bad one.

9 Is the man continent who abides by any and every rule and any and every choice, or the man who abides by the right choice, and is he incontinent who abandons any and every choice and any and every rule, or he who abandons the rule that is not false and the choice that is right; this is how we put it before in our statement of

the problem. Or is it incidentally any and every choice but *per se* the true rule and the right choice by which the one abides and the other does not? If any one chooses or pursues this for the sake of that, *per se* he pursues and chooses the latter, but incidentally the former. But when we speak without qualification we mean what is *per se*. Therefore in a sense the one abides by, and the other abandons, any and every opinion; but without qualification, the true opinion.

There are some who are apt to abide by their opinion, who are called strong-headed, viz. those who are hard to persuade in the first instance and are not easily persuaded to change; these have some likeness to the continent man, as the prodigal is in a way like the liberal man and the rash man like the confident man; but they are different in many respects. For it is to passion and appetite that the one will not yield, since on occasion the continent man *will* be easy to persuade; but it is to argument that the others refuse to yield, for they do form appetites and many of them are led by their pleasures. Now the people who are strong-headed are the opinionated, the ignorant, and the boorish – the opinionated being influenced by pleasure and pain; for they delight in the victory they gain if they are not persuaded to change, and are pained if their decisions become null and void as decrees sometimes do; so that they are liker the incontinent than the continent man.

But there are some who fail to abide by their resolutions, not as a result of incontinence, e.g. Neoptolemus in Sophocles' *Philoctetes*; yet it was for the sake of pleasure that he did not stand fast – but a noble pleasure; for telling the truth was noble to him, but he had been persuaded by Odysseus to tell the lie. For not every one who does anything for the sake of pleasure is either self-indulgent or bad or incontinent, but he who does it for a disgraceful pleasure.

Since there is also a sort of man who takes less delight than he should in bodily things, and does not abide by the rule, he who is intermediate between him and the incontinent man is the continent man; for the incontinent man fails to abide by the rule because he delights too much in them, and this man because he delights in them too little; while the continent man abides by the rule and does not change on either account. Now if continence is good, both the contrary states must be bad, as they actually appear to be;

Book VII.9

but because the other extreme is seen in few people and seldom, as temperance is thought to be contrary only to self-indulgence, so is continence to incontinence.

Since many names are applied analogically, it is by analogy that we have come to speak of the 'continence' of the temperate man; for both the continent man and the temperate man are such as to do nothing contrary to the rule for the sake of the bodily pleasures, but the former has and the latter has not bad appetites, and the latter is such as not to feel pleasure contrary to the rule, while the former is such as to feel pleasure but not to be led by it. And the incontinent and the self-indulgent man are also like one another; they are different, but both pursue bodily pleasures – the latter, however, also thinking that he ought to do so, while the former does not think this.

10 Nor can the same man have practical wisdom and be incontinent; for it has been shown that a man is at the same time practically wise, and good in respect of character. Further, a man has practical wisdom not by knowing only but by being able to act; but the incontinent man is unable to act – there is, however, nothing to prevent a *clever* man from being incontinent; this is why it is sometimes actually thought that some people have practical wisdom but are incontinent, viz. because cleverness and practical wisdom differ in the way we have described in our first discussions, and are near together in respect of their reasoning, but differ in respect of their purpose – nor yet is the incontinent man like the man who knows and is contemplating a truth, but like the man who is asleep or drunk. And he acts willingly (for he acts in a sense with knowledge both of what he does and of the end to which he does it), but is not wicked, since his purpose is good; so that he is half-wicked. And he is not a criminal; for he does not act of malice aforethought; of the two types of incontinent man the one does not abide by the conclusions of his deliberation, while the excitable man does not deliberate at all. And thus the incontinent man is like a city which passes all the right decrees and has good laws, but makes no use of them, as in Anaxandrides' jesting remark,

> 'The city willed it, that cares nought for laws';

but the wicked man is like a city that uses its laws, but has wicked laws to use.

Now incontinence and continence are concerned with that which is in excess of the state characteristic of most men; for the continent man abides by his resolutions more and the incontinent man less than most men can.

Of the forms of incontinence, that of excitable people is more curable than that of those who deliberate but do not abide by their decisions, and those who are incontinent through habituation are more curable than those in whom incontinence is innate; for it is easier to change a habit than to change one's nature; even habit is hard to change just because it is like nature, as Evenus says:

> I say that habit's but long practice, friend,
> And this becomes men's nature in the end.

We have now stated what continence, incontinence, endurance, and softness are, and how these states are related to each other.

11

The study of pleasure and pain belongs to the province of the political philosopher; for he is the architect of the end, with a view to which we call one thing bad and another good without qualification. Further, it is one of our necessary tasks to consider them; for not only did we lay it down that moral virtue and vice are concerned with pains and pleasures, but most people say that happiness involves pleasure; this is why the blessed man is called by a name derived from a word meaning enjoyment.

Now (1) some people think that no pleasure is a good, either in itself or incidentally, since the good and pleasure are not the same; (2) others think that some pleasures are good but that most are bad. (3) Again there is a third view, that even if all pleasures are goods, yet the best thing in the world cannot be pleasure. (1) The reasons given for the view that pleasure is not a good at all are (a) that every pleasure is a perceptible process to a natural state, and that no process is of the same kind as its end, e.g. no process of building of the same kind as a house. (b) A temperate man avoids pleasures. (c) A man of practical wisdom pursues what is free from pain, not what is pleasant. (d) The pleasures are a hindrance to thought, and the more so the more one delights in them, e.g. in sexual pleasure; for no one could think of anything while absorbed in this. (c) There is no art of pleasure; but every good is the product of some art. (f) Children and the brutes pursue pleasures. (2) The reasons for the view that not all pleasures are good are that (a) there are pleasures that are actually base and objects of reproach, and (b) there are harmful pleasures; for some pleasant things are unhealthy. (3) The reason for the view that the best thing in the world is not pleasure is that pleasure is not an end but a process.

12 These are pretty much the things that are said. That it does not follow from these grounds that pleasure is not a good, or even the chief good, is plain from the following considerations. (A) (a) First, since that which is good may be so in either of two senses (one thing good simply and another good for a particular person), natural constitutions and states of being, and therefore also the corresponding movements and processes, will be correspondingly divisible. Of those which are thought to be bad some will be bad if taken without qualification but not bad for a particular person, but worthy of his choice, and some will not be worthy of choice even for a particular person, but only at a particular time and for a short period, though not without qualification; while others are not even pleasures, but seem to be so, viz. all those which involve pain and whose end is curative, e.g. the processes that go on in sick persons.

(b) Further, one kind of good being activity and another being state, the processes that restore us to our natural state are only incidentally pleasant; for that matter the activity at work in the appetites for them is the activity of so much of our state and nature as has remained unimpaired; for there are actually pleasures that involve *no* pain or appetite (e.g. those of contemplation), the nature in such a case not being defective at all. That the others are incidental is indicated by the fact that men do not enjoy the same pleasant objects when their nature is in its settled state as they do when it is being replenished, but in the former case they enjoy the things that are pleasant without qualification, in the latter the contraries of these as well; for then they enjoy even sharp and bitter things, none of which is pleasant either by nature or without qualification. The states they produce, therefore, are not pleasures naturally or without qualification; for as pleasant things differ, so do the pleasures arising from them.

(c) Again, it is not necessary that there should be something else better than pleasure, as some say the end is better than the process; for pleasures are not processes nor do they all involve process – they are activities and ends; nor do they arise when we are becoming something, but when we are exercising some faculty; and not all pleasures have an end different from themselves, but only the pleasures of persons who are being led to the perfecting of their nature. This is why it is not right to say that pleasure is perceptible process, but it should rather be called activity of the natural state, and instead of 'perceptible' 'unimpeded'. It is thought by *some* people to be process just because they think it is in the strict sense *good*; for they think that activity is process, which it is not.

(B) The view that pleasures are bad because some pleasant things are unhealthy is like saying that healthy things are bad because some healthy things are bad for money-making; both are bad in the respect mentioned, but they are not *bad* for *that* reason – indeed, thinking itself is sometimes injurious to health.

Neither practical wisdom nor any state of being is impeded by the pleasure arising from it; it is foreign pleasures that impede, for the pleasures arising from thinking and learning will make us think and learn all the more.

(C) The fact that no pleasure is the product of any art arises naturally enough; there is no art of any other activity either, but only of the corresponding faculty; though for that matter the arts of the perfumer and the cook *are* thought to be arts of pleasure.

(D) The arguments based on the grounds that the temperate man avoids pleasure and that the man of practical wisdom pursues the painless life, and that children and the brutes pursue pleasure, are all refuted by the same consideration. We have pointed out in what sense pleasures are good without qualification and in what sense some are not good; now both the brutes and children pursue pleasures of the latter kind (and the man of practical wisdom pursues tranquil freedom from that kind), viz. those which imply appetite and pain, i.e. the bodily pleasures (for it is these that are of this nature) and the excesses of them, in respect of which the self-indulgent man is self-indulgent. This is why the temperate man avoids these pleasures; for even he *has* pleasures of his own.

13 But further (E) it is agreed that pain is bad and to be avoided; for some pain is without qualification bad, and other pain is bad because it is in some respect an impediment to us. Now the contrary of that which is to be avoided, *qua* something to be avoided and bad, is good. Pleasure, then, is necessarily a good. For the answer of Speusippus, that pleasure is contrary both to pain and to good, as the greater is contrary both to the less and to the equal, is not successful; since he would not say that pleasure is essentially just a species of evil.

And (F) if certain pleasures are bad, that does not prevent the chief good from being some pleasure, just as the chief good may be some form of knowledge though certain kinds of knowledge are bad. Perhaps it is even necessary, if each disposition has unimpeded activities, that, whether the activity (if unimpeded) of all our dispositions or that of some one of them is happiness, this should be the thing most worthy of our choice; and this activity is pleasure. Thus the chief good would be some pleasure, though most pleasures might perhaps be bad without qualification. And for this reason all men think that the happy life is pleasant and weave pleasure into their ideal of happiness – and reasonably too; for no activity is perfect when it is impeded, and happiness is a perfect thing; this is why the happy man needs the goods of the body and external goods, i.e. those of fortune, viz. in order that he may not be impeded in these ways. Those who say that the victim on the rack or the man who falls into great misfortunes is happy if he is good, are, whether they mean to or not, talking nonsense. Now because we need fortune as well as other things, some people think good fortune the same thing as happiness; but it is not that, for even good fortune itself when in excess is an impediment, and perhaps should then be no longer called good fortune; for its limit is fixed by reference to happiness.

And indeed the fact that all things, both brutes and men, pursue pleasure is an indication of its being somehow the chief good:

> No voice is wholly lost that many peoples . . .

But since no one nature or state either is or is thought the best for all, neither do all pursue the same pleasure; yet all pursue pleasure. And perhaps they actually pursue not the pleasure they think they pursue nor that which they would say they pursue, but the same pleasure; for all things have by nature something divine in them. But the bodily pleasures have appropriated the name both because we oftenest steer our course for them and because all men share in them; thus because they alone are familiar, men think there are no others.

It is evident also that if pleasure, i.e. the activity of our faculties, is not a good, it will not be the case that the happy man lives a pleasant life; for to what end should he need pleasure, if it is not a good but the happy man may even live a painful life? For pain is neither an evil nor a good, if pleasure is not; why then should he avoid it? Therefore, too, the life of the good man will not be pleasanter than that of any one else, if his activities are not more pleasant.

(G) With regard to the bodily pleasures, those who say that *some* 14 pleasures are very much to be chosen, viz. the noble pleasures, but not the bodily pleasures, i.e. those with which the self-indulgent man is concerned, must consider why, then, the contrary pains are bad. For the contrary of bad is good. Are the necessary pleasures good in the sense in which even that which is not bad is good? Or are they good up to a point? Is it that where you have states and processes of which there cannot be too much, there cannot be too much of the corresponding pleasure, and that where there can be too much of the one there can be too much of the other also? Now there can be too much of bodily goods, and the bad man is bad by virtue of pursuing the excess, not by virtue of pursuing the necessary pleasures (for *all* men enjoy in some way or other both dainty foods and wines and sexual intercourse, but not all men do as they ought). The contrary is the case with pain; for he does not avoid the excess of it, he avoids it altogether; and this is peculiar to him, for the alternative to excess of pleasure is not pain, except to the man who pursues this excess.

Since we should state not only the truth, but also the cause of error — for this contributes towards producing conviction, since

Book VII.14

when a reasonable explanation is given of why the false view appears true, this tends to produce belief in the true view – therefore we must state why the bodily pleasures appear the more worthy of choice. (*a*) Firstly, then, it is because they expel pain; owing to the excesses of pain that men experience, they pursue excessive and in general bodily pleasure as being a cure for the pain. Now curative agencies produce intense feeling – which is the reason why they are pursued – because they show up against the contrary pain. (Indeed pleasure is thought not to be good for these two reasons, as has been said, viz. that (α) some of them are activities belonging to a bad nature – either congenital, as in the case of a brute, or due to habit, i.e. those of bad men; while (β) others are meant to cure a defective nature, and it is better to be in a healthy state than to be getting into it, but these arise during the process of being made perfect and are therefore only incidentally good.) (*b*) Further, they are pursued because of their violence by those who cannot enjoy other pleasures. (At all events they go out of their way to manufacture thirsts somehow for themselves. When these are harmless, the practice is irreproachable; when they are hurtful, it is bad.) For they have nothing else to enjoy, and, besides, a neutral state is painful to many people because of their nature. For the animal is always in travail, as the students of natural science also testify, saying that sight and hearing are painful; but we have become used to this, as they maintain. Similarly, while, in youth, people are, owing to the growth that is going on, in a situation like that of drunken men, and youth is pleasant, on the other hand people of excitable nature always need relief; for even their body is ever in torment owing to its special composition, and they are always under the influence of violent desire; but pain is driven out both by the contrary pleasure, and by any chance pleasure if it be strong; and for these reasons they become self-indulgent and bad. But the pleasures that do not involve pains do not admit of excess; and these are among the things pleasant by nature and not incidentally. By things pleasant incidentally I mean those that act as cures (for because as a result people are cured, through some action of the part that remains healthy, for this reason the process is thought pleasant); by things naturally pleasant I mean those that stimulate the action of the healthy nature.

There is no one thing that is always pleasant, because our nature is not simple but there is another element in us as well, inasmuch as we are perishable creatures, so that if the one element does something, this is unnatural to the other nature, and when the two elements are evenly balanced, what is done seems neither painful nor pleasant; for if the nature of anything were simple, the same action would always be most pleasant to it. This is why God always enjoys a single and simple pleasure; for there is not only an activity of movement but an activity of immobility, and pleasure is found more in rest than in movement. But 'change in all things is sweet', as the poet says, because of some vice; for as it is the vicious man that is changeable, so the nature that needs change is vicious; for it is not simple nor good.

We have now discussed continence and incontinence, and pleasure and pain, both what each is and in what sense some of them are good and others bad; it remains to speak of friendship.

Book IX

chapters 4, 8, 9

4 Friendly relations with one's neighbours, and the marks by which friendships are defined, seem to have proceeded from a man's relations to himself. For (1) we define a friend as one who wishes and does what is good, or seems so, for the sake of his friend, or (2) as one who wishes his friend to exist and live, for his sake, which mothers do to their children, and friends do who have come into conflict. And (3) others define him as one who lives with and (4) has the same tastes as another; or (5) one who grieves and rejoices with his friend; and this too is found in mothers most of all. It is by some one of these characteristics that friendship too is defined.

Now each of these is true of the good man's relation to himself (and of all other men in so far as they think themselves good; virtue and the good man seem, as has been said, to be the measure of every class of things). For his opinions are harmonious, and he desires the same things with all his soul; and therefore he wishes for himself what is good and what seems so, and does it (for it is characteristic of the good man to work out the good), and does so for his own sake (for he does it for the sake of the intellectual element in him, which is thought to be the man himself); and he wishes himself to live and be preserved, and especially the element by virtue of which he thinks. For existence is good to the virtuous man, and each man wishes himself what is good, while no one chooses to possess the whole world if he has first to become some one else (for that matter, even now God possesses the good); he wishes for this only on condition of being whatever he is; and the element that thinks would seem to be the individual man, or to be so more than any other element in him. And such a man wishes to live with himself; for he does so with pleasure, since the memories of his past acts are delightful and his hopes for the future are good, and therefore pleasant. His mind is well stored too with subjects of contemplation. And he grieves and rejoices, more than any other, with himself; for the same thing is always painful, and the same thing always pleasant, and not one thing at one time and another at another; he has, so to speak, nothing to repent of.

Therefore, since each of these characteristics belongs to the good man in relation to himself, and he is related to his friend as to himself (for his friend is another self), friendship too is thought to be one of these attributes, and those who have these attributes to be friends. Whether there is or is not friendship between a man and himself is a question we may dismiss for the present; there would seem to be friendship in so far as he is two or more, to judge from the afore-mentioned attributes of friendship, and from the fact that the extreme of friendship is likened to one's love for oneself.

But the attributes named seem to belong even to the majority of men, poor creatures though they may be. Are we to say then that in so far as they are satisfied with themselves and think they are good, they share in these attributes? Certainly no one who is thoroughly bad and impious has these attributes, or even seems to do so. They hardly belong even to inferior people; for they are at variance with themselves, and have appetites for some things and rational desires for others. This is true, for instance, of incontinent people; for they choose, instead of the things they themselves think good, things that are pleasant but hurtful; while others again, through cowardice and laziness, shrink from doing what they think best for themselves. And those who have done many terrible deeds and are hated for their wickedness even shrink from life and destroy themselves. And wicked men seek for people with whom to spend their days, and shun themselves; for they remember many a grievous deed, and anticipate others like them, when they are by themselves, but when they are with others they forget. And having nothing lovable in them they have no feeling of love to themselves. Therefore also such men do not rejoice or grieve with themselves; for their soul is rent by faction, and one element in it by reason of its wickedness grieves when it abstains from certain acts, while the other part is pleased, and one draws them this way and the other that, as if they were pulling them in pieces. If a man cannot at the same time be pained and pleased, at all events after a short time he is pained *because* he was pleased, and he could have wished that these things had not been pleasant to him; for bad men are laden with repentance.

Therefore the bad man does not seem to be amicably disposed even to himself, because there is nothing in him to love; so that if to be thus is the height of wretchedness, we should strain every nerve to avoid wickedness and should endeavour to be good; for so and only so can one be either friendly to oneself or a friend to another.

8 The question is also debated, whether a man should love himself most, or some one else. People criticize those who love themselves most, and call them self-lovers, using this as an epithet of disgrace, and a bad man seems to do everything for his own sake, and the more so the more wicked he is – and so men reproach him, for instance, with doing nothing of his own accord – while the good man acts for honour's sake, and the more so the better he is, and acts for his friend's sake, and sacrifices his own interest.

But the facts clash with these arguments, and this is not surprising. For men say that one ought to love best one's best friend, and a man's best friend is one who wishes well to the object of his wish for his sake, even if no one is to know of it; and these attributes are found most of all in a man's attitude towards himself, and so are all the other attributes by which a friend is defined; for, as we have said, it is from this relation that all the characteristics of friendship have extended to our neighbours. All the proverbs, too, agree with this, e.g. 'a single soul', and 'what friends have is common property', and 'friendship is equality', and 'charity begins at home'; for all these marks will be found most in a man's relation to himself; he is his own best friend and therefore ought to love himself best. It is therefore a reasonable question, which of the two views we should follow; for both are plausible.

Perhaps we ought to mark off such arguments from each other and determine how far and in what respects each view is right. Now if we grasp the sense in which each school uses the phrase 'lover of self', the truth may become evident. Those who use the term as one of reproach ascribe self-love to people who assign to themselves the greater share of wealth, honours, and bodily pleasures; for these are what most people desire, and busy themselves about as though they were the best of all things, which is the reason, too, why they become objects of competition. So those who are grasping with regard to these things gratify their appetites and in general their feelings and the irrational element of the soul; and most men are of this nature (which is the reason why the epithet has come to be used as it is – it takes its meaning from the prevailing type of self-love, which is a bad one); it is just, therefore, that men who are lovers of self in this way are reproached for being so. That it is those who give themselves the preference in regard to objects of this sort that most people usually call lovers of self is plain; for if a man were always anxious that he himself, above all things, should act justly, temperately, or in accordance with any other of the virtues, and in general were always to try to secure for himself the honourable course, no one will call such a man a lover of self or blame him.

But such a man would seem more than the other a lover of self; at all events he assigns to himself the things that are noblest and best, and gratifies the most authoritative element in himself and in all things obeys this; and just as a city or any other systematic whole is most properly identified with the most authoritative element in it, so is a man; and therefore the man who loves this and gratifies it is most of all a lover of self. Besides, a man is said to have or not to have self-control according as his reason has or has not the control, on the assumption that this is the man himself; and the things men have done on a rational principle are thought most properly their own acts and voluntary acts. That this is the man himself, then, or is so more than anything else, is plain, and also that the good man loves most this part of him. Whence it follows that he is most truly a lover of self, of another type than that which is a matter of reproach, and as different from that as living according to a rational principle is from living as passion dictates, and desiring what is noble from desiring what seems advantageous. Those, then, who busy themselves in an exceptional degree with noble actions all men approve and praise; and if *all* were to strive towards what is noble and strain every nerve to do the noblest deeds, everything would be as it should be for the common weal, and every one would secure for himself the goods that are greatest, since virtue is the greatest of goods.

Therefore the good man should be a lover of self (for he will both himself profit by doing noble acts, and will benefit his fellows), but the wicked man should not; for he will hurt both himself and his neighbours, following as he does evil passions. For the wicked man, what he does clashes with what he ought to do, but what the good man ought to do he does; for reason in each of its possessors chooses what is best for itself, and the good man obeys his reason. It is true of the good man too that he does many acts for the sake of his friends and his country, and if necessary dies for them; for he will throw away both wealth and honours and in general the goods that are objects of competition, gaining for himself nobility; since he would prefer a short period of intense pleasure to a long one of mild enjoyment, a twelvemonth of noble life to many years of humdrum existence, and one great and noble action to many trivial ones. Now those who die for others doubtless attain this result; it is therefore a great prize that they choose for themselves. They will throw away wealth too on condition that their friends will gain more; for while a man's friend gains wealth he himself achieves nobility; he is therefore assigning the greater good to himself. The same too is true of honour and office; all these things he will sacrifice to his friend; for this is noble and laudable for himself. Rightly then is he thought to be good, since he chooses nobility before all else. But he may even give up actions to his friend; it may be nobler to become the cause of his friend's acting than to act himself. In all the actions, therefore, that men are praised for, the good man is seen to assign himself the greater share in what is noble. In this sense, then, as has been said, a man should be a lover of self; but in the sense in which most men are so, he ought not.

9 It is also disputed whether the happy man will need friends or not. It is said that those who are supremely happy and self-sufficient have no need of friends; for they have the things that are good, and therefore being self-sufficient they need nothing further, while a friend, being another self, furnishes what a man cannot provide by his own effort; whence the saying 'when fortune is kind, what need of friends?' But it seems strange, when one assigns all good things to the happy man, not to assign friends, who are thought

the greatest of external goods. And if it is more characteristic of a friend to do well by another than to be well done by, and to confer benefits is characteristic of the good man and of virtue, and it is nobler to do well by friends than by strangers, the good man will need people to do well by. This is why the question is asked whether we need friends more in prosperity or in adversity, on the assumption that not only does a man in adversity need people to confer benefits on him, but also those who are prospering need people to do well by. Surely it is strange, too, to make the supremely happy man a solitary; for no one would choose the whole world on condition of being alone, since man is a political creature and one whose nature is to live with others. Therefore even the happy man lives with others; for he has the things that are by nature good. And plainly it is better to spend his days with friends and good men than with strangers or any chance persons. Therefore the happy man needs friends.

What then do holders of the first view mean, and in what respect are they right? Is it that most men identify friends with useful people? Of such friends indeed the supremely happy man will have no need, since he already has the things that are good; nor will he need those whom one makes one's friends because of their pleasantness, or he will need them only to a small extent (for his life, being pleasant, has no need of adventitious pleasure); and because he does not need *such* friends he is thought not to need friends.

But this is surely not true. For we have said at the outset that happiness is an activity; and activity plainly comes into being and is not present at the start like a piece of property. If (1) happiness lies in living and being active, and the good man's activity is virtuous and pleasant in itself, as we have said at the outset, and (2) a thing's being one's own is one of the attributes that make it pleasant, and (3) we can contemplate our neighbours better than ourselves and their actions better than our own, and if the actions of virtuous men who are their friends are pleasant to good men (since these have both the attributes that are naturally pleasant), - if this be so, the supremely happy man will need friends of this sort, since his purpose is to contemplate worthy actions and actions that are his own, and the actions of a good man who is his friend have both these qualities.

Further, men think that the happy man ought to live pleasantly. Now if he were a solitary, life would be hard for him; for by oneself it is not easy to be continuously active; but with others and towards others it is easier. With others therefore his activity will be more continuous, and it is in itself pleasant, as it ought to be for the man who is supremely happy; for a good man *qua* good delights in virtuous actions and is vexed at vicious ones, as a musical man enjoys beautiful tunes but is pained at bad ones. A certain training in virtue arises also from the company of the good, as Theognis has said before us.

If we look at it more scientifically, a virtuous friend seems to be naturally desirable for a virtuous man. For that which is good by nature, we have said, is for the virtuous man good and pleasant in itself. Now life is defined in the case of animals by the power of perception, in that of man by the power of perception or thought; and a power is defined by reference to the corresponding activity, which is the essential thing; therefore life seems to be essentially the act of perceiving or thinking. And life is among the things that are good and pleasant in themselves, since it is determinate and the determinate is of the nature of the good; and that which is good by nature is also good for the virtuous man (which is the reason why life seems pleasant to all men); but we must not apply this to a wicked and corrupt life nor to a life spent in pain; for such a life is indeterminate, as are its attributes. The nature of pain will become plainer in what follows. But if life itself is good and pleasant (which it seems to be, from the very fact that all men desire it, and particularly those who are good and supremely happy; for to such men life is most desirable, and their existence is the most supremely happy); and if he who sees perceives that he sees, and he who hears, that he hears, and he who walks, that he walks, and in the case of all other activities similarly there is something which perceives that we are active, so that if we perceive, we perceive that we perceive, and if we think, that we think; and if to perceive that we perceive or think is to perceive that we exist (for existence was defined as perceiving or thinking); and if perceiving that one lives is in itself one of the things that are pleasant (for life is by nature good, and to perceive what is good present in oneself is pleasant); and if life is desirable, and particularly so for good men, because to them existence is good and pleasant (for they are pleased at the consciousness of the presence in them of what is in itself good); and if as the virtuous man is to himself, he is to his friend also (for his friend is another self): – if all this be true, as his own being is desirable for each man, so, or almost so, is that of his friend. Now his being was seen to be desirable because he perceived his own goodness, and such perception is pleasant in itself. He needs, therefore, to be conscious of the existence of his friend as well, and this will be realized in their living together and sharing in discussion and thought; for this is what living together would seem to mean in the case of man, and not, as in the case of cattle, feeding in the same place.

If, then, being is in itself desirable for the supremely happy man (since it is by its nature good and pleasant), and that of his friend is very much the same, a friend will be one of the things that are desirable. Now that which is desirable for him he must have, or he will be deficient in this respect. The man who is to be happy will therefore need virtuous friends.

Book X

1 AFTER these matters we ought perhaps next to discuss pleasure. For it is thought to be most intimately connected with our human nature, which is the reason why in educating the young we steer them by the rudders of pleasure and pain; it is thought, too, that to enjoy the things we ought and to hate the things we ought has the greatest bearing on virtue of character. For these things extend right through life, with a weight and power of their own in respect both to virtue and to the happy life, since men choose what is pleasant and avoid what is painful; and such things, it will be thought, we should least of all omit to discuss, especially since they admit of much dispute. For some say pleasure is the good, while others, on the contrary, say it is thoroughly bad – some no doubt being persuaded that the facts are so, and others thinking it has a better effect on our life to exhibit pleasure as a bad thing even if it is not; for most people (they think) incline towards it and are the slaves of their pleasures, for which reason they ought to lead them in the opposite direction, since thus they will reach the middle state. But surely this is not correct. For arguments about matters concerned with feelings and actions are less reliable than facts; and so when they clash with the facts of perception they are despised, and discredit the truth as well; if a man who runs down pleasure is once seen to be aiming at it, his inclining towards it is thought to imply that it is all worthy of being aimed at; for most people are not good at drawing distinctions. True arguments seem, then, most useful, not only with a view to knowledge, but with a view to life also; for since they harmonize with the facts they are believed, and so they stimulate those who understand them to live according to them. – Enough of such questions; let us proceed to review the opinions that have been expressed about pleasure.

2 Eudoxus thought pleasure was the good because he saw all things, both rational and irrational, aiming at it, and because in all things that which is the object of choice is what is excellent, and that which is most the object of choice the greatest good; thus the fact

that all things moved towards the same object indicated that this was for all things the chief good (for each thing, he argued, finds its own good, as it finds its own nourishment); and that which is good for all things and at which all aim was *the* good. His arguments were credited more because of the excellence of his character than for their own sake; he was thought to be remarkably temperate and therefore it was thought that he was not saying what he did say as a friend of pleasure, but that the facts really were so. He believed that the same conclusion followed no less plainly from a study of the contrary of pleasure; pain was in itself an object of aversion to all things, and therefore its contrary must be similarly an object of choice. And again that is most an object of choice which we choose not because or for the sake of something else, and pleasure is admittedly of this nature; for no one asks to what end he is pleased, thus implying that pleasure is in itself an object of choice. Further, he argued that pleasure when added to any good, e.g. to just or temperate action, makes it more worthy of choice, and that it is only by itself that the good can be increased.

This argument seems to show it to be one of the goods, and no more a good than any other; for every good is more worthy of choice along with another good than taken alone. And so it is by an argument of this kind that Plato proves the good *not* to be pleasure; he argues that the pleasant life is more desirable with wisdom than without, and that if the mixture is better, pleasure is not the good; for the good cannot become more desirable by the addition of anything to it. Now it is clear that nothing else, any more than pleasure, can be the good if it is made more desirable by the addition of any of the things that are good in themselves. What, then, is there that satisfies this criterion, which at the same time we can participate in? It is something of this sort that we are looking for.

Those who object that that at which all things aim is not necessarily good are, we may surmise, talking nonsense. For we say that that which every one thinks really is so; and the man who attacks this conviction will hardly have anything more convincing to maintain instead. If it were irrational creatures that desired the things in question, there might be something in what they say; but if intelligent creatures do so as well, how can there be anything in it? But perhaps even in inferior creatures there is some natural good stronger than themselves which aims at their proper good.

Nor does the argument about the contrary of pleasure seem to be correct. They say that if pain is an evil it does not follow that pleasure is a good; for evil is opposed to evil and at the same time both are opposed to the neutral state – which is correct enough but does not apply to the things in question. For if both pleasure and pain belonged to the class of evils they ought both to be objects of aversion, while if they belonged to the class of neutrals neither should be an object of aversion or they should both be equally so; but in fact people evidently avoid the one as evil and choose the other as good; that then must be the nature of the opposition between them.

3 Nor again, if pleasure is not a quality, does it follow that it is not a good; for the activities of virtue are not qualities either, nor is happiness.

They say, however, that the good is determinate, while pleasure is indeterminate, because it admits of degrees. Now if it is from the feeling of pleasure that they judge thus, the same will be true of justice and the other virtues, in respect of which we plainly say that people of a certain character are so more or less, and act more or less in accordance with these virtues; for people may be more just or brave, and it is possible also to act justly or temperately more or less. But if their judgement is based on the various pleasures, surely they are not stating the real cause, if in fact some pleasures are unmixed and others mixed. Again, just as health admits of degrees without being indeterminate, why should not pleasure? The same proportion is not found in all things, nor a single proportion always in the same thing, but it may be relaxed and yet persist up to a point, and it may differ in degree. The case of pleasure also may therefore be of this kind.

Again, they assume that the good is perfect while movements and comings into being are imperfect, and try to exhibit pleasure as being a movement and a coming into being. But they do not seem to be right even in saying that it is a movement. For speed and slowness are thought to be proper to every movement, and if a movement, e.g. that of the heavens, has not speed or slowness in itself, it has it in relation to something else; but of pleasure neither of these things is true. For while we may *become* pleased quickly as we may become angry quickly, we cannot *be* pleased quickly, not even in relation to some one else, while we *can* walk, or grow, or the like, quickly. While, then, we can change quickly or slowly into a state of pleasure, we cannot quickly exhibit the activity of pleasure, i.e. be pleased. Again, how can it be a coming into being? It is not thought that any chance thing can come out of any chance thing, but that a thing is dissolved into that out of which it comes into being; and pain would be the destruction of that of which pleasure is the coming into being.

They say, too, that pain is the lack of that which is according to nature, and pleasure is replenishment. But these experiences are bodily. If then pleasure is replenishment with that which is according to nature, that which feels pleasure will be that in which the replenishment takes place, i.e. the body; but that is not thought to be the case; therefore the replenishment is not pleasure, though one would be pleased when replenishment was taking place, just as one would be pained if one was being operated on. This opinion seems to be based on the pains and pleasures connected with nutrition; on the fact that when people have been short of food and have felt pain beforehand they are pleased by the replenishment. But this does not happen with all pleasures; for the pleasures of learning and, among the sensuous pleasures, those of smell, and also many sounds and sights, and memories and hopes, do not presuppose pain. Of what then will these be the coming into being? There has not been lack of anything of which there might be a replenishment.

In reply to those who bring forward the disgraceful pleasures one may say that these are not pleasant; if things are pleasant to people of vicious constitution, we must not suppose that they are also pleasant to others than these, just as we do not reason so about the things that are wholesome or sweet or bitter to sick people, or ascribe whiteness to the things that seem white to those suffering from a disease of the eye. Or one might answer thus – that the pleasures are desirable, but not from *these* sources, as wealth is desirable, but not as the reward of betrayal, and health, but not at the cost of eating anything and everything. Or perhaps pleasures differ in kind; for those derived from noble sources are different from those derived from base sources, and one cannot get the pleasure of the just man without being just, nor that of the musical man without being musical, and so on.

The fact, too, that a friend is different from a flatterer seems to make it plain that pleasure is not a good or that pleasures are different in kind; for the one is thought to consort with us a view to the good, the other with a view to our pleasure, and the one is reproached for his conduct while the other is praised on the ground that he consorts with us for different ends. And no one would choose to live with the intellect of a child throughout his life, however much he were to be pleased at the things that children are pleased at, nor to get enjoyment by doing some most disgraceful deed, though he were never to feel any pain in consequence. And there are many things we should be keen about even if they brought no pleasure, e.g. seeing, remembering, knowing, possessing the virtues. If pleasures necessarily do accompany these, that makes no odds; we should choose these even if no pleasure resulted. It seems to be clear, then, that neither is pleasure the good nor is all pleasure desirable, and that some pleasures *are* desirable in themselves, differing in kind or in their sources from the others. So much for the things that are said about pleasure and pain.

4 What pleasure is, or what kind of thing it is, will become plainer if we take up the question again from the beginning. Seeing seems to be at any moment complete, for it does not lack anything which coming into being later will complete its form; and pleasure also seems to be of this nature. For it is a whole, and at no time can one find a pleasure whose form will be completed if the pleasure lasts longer. For this reason, too, it is not a movement. For every movement (e.g. that of building) takes time and is for the sake of an end, and is complete when it has made what it aims at. It is complete, therefore, only in the whole time or at that final moment. In their parts and during the time they occupy, all movements are incomplete, and are different in kind from the whole movement and from each other. For the fitting together of the

stones is different from the fluting of the column, and these are both different from the making of the temple; and the making of the temple is complete (for it lacks nothing with a view to the end proposed), but the making of the base or of the triglyph is incomplete; for each is the making of only a part. They differ in kind, then, and it is not possible to find at any and every time a movement complete in form, but if at all, only in the whole time. So, too, in the case of walking and all other movements. For if locomotion is a movement from here to there, it, too, has differences in kind — flying, walking, leaping, and so on. And not only so, but in walking itself there are such differences; for the whence and whither are not the same in the whole racecourse and in a part of it, nor in one part and in another, nor is it the same thing to traverse this line and that; for one traverses not only a line but one which is in a place, and this one is in a different place from that. We have discussed movement with precision in another work, but it seems that it is not complete at any and every time, but that the many movements are incomplete and different in kind, since the whence and whither give them their form. But of pleasure the form is complete at any and every time. Plainly, then, pleasure and movement must be different from each other, and pleasure must be one of the things that are whole and complete. This would seem to be the case, too, from the fact that it is not possible to move otherwise than in time, but it *is* possible to be pleased; for that which takes place in a moment is a whole.

From these considerations it is clear, too, that these thinkers are not right in saying there is a movement or a coming into being *of* pleasure. For these cannot be ascribed to all things, but only to those that are divisible and not wholes; there is no coming into being of seeing nor of a point nor of a unit, nor is any of these a movement or coming into being; therefore there is no movement or coming into being of pleasure either; for it is a whole.

Since every sense is active in relation to its object, and a sense which is in good condition acts perfectly in relation to the most beautiful of its objects (for perfect activity seems to be ideally of this nature; whether we say that *it* is active, or the organ in which it resides, may be assumed to be immaterial), it follows that in the case of each sense the best activity is that of the best-conditioned

Book X.4

organ in relation to the finest of its objects. And this activity will be the most complete and pleasant. For, while there is pleasure in respect of any sense, and in respect of thought and contemplation no less, the most complete is pleasantest, and that of a well-conditioned organ in relation to the worthiest of its objects is the most complete; and the pleasure completes the activity. But the pleasure does not complete it in the same way as the combination of object and sense, both good, just as health and the doctor are not in the same way the cause of a man's being healthy. (That pleasure is produced in respect of each sense is plain; for we speak of sights and sounds as pleasant. It is also plain that it arises most of all when both the sense is at its best and it is active in reference to an object which corresponds; when both object and perceiver are of the best there will always be pleasure, since the requisite agent and patient are both present.) Pleasure completes the activity not as the corresponding permanent state does, by its immanence, but as an end which supervenes as the bloom of youth does on those in the flower of their age. So long, then, as both the intelligible or sensible object and the discriminating or contemplative faculty are as they should be, the pleasure will be in the activity; for when both the passive and the active factor are unchanged and are related to each other in the same way, the same result naturally follows.

How, then, is it that no one is continuously pleased? Is it that we grow weary? Certainly all human things are incapable of continuous activity. Therefore pleasure also is not continuous; for it accompanies activity. Some things delight us when they are new, but later do so less, for the same reason; for at first the mind is in a state of stimulation and intensely active about them, as people are with respect to their vision when they look hard at a thing, but afterwards our activity is not of this kind, but has grown relaxed; for which reason the pleasure also is dulled.

One might think that all men desire pleasure because they all aim at life; life is an activity, and each man is active about those things and with those faculties that he loves most; e.g. the musician is active with his hearing in reference to tunes, the student with his mind in reference to theoretical questions, and so on in each case; now pleasure completes the activities, and therefore life, which they desire. It is with good reason, then, that they aim at pleasure too, since for every one it completes life, which is desirable. But whether we choose life for the sake of pleasure or pleasure for the sake of life is a question we may dismiss for the present. For they seem to be bound up together and not to admit of separation, since without activity pleasure does not arise, and every activity is completed by the attendant pleasure.

For this reason pleasures seem, too, to differ in kind. For things different in kind are, we think, completed by different things (we see this to be true both of natural objects and of things produced by art, e.g. animals, trees, a painting, a sculpture, a house, an implement); and, similarly, we think that activities differing in kind are completed by things differing in kind. Now the activities of thought differ from those of the senses, and both differ among themselves, in kind; so, therefore, do the pleasures that complete them.

This may be seen, too, from the fact that each of the pleasures is bound up with the activity it completes. For an activity is intensified by its proper pleasure, since each class of things is better judged of and brought to precision by those who engage in the activity with pleasure; e.g. it is those who enjoy geometrical thinking that become geometers and grasp the various propositions better, and, similarly, those who are fond of music or of building, and so on, make progress in their proper function by enjoying it; so the pleasures intensify the activities, and what intensifies a thing is proper to it, but things different in kind have properties different in kind.

This will be even more apparent from the fact that activities are hindered by pleasures arising from other sources. For people who are fond of playing the flute are incapable of attending to arguments if they overhear some one playing the flute, since they enjoy flute-playing more than the activity in hand; so the pleasure connected with flute-playing destroys the activity concerned with argument. This happens, similarly, in all other cases, when one is active about two things at once; the more pleasant activity drives out the other, and if it is much more pleasant does so all the more, so that one even ceases from the other. This is why when we enjoy anything very much we do not throw ourselves into anything else, and do one thing only when we are not much pleased by another; e.g. in the theatre the people who eat sweets do so most when the actors are poor. Now since activities are made precise and more enduring and better by their proper pleasure, and injured by alien pleasures, evidently the two kinds of pleasure are far apart. For alien pleasures do pretty much what proper pains do, since activities are destroyed by their proper pains; e.g. if a man finds writing or doing sums unpleasant and painful, he does not write, or does not do sums, because the activity is painful. So an activity suffers contrary effects from its proper pleasures and pains, i.e. from those that supervene on it in virtue of its own nature. And alien pleasures have been stated to do much the same as pain; they destroy the activity, only not to the same degree.

Now since activities differ in respect of goodness and badness, and some are worthy to be chosen, others to be avoided, and others neutral, so, too, are the pleasures; for to each activity there is a proper pleasure. The pleasure proper to a worthy activity is good and that proper to an unworthy activity bad; just as the appetites for noble objects are laudable, those for base objects culpable. But the pleasures involved in activities are more proper to them than the desires; for the latter are separated both in time and in nature, while the former are close to the activities, and so hard to distinguish from them that it admits of dispute whether the activity is not the same as the pleasure. (Still, pleasure does not seem to *be* thought or perception – that would be strange; but because they are not found apart they appear to some people the same.) As activities are different, then, so are the corresponding pleasures. Now sight is superior to touch in purity, and hearing and smell to taste; the pleasures, therefore, are similarly superior, and those of thought superior to these, and within each of the two kinds some are superior to others.

Each animal is thought to have a proper pleasure, as it has a proper function; viz. that which corresponds to its activity. If we survey them species by species, too, this will be evident; horse, dog, and man have different pleasures, as Heraclitus says 'asses would prefer sweepings to gold'; for food is pleasanter than gold to asses. So the pleasures of creatures different in kind differ in kind, and it is plausible to suppose that those of a single species do not differ. But they vary to no small extent, in the case of men at least; the same things delight some people and pain others, and are painful and odious to some, and pleasant to and liked by others. This happens, too, in the case of sweet things; the same things do not seem sweet to a man in a fever and a healthy man – nor hot to a weak man and one in good condition. The same happens in other cases. But in all such matters that which appears to the good man is thought to be really so. If this is correct, as it seems to be, and virtue and the good man as such are the measure of each thing, those also will be pleasures which appear so to him, and those things pleasant which he enjoys. If the things he finds tiresome seem pleasant to some one, that is nothing surprising; for men may be ruined and spoilt in many ways; but the things are not pleasant, but only pleasant to these people and to people in this condition. Those which are admittedly disgraceful plainly should not be said to be pleasures, except to a perverted taste; but of those that are thought to good what kind of pleasure or what pleasure should be said to be that proper to man? Is it not plain from the corresponding activities? The pleasures follow these. Whether, then, the perfect and supremely happy man has one or more activities, the pleasures that perfect these will be said in the strict sense to be pleasures proper to man, and the rest will be so in a secondary and fractional way, as are the activities.

Now that we have spoken of the virtues, the forms of friendship, and the varieties of pleasure, what remains is to discuss in outline the nature of happiness, since this is what we state the end of human affairs to be. Our discussion will be the more concise if we first sum up what we have said already. We said, then, that it is not a disposition; for if it were it might belong to some one who was asleep throughout his life, living the life of a plant, or, again, to some one who was suffering the greatest misfortunes. If these implications are unacceptable, and we must rather class happiness as an activity, as we have said before, and if some activities are necessary, and desirable for the sake of something else, while others are so in themselves, evidently happiness must be placed among those desirable in themselves, not among those desirable for the sake of something else; for happiness does not lack anything, but is self-sufficient. Now those activities are desirable in themselves from which nothing is sought beyond the activity. And of this nature virtuous actions are thought to be; for to do noble and good deeds is a thing desirable for its own sake.

Pleasant amusements also are thought to be of this nature; we choose them not for the sake of other things; for we are injured rather than benefited by them, since we are led to neglect our bodies and our property. But most of the people who are deemed happy take refuge in such pastimes, which is the reason why those who are ready-witted at them are highly esteemed at the courts of tyrants; they make themselves pleasant companions in the tyrants' favourite pursuits, and that is the sort of man they want. Now these things are thought to be of the nature of happiness because people in despotic positions spend their leisure in them, but perhaps such people prove nothing; for virtue and reason, from which good activities flow, do not depend on despotic position; nor, if these people, who have never tasted pure and generous pleasure, take refuge in the bodily pleasures, should these for that reason be thought more desirable; for boys, too, think the things that are valued among themselves are the best. It is to be expected, then, that, as different things seem valuable to boys and to men, so they should to bad men and to good. Now, as we have often maintained, those things are both valuable and pleasant which are such to the good man; and to each man the activity in accordance with his own disposition is most desirable, and, therefore, to the good man that which is in accordance with virtue. Happiness, therefore, does not lie in amusement; it would, indeed, be strange if the end were amusement, and one were to take trouble and suffer hardship all one's life in order to amuse oneself. For, in a word, everything that we choose we choose for the sake of something else — except happiness, which is an end. Now to exert oneself and work for the sake of amusement seems silly and utterly childish. But to amuse oneself in order that one may exert oneself, as Anacharsis puts it, seems right; for amusement is a sort of relaxation, and we need relaxation because we cannot work continuously. Relaxation, then, is not an end; for it is taken for the sake of activity.

The happy life is thought to be virtuous; now a virtuous life requires exertion, and does not consist in amusement. And we say that serious things are better than laughable things and those connected with amusement, and that the activity of the better of any two things – whether it be two elements of our being or two men – is the more serious; but the activity of the better is *ipso facto* superior and more of the nature of happiness. And any chance person – even a slave – can enjoy the bodily pleasures no less than the best man; but no one assigns to a slave a share in happiness – unless he assigns to him also a share in human life. For happiness does not lie in such occupations, but, as we have said before, in virtuous activities.

If happiness is activity in accordance with virtue, it is reasonable that it should be in accordance with the highest virtue; and this will be that of the best thing in us. Whether it be reason or something else that is this element which is thought to be our natural ruler and guide and to take thought of things noble and divine, whether it be itself also divine or only the most divine element in us, the activity of this in accordance with its proper virtue will be perfect happiness. That this activity is contemplative we have already said.

Now this would seem to be in agreement both with what we said before and with the truth. For, firstly, this activity is the best (since not only is reason the best thing in us, but the objects of reason are the best of knowable objects); and, secondly, it is the most continuous, since we can contemplate truth more continuously than we can *do* anything. And we think happiness has pleasure mingled with it, but the activity of philosophic wisdom is admittedly the pleasantest of virtuous activities; at all events the pursuit of it is thought to offer pleasures marvellous for their purity and their enduringness, and it is to be expected that those who know will pass their time more pleasantly than those who inquire. And the self-sufficiency that is spoken of must belong most to the contemplative activity. For while a philosopher, as well as a just man or one possessing any other virtue, needs the necessaries of life, when they are sufficiently equipped with things of that sort the just man needs people towards whom and with whom he shall act justly, and the temperate man, the brave man, and

Book X.7

each of the others is in the same case, but the philosopher, even when by himself, can contemplate truth, and the better the wiser he is; he can perhaps do so better if he has fellow-workers, but still he is the most self-sufficient. And this activity alone would seem to be loved for its own sake; for nothing arises from it apart from the contemplating, while from practical activities we gain more or less apart from the action. And happiness is thought to depend on leisure; for we are busy that we may have leisure, and make war that we may live in peace. Now the activity of the practical virtues is exhibited in political or military affairs, but the actions concerned with these seem to be unleisurely. Warlike actions are completely so (for no one chooses to be at war, or provokes war, for the sake of being at war; any one would seem absolutely murderous if he were to make enemies of his friends in order to bring about battle and slaughter); but the action of the statesman is also unleisurely, and – apart from the political action itself – aims at despotic power and honours, or at all events happiness, for him and his fellow citizens – a happiness different from political action, and evidently sought as being different. So if among virtuous actions political and military actions are distinguished by nobility and greatness, and these are unleisurely and aim at an end and are not desirable for their own sake, but the activity of reason, which is contemplative, seems both to be superior in serious worth and to aim at no end beyond itself, and to have its pleasure proper to itself (and this augments the activity), and the self-sufficiency, leisureliness, unweariedness (so far as this is possible for man), and all the other attributes ascribed to the supremely happy man are evidently those connected with this activity, it follows that this will be the complete happiness of man, if it be allowed a complete term of life (for none of the attributes of happiness is *in*complete).

But such a life would be too high for man; for it is not in so far as he is man that he will live so, but in so far as something divine is present in him; and by so much as this is superior to our composite nature is its activity superior to that which is the exercise of the other kind of virtue. If reason is divine, then, in comparison with man, the life according to it is divine in comparison with human life. But we must not follow those who advise us, being men, to think of human things, and, being mortal, of mortal things, but must, so far as we can, make ourselves immortal, and strain every nerve to live in accordance with the best thing in us; for even if it be small in bulk, much more does it in power and worth surpass everything. And this would seem actually to *be* each man, since it is the authoritative and better part of him. It would be strange, then, if he were to choose not the life of himself but that of something else. And what we said before will apply now; that which is proper to each thing is by nature best and most pleasant for each thing; for man, therefore, the life according to reason is best and pleasantest, since reason more than anything else *is* man. This life therefore is also the happiest.

But in a secondary degree the life in accordance with the other kind of virtue is happy; for the activities in accordance with this befit our human estate. Just and brave acts, and other virtuous acts, we do in relation to each other, observing our respective duties with regard to contracts and services and all manner of actions and with regard to passions; and all of these seem to be typically human. Some of them seem even to arise from the body, and virtue of character to be in many ways bound up with the passions. Practical wisdom, too, is linked to virtue of character, and this to practical wisdom, since the principles of practical wisdom are in accordance with the moral virtues and rightness in morals is in accordance with practical wisdom. Being connected with the passions also, the moral virtues must belong to our composite nature; and the virtues of our composite nature are human; so, therefore, are the life and the happiness which correspond to these. The excellence of the reason is a thing apart; we must be content to say this much about it, for to describe it precisely is a task greater than our purpose requires. It would seem, however, also to need external equipment but little, or less than moral virtue does. Grant that both need the necessaries, and do so equally, even if the statesman's work is the more concerned with the body and things of that sort; for there will be little difference there; but in what they need for the exercise of their activities there will be much difference. The liberal man will need money for the doing of his liberal deeds, and the just man too will need it for the returning of services (for wishes are hard to discern, and even people who are not just *pretend* to wish to act justly); and the brave man will need power if he is to accomplish any of the acts that correspond to his virtue, and the temperate man will need opportunity; for how else is either he or any of the others to be recognized? It is debated, too, whether the purpose or the deed is more essential to virtue, which is assumed to involve both; it is surely clear that its perfection involves both; but for deeds many things are needed, and more, the greater and nobler the deeds are. But the man who is contemplating the truth needs no such thing, at least with a view to the exercise of his activity; indeed they are, one may say, even hindrances, at all events to his contemplation; but in so far as he is a man and lives with a number of people, he chooses to do virtuous acts; he will therefore need such aids to living a human life.

But that perfect happiness is a contemplative activity will appear from the following consideration as well. We assume the gods to be above all other beings blessed and happy; but what sort of actions must we assign to them? Acts of justice? Will not the gods seem absurd if they make contracts and return deposits, and so on? Acts of a brave man, then, confronting dangers and running risks because it is noble to do so? Or liberal acts? To whom will they give? It will be strange if they are really to have money or anything of the kind. And what would their temperate acts be? Is not such praise tasteless, since they have no bad appetites? If we were to run through them all, the circumstances of action would be found trivial and unworthy of gods. Still, every one supposes that they *live* and therefore that they are active; we cannot suppose them to sleep like Endymion. Now if you take away from a living being action, and still more production, what is left but contemplation? Therefore the activity of God, which surpasses all others in blessedness, must be contemplative; and of human activities, therefore, that which is most akin to this must be most of the nature of happiness.

This is indicated, too, by the fact that the other animals have no share in happiness, being completely deprived of such activity. For while the whole life of the gods is blessed, and that of men too in so far as some likeness of such activity belongs to them, none of the other animals is happy, since they in no way share in contemplation. Happiness extends, then, just so far as contemplation does, and those to whom contemplation more fully belongs are more truly happy, not as a mere concomitant but in virtue of the contemplation; for this is in itself precious. Happiness, therefore, must be some form of contemplation.

But, being a man, one will also need external prosperity; for our nature is not self-sufficient for the purpose of contemplation, but our body also must be healthy and must have food and other attention. Still, we must not think that the man who is to be happy will need many things or great things, merely because he cannot be supremely happy without external goods; for self-sufficiency and action do not involve excess, and we can do noble acts without ruling earth and sea; for even with moderate advantages one can act virtuously (this is manifest enough; for private persons are thought to do worthy acts no less than despots—indeed even more); and it is enough that we should have so much as that; for the life of the man who is active in accordance with virtue will be happy. Solon, too, was perhaps sketching well the happy man when he described him as moderately furnished with externals but as having done (as Solon thought) the noblest acts, and lived temperately; for one can with but moderate possessions do what one ought. Anaxagoras also seems to have supposed the happy man not to be rich nor a despot, when he said that he would not be surprised if the happy man were to seem to most people a strange person; for they judge by externals, since these are all they perceive. The opinions of the wise seem, then, to harmonize with our arguments. But while even such things carry some conviction, the truth in practical matters is discerned from the facts of life; for these are the decisive factor. We must therefore survey what we have already said, bringing it to the test of the facts of life, and if it harmonizes with the facts we must accept it, but if it clashes with them we must suppose it to be mere theory. Now he who exercises his reason and cultivates it seems to be both in the best state of mind and most dear to the gods. For if the gods have any care for human affairs, as they are thought to have, it would be reasonable both that they should delight in that which was best and most akin to them (i.e. reason) and that they should reward those who love and honour this most, as caring for the things that are dear to them and acting both rightly and nobly. And that all these attributes belong most of all to the philosopher is manifest. He, therefore, is the dearest to the gods. And he who is that will presumably be also the happiest; so that in this way too the philosopher will more than any other be happy.

9 If these matters and the virtues, and also friendship and pleasure, have been dealt with sufficiently in outline, are we to suppose that our programme has reached its end? Surely, as the saying goes, where there are things to be done the end is not to survey and recognize the various things, but rather to do them; with regard to virtue, then, it is not enough to know, but we must try to have and use it, or try any other way there may be of becoming good. Now if arguments were in themselves enough to make men good, they would justly, as Theognis says, have won very great rewards, and such rewards should have been provided; but as things are, while they seem to have power to encourage and stimulate the generous-minded among our youth, and to make a character which is gently born, and a true lover of what is noble, ready to be possessed by virtue, they are not able to encourage the many to nobility and goodness. For these do not by nature obey the sense of shame, but only fear, and do not abstain from bad acts because of their baseness but through fear of punishment; living by passion they pursue their own pleasures and the means to them, and avoid the opposite pains, and have not even a conception of what is noble and truly pleasant, since they have never tasted it. What argument would remould such people? It is hard, if not impossible, to remove by argument the traits that have long since been incorporated in the character; and perhaps we must be content if, when all the influences by which we are thought to become good are present, we get some tincture of virtue.

Now some think that we are made good by nature, others by habituation, others by teaching. Nature's part evidently does not depend on us, but as a result of some divine causes is present in those who are truly fortunate; while argument and teaching, we may suspect, are not powerful with all men, but the soul of the student must first have been cultivated by means of habits for noble joy and noble hatred, like earth which is to nourish the seed. For he who lives as passion directs will not hear argument that dissuades him, nor understand it if he does; and how can we persuade one in such a state to change his ways? And in general passion seems to yield not to argument but to force. The character, then, must somehow be there already with a kinship to virtue, loving what is noble and hating what is base.

But it is difficult to get from youth up a right training for virtue if one has not been brought up under right laws; for to live temperately and hardily is not pleasant to most people, especially when they are young. For this reason their nurture and occupations should be fixed by law; for they will not be painful when they have become customary. But it is surely not enough that when they are young they should get the right nurture and attention; since they must, even when they are grown up, practise and be habituated to them, we shall need laws for this as well, and generally speaking to cover the whole of life; for most people obey necessity rather than argument, and punishments rather than the sense of what is noble.

This is why some think that legislators ought to stimulate men to virtue and urge them forward by the motive of the noble, on the assumption that those who have been well advanced by the formation of habits will attend to such influences; and that punishments and penalties should be imposed on those who disobey and are of inferior nature, while the incurably bad should be completely banished. A good man (they think), since he lives with his mind fixed on what is noble, will submit to argument, while a bad man, whose desire is for pleasure, is corrected by pain like a beast of burden. This is, too, why they say the pains inflicted should be those that are most opposed to the pleasures such men love.

However that may be, if (as we have said) the man who is to be good must be well trained and habituated, and go on to spend his time in worthy occupations and neither willingly nor unwillingly do bad actions, and if this can be brought about if men live in accordance with a sort of reason and right order, provided this has force, – if this be so, the paternal command indeed has not the required force or compulsive power (nor in general has the command of one man, unless he be a king or something similar), but the law *has* compulsive power, while it is at the same time a rule proceeding from a sort of practical wisdom and reason. And while people hate *men* who oppose their impulses, even if they oppose them rightly, the law in its ordaining of what is good is not burdensome.

In the Spartan state alone, or almost alone, the legislator seems to have paid attention to questions of nurture and occupations; in most states such matters have been neglected, and each man lives as he pleases, Cyclops-fashion, 'to his own wife and children dealing law'. Now it is best that there should be a public and proper care for such matters; but if they are neglected by the community it would seem right for each man to help his children and friends towards virtue, and that they should have the power, or at least the will, to do this.

It would seem from what has been said that he can do this better if he makes himself capable of leglislating. For public control is plainly effected by laws, and good control by good laws; whether written or unwritten would seem to make no difference, nor whether they are laws providing for the education of individuals or of groups – any more than it does in the case of music or gymnastics and other such pursuits. For as in cities laws and prevailing types of character have force, so in households do the injunctions and the habits of the father, and these have even more because of the tie of blood and the benefits he confers; for the children start with a natural affection and disposition to obey. Further, private education has an advantage over public, as private medical treatment has; for while in general rest and abstinence from food are good for a man in a fever, for a particular man they may not be; and a boxer presumably does not prescribe the same style of fighting to all his pupils. It would seem, then, that the detail is worked out with more precision if the control is private; for each person is more likely to get what suits his case.

But the details can be best looked after, one by one, by a doctor or gymnastic instructor or any one else who has the general knowledge of what is good for every one or for people of a certain kind (for the sciences both are said to be, and are, concerned with what is universal); not but what some particular detail may perhaps be well looked after by an unscientific person, if he has studied accurately in the light of experience what happens in each case, just as some people seem to be their own best doctors, though they could give no help to any one else. None the less, it will perhaps be agreed that if a man does wish to become master of an art or science he must go to the universal, and come to know it as well as possible; for, as we have said, it is with this that the sciences are concerned.

And surely he who wants to make men, whether many or few, better by his care must try to become capable of legislating, if it is through laws that we can become good. For to get any one whatever – any one who is put before us – into the right condition is not for the first chance comer; if any one can do it, it is the man who knows, just as in medicine and all other matters which give scope for care and prudence.

Must we not, then, next examine whence or how one can learn how to legislate? Is it, as in all other cases, from statesmen? Certainly it was thought to be a part of statesmanship. Or is a difference apparent between statesmanship and the other sciences and arts? In the others the same people are found offering to teach the arts and practising them, e.g. doctors or painters; but while the sophists profess to teach politics, it is practised not by any of them but by the politicians, who would seem to do so by dint of a certain skill and experience rather than of thought; for they are not found either writing or speaking about such matters (though it were a nobler occupation perhaps than composing speeches for the law-courts and the assembly), nor again are they found to have made statesmen of their own sons or any other of their friends. But it was to be expected that they should if they could; for there is nothing better than such a skill that they could have left to their cities, or could prefer to have for themselves, or, therefore, for those dearest to them. Still, experience seems to contribute not a little; else they could not have become politicians by familiarity with politics; and so it seems that those who aim at knowing about the art of politics need experience as well.

But those of the sophists who profess the art seem to be very far from teaching it. For, to put the matter generally, they do not even know what kind of thing it is nor what kinds of things it is about; otherwise they would not have classed it as identical with

Book X.9

rhetoric or even inferior to it, nor have thought it easy to legislate by collecting the laws that are thought well of; they say it is possible to select the best laws, as though even the selection did not demand intelligence and as though right judgement were not the greatest thing, as in matters of music. For while people experienced in any department judge rightly the works produced in it, and understand by what means or how they are achieved, and what harmonizes with what, the inexperienced must be content if they do not fail to see whether the work has been well or ill made – as in the case of painting. Now laws are as it were the 'works' of the political art; how then can one learn from them to be a legislator, or judge which are best? Even medical men do not seem to be made by a study of text-books. Yet people try, at any rate, to state not only the treatments, but also how particular classes of people can be cured and should be treated – distinguishing the various habits of body; but while this seems useful to experienced people, to the inexperienced it is valueless. Surely, then, while collections of laws, and of constitutions also, may be serviceable to those who can study them and judge what is good or bad and what enactments suit what circumstances, those who go through such collections without a practised faculty will not have right judgement (unless it be as a spontaneous gift of nature), though they may perhaps become more intelligent in such matters.

Now our predecessors have left the subject of legislation to us unexamined; it is perhaps best, therefore, that we should ourselves study it, and in general study the question of the constitution, in order to complete to the best of our ability our philosophy of human nature. First, then, if anything has been said well in detail by earlier thinkers, let us try to review it; then in the light of the constitutions we have collected let us study what sorts of influence preserve and destroy states, and what sorts preserve or destroy the particular kinds of constitution, and to what causes it is due that some are well and others ill administered. When these have been studied we shall perhaps be more likely to see with a comprehensive view, which constitution is best, and how each must be ordered, and what laws and customs it must use, if it is to be at its best. Let us make a beginning of our discussion.

EUDEMIAN ETHICS

EUDEMIAN ETHICS

Book I

1 THE man who stated his judgement in the god's precinct in **1214a** Delos made an inscription on the propylaeum to the temple of Leto, in which he separated from one another the good, the beautiful, and the pleasant as not all properties of the same thing; he wrote, 'Most beautiful is what is most just, but best is health, 5 and pleasantest the obtaining of what one desires.' But let us disagree with him; for happiness is at once the most beautiful and best of all things and also the pleasantest.

Now about each thing and kind there are many views that are 10 disputed and need investigation; of these some are concerned with knowledge only, some with the acquisition of things and the performance of acts as well. About those which involve speculative philosophy only we must at a suitable opportunity say what is relevant to that study. But first we must consider in what the 15 happy life consists and how it is to be acquired, whether all who receive the epithet 'happy' become so by nature (as we become tall, short, or of different complexions), or by teaching (happiness being a sort of science), or by some sort of discipline – for men 20 acquire many qualities neither by nature nor by teaching but by habituation, bad qualities if they are habituated to the bad, good if to the good. Or do men become happy in none of these ways, but either – like those possessed by nymphs or deities – through a sort of divine influence, being as it were inspired, or through 25 chance? For many declare happiness to be identical with good luck.

That men, then, possess happiness through all or some or one of these causes is evident; for practically all cases of becoming fall under these principles – for all acts arising from thought may be included among acts that arise from knowledge. Now to be 30 happy, to live blissfully and beautifully, must consist mainly in three things, which seem most desirable; for some say prudence is the greatest good, some virtue, and some pleasure. Some also dispute about the magnitude of the contribution made by each of these elements to happiness, some declaring the contribution of one to be greater, some that of another, – these regarding prudence as a greater good than virtue, those the opposite, while others regard pleasure as a greater good than either: and some consider the happy life to be compounded of all or of two of these, while others hold it to consist in one of them alone.

First then about these things we must enjoin every one that has the power to live according to his own choice to set up for himself some object for the beautiful life to aim at, (whether honour or reputation or wealth or culture), with reference to which he will then do all his acts, since not to have one's life organized in view of some end is a mark of much folly. Then above all we must first define to ourselves without hurry or carelessness in which of our belongings the happy life is lodged, and what are the indispensable conditions of its attainment – for health is not the same as the indispensable conditions of health; and so it is with many other things, e.g. the beautiful life and its indispensable conditions are not identical. Of such things some are not peculiar to health or even to life, but common – to speak broadly – to all dispositions and actions, e.g. without breathing or being awake or having the power of movement we could enjoy neither good nor evil; but some are indispensable conditions in a more special sense and peculiar to each kind of thing, and these it is specially important to observe; e.g. the eating of meat and walking after meals are more peculiarly the indispensable conditions of a good physical state than the more general conditions mentioned above. For herein is the cause of the disputes about happy living, its nature and causes; for some take to be elements in happiness what are merely its indispensable conditions.

To examine then all the views held about happiness is superfluous, for children, sick people, and the insane all have views, but no sane person would dispute over them; for such persons need not argument but years in which they may change, or else medical or political correction – for medicine, no less than stripes, is a correction. Similarly we have not to consider the views of the multitude (for they talk without consideration about almost everything, and most about happiness); for it is absurd to apply argument to those who need not argument but suffering. But since every study has its special problems, evidently there are such relating to the best life and best existence; the opinions then that put these difficulties it is well to examine, for a disputant's refutation of what is opposed to his argument is a demonstration of the argument itself.

Further, it is proper not to neglect these considerations, especially with a view to that at which all inquiry should be directed, viz. the causes that enable us to share in the good and beautiful life – if any one finds it invidious to call it the blessed life – and with a view to the hope we may have of attaining each good. For if the beautiful life consists in what is due to fortune or nature, it would be something that many cannot hope for, since its acquisition is not in their power, nor attainable by their care or activity; but if it depends on the individual and his personal acts being of a certain character, then the supreme good would be both more general and more divine, more general because more would be able to possess it, more divine because happiness would then be the prize offered to those who make themselves and their acts of a certain character.

4 Most of the doubts and difficulties raised will become clear, if we define well what we ought to think happiness to be, whether that it consists merely in having the soul of a certain character – as some of the sages and older writers thought – or whether the man must indeed be of a certain character, but it is even more necessary that his acts should be of a certain character.

Now if we make a division of the kinds of life, some do not even pretend to this sort of well-being, being only pursued for the sake of what is necessary, e.g. those concerned with vulgar arts, or with commercial or servile occupations – by vulgar I mean arts pursued only with a view to reputation, by servile those which are sedentary and wage-earning, by commercial those connected with buying in markets and huckstering in shops. But there are also three goods directed to a happy employment of life, those which we have above called the three greatest of human goods, virtue, prudence, and pleasure. We thus see that there are three lives which all those choose who have power, viz. the lives of 'the political man', the philosopher, the voluptuary; for of these the philosopher intends to occupy himself with prudence and contemplation of truth, the 'political man' with noble acts (i.e. those springing from virtue), the voluptuary with bodily pleasures. Therefore the latter calls a different person happy, as was indeed said before. Anaxagoras of Clazomenae being asked, 'Who was the happiest of men?' answered, 'None of those you suppose, but one who would appear a strange being to you,' because he saw that the questioner thought it impossible for one not great and beautiful or rich to deserve the epithet 'happy', while he himself perhaps thought that the man who lived painlessly and pure of injustice or else engaged in some divine contemplation was really, as far as a man may be, blessed.

About many other things it is difficult to judge well, but most difficult about that on which judgement seems to all easiest and the knowledge of it in the power of any man – viz. what of all that is found in living is desirable, and what, if attained, would satisfy our desire. For there are many circumstances that make men fling away life, as disease, excessive pain, storms, so that it is clear that, if one were given the power of choice, not to be born at all would, as far at least as these reasons go, have been desirable. Further, the life we lead as children is not desirable, for no one in his senses would consent to return again to this. Further, many incidents involving neither pleasure nor pain or involving pleasure but not of a noble kind are such that, as far as they are concerned, non-existence is preferable to life. And generally, if one were to bring together all that all men do and undergo but not willingly because not for its own sake, and were to add to this an infinite duration, one would none the more on account of these experiences choose to live rather than not to live. But further, neither for the pleasure of eating alone or that of sex, if all the other pleasures were removed that knowing or seeing or any other sense provides men with, would a single man value life, unless he were utterly servile. For it is clear that to the man making this choice there would be no difference between being born

Book I.5

a brute and a man; at any rate the ox in Egypt, which they reverence as Apis, in most of such matters has more licence than many monarchs. We may say the same of the pleasure of sleeping. For what is the difference between sleeping an unbroken sleep from one's first day to one's last, say for a thousand or any number of years, and living the life of a plant? Plants at any rate seem to possess this sort of life, and similarly children; for children, too, continue having their nature from their first coming into being in their mother's womb, but sleep the entire time. It is clear then from these considerations that men, though they look, fail to see what is well-being, what is the good in life.

And so they tell us that Anaxagoras answered a man who was raising problems of this sort and asking why one should choose rather to be born than not – 'for the sake of viewing the heavens and the whole order of the universe'. He, then, thought the choice of life for the sake of some sort of knowledge to be precious; but those who felicitate Sardanapallus or Smindyrides the Sybarite or any other of those who live the voluptuary's life, these seem all to place happiness in the feeling of pleasure. But others would rather choose virtuous deeds than either any sort of wisdom or sensual pleasures; at any rate some choose these not only for the sake of reputation, but even when they are not going to win credit by them. But most 'political' men are not truly so called; they are not in truth 'political', for the 'political' man is one who chooses noble acts for their own sake, while most take up the 'political' life for the sake of money and greed.

From what has been said, then, it is clear that all connect happiness with one or other of three lives, the 'political', the philosophic, and the voluptuary's. Now among these the nature and quality and sources of the pleasure of the body and sensual enjoyment are clear, so that we have not to inquire what such pleasures are, but whether they tend to happiness or not and how they tend, and whether – supposing it right to attach to the noble life certain pleasures – it is right to attach these, or whether some other sort of participation in these is a necessity, but the pleasures through which men rightly think the happy man to live pleasantly and not merely painlessly are different.

But about these let us inquire later. First let us consider about virtue and prudence, the nature of each, and whether they are parts of the good life either in themselves or through the actions that arise from them, since all — or at least all important thinkers — connect happiness with these.

Socrates, then, the elder, thought the knowledge of virtue to be the end, and used to inquire what is justice, what bravery and each of the parts of virtue; and his conduct was reasonable, for he thought all the virtues to be kinds of knowledge, so that to know justice and to be just came simultaneously; for the moment that we have learned geometry or architecture we are architects or geometers. Therefore he inquired what virtue is, not how or from what it arises. This is correct with regard to theoretical knowledge, for there is no other part of astronomy or physics or geometry except knowing and contemplating the nature of the things which are the subjects of those sciences; though nothing prevents them from being in an incidental way useful to us for much that we cannot do without. But the end of the productive sciences is different from science and knowledge, e.g. health from medical science, law and order (or something of the sort) from political science. Now to know anything that is noble is itself noble; but regarding virtue, at least, not to know what it is, but to know out of what it arises is most precious. For we do not wish to know what bravery is but to be brave, nor what justice is but to be just, just as we wish to be in health rather than to know what being in health is, and to have our body in good condition rather than to know what good condition is.

About all these matters we must try to get conviction by argument, using perceived facts as evidence and illustration. It would be best that all men should clearly concur with what we are going to say, but if that is unattainable, then that all should in some way at least concur. And this if led on they will do, for every man has some contribution to make to the truth, and with this as a starting-point we must give some sort of proof about these matters. For by advancing from true but obscure statements we shall arrive at clear ones, always replacing the usual confused statement by more real knowledge. Now in every inquiry there is a difference between philosophic and unphilosophic argument; therefore we should not think even in political philosophy that the sort of consideration which not only makes the nature of the thing evident but also its cause is superfluous; for such consideration is in every inquiry the truly philosophic method. But this needs much caution. For there are some who, because it is thought to be the mark of a philosopher to make no arbitrary statement but always to give a reason, often without its being noticed give reasons foreign to the subject and idle – this they do sometimes from ignorance, sometimes because they are charlatans – by which reasons even men experienced and able to act are trapped by those who neither have nor are capable of having practical and constructive thought. And this happens to them from want of culture; for inability in regard to each matter to distinguish reasonings appropriate to the subject from those foreign to it is want of culture. And it is well to criticize separately the reason that gives the cause and the conclusion, both because of what has just been said, viz. that one should attend not merely to what is inferred by argument, but often attend more to perceived facts – whereas now when men are unable to see a flaw in the argument they are compelled to believe what has been said, and because often that which seems to have been shown by argument is true indeed, but not for the cause which the argument assigns; for one may prove truth by means of falsehood, as is clear from the *Analytics*.

7 After these further preliminary remarks let us start on our discourse from what we have called the first confused statements, and then seek to discover a clear judgement about the nature of happiness. Now this is admitted to be the greatest and best of human goods – we say human, for there might perhaps be a happiness peculiar to some superior being, e.g. a god; for of the other animals, which are inferior in their nature to men, none have a right to the epithet 'happy'; for no horse, bird, or fish is happy, nor anything the name of which does not imply some share of a divine element in its nature; but in virtue of some other sort of participation in good things some have a better life, some a worse.

But we must see later that this is so. At present we say that of goods some are within the range of human action, some not; and this we say because some things – and therefore also some good things – are incapable of change, yet these are perhaps as to their nature the best. Some things, again, are within the range of action, but only to beings superior to us. But since 'within the range of action' is an ambiguous phrase – for both that for the sake of which we act and the things we do for its sake have to do with actions, and thus we put among things within the range of action both health and wealth and the acts done for the sake of these ends, i.e. health-giving and money-making ones – it is clear that we must regard happiness as the best of what is within the range of action for man.

We must then examine what is the best, and in how many senses 8 we use the word. The answer is principally contained in three views. For men say that the good *per se* is the best of all things, the good *per se* being that whose property is to be the first good and the cause by its presence in other things of their being good. Both of which attributes, they claim, belong to the Idea of good (I mean by 'both' that of being the first good and also the cause of other things being good by its presence in them). For good is predicated of this Idea most truly (other things being good by participation in and likeness to this); and this is the first good. For the destruction of that which is participated in involves also the destruction of that which participates in the Idea and is named from its participation in it; but this is the relation of the first to the later. So that the Idea of good is the good *per se*; for this is also (they say) separable from what participates in it, like all other Ideas.

The discussion, however, of this view belongs necessarily to another inquiry and one for the most part more logical, for arguments that are at once destructive and general belong to no other science but logic. But if we must speak briefly about these matters, we say first that it is to speak abstractly and idly to assert that there is an Idea whether of good or of anything whatever – this has been considered in many ways both in our popular and in our philosophic discussions. Next, however much there are Ideas and in particular an Idea of good, it is perhaps useless with a view to a good life and to action. For the good has many senses, as numerous as those of being. For being, as we have divided it in other works,

Book I.8

signifies now what a thing is, now quality, now quantity, now time, and in addition it sometimes consists in being changed, sometimes in effecting change; and the good is found in each of these modes, in substance as mind and God, in quality as justice, in quantity as moderation, in time as opportunity, while as examples of it in change we have that which teaches and that which is being taught. As then being is not one in all that we have just mentioned, so neither is good; nor is there one science either of being or of the good. Not even things named good in the same category are the objects of a single science, e.g. opportunity or moderation, but one science studies one kind of opportunity or moderation, and another another. Thus opportunity and moderation in regard to food are studied by medicine and gymnastics, in military matters by the art of strategy, and similarly with other sorts of action. So it can hardly be the province of one science to study the good *per se*.

Further, in things having a natural succession, a prior and a posterior, there is no common element beyond, and, further, separable from, them, for then there would be something prior to the first. For the common and separable element would be prior, because with its destruction the first would be destroyed as well; e.g. if the double is the first of the multiples, then the universal multiple cannot be separable, for it would be prior to the double, if the common element turns out to be the Idea, as it would be if one made the common element separable. For if justice is good, and so also is bravery, there is then, they say, a good *per se*, for which they add '*per se*' to the general definition; but what could this mean except that it is 'eternal' and 'separable'? But what is white for many days is no whiter than that which is white for a single day; so not even the common good would be identical with 'the Idea', for it is the common property of all.

But we should show the nature of the good *per se* in the opposite way to that now used. For now from what is not agreed to possess the good they demonstrate the things admitted to be good, e.g. from numbers they demonstrate that justice and health are goods, for they are arrangements and numbers, and it is assumed that goodness is a property of numbers and units because unity is the good itself. But they ought, from what are admitted to be goods, e.g. health, strength, and temperance, to demonstrate that beauty is present even more in the changeless; for all these things in the sensible world are order and rest; but if so, then the changeless is still more beautiful, for it has these attributes still more. And it is a bold way to demonstrate that unity is the good *per se* to say that numbers aim at it; for no one says distinctly how they do so, but the saying is altogether too unqualified. And how can one suppose that there is desire where there is no life? One should consider seriously about this and not assume without reasons what it is not easy to believe even with reasons. And to say that all existing things desire some one good is not true; for each seeks its own special good, the eye vision, the body health, and so on.

There are then these difficulties in the way of there being a good *per se*; further, it would be useless to political philosophy, which, like all others, has its particular good, e.g. as gymnastic has good bodily condition.

And similarly neither is good as a universal either the good *per se* (for it might belong even to a small good) or practicable; for medicine does not consider how to procure an attribute that may be an attribute of *anything*, but how to procure health; and so each of the other arts. But 'good' is ambiguous, and there is in it a noble part, and part is practicable but the rest not so. The sort of good that is practicable is an object aimed at, but not the good in things unchanging.

It is clear, then, that neither the Idea of good nor the good as universal is the good *per se* that we are actually seeking; for the one is unchangeable and not practical, and the other though changeable is still not practical. But the object aimed at as end is best, and the cause of all that comes under it, and first of all goods. This then must be the good *per se*, the end of all human action. And this is what comes under the master-art of all, which is politics, economics, and prudence; for these mental habits differ from all other by their being of this nature; whether they differ from one another must be stated later. And that the end is the cause of all that comes under it, the method of teaching shows; for the teacher first defines the end and thence shows of each of the other things that it is good; for the end aimed at is the cause. E.g. since to be in health is so and so, so and so must needs be what conduces to it; the wholesome is the efficient cause of health and yet only of its actual existence; it is not the cause of health being good. Further, no one demonstrates that health is good (except he is a sophist and no doctor, but one who produces deceptive arguments from inappropriate considerations), any more than any other principle.

Book II

chapters 1, 6-11

1   AFTER this let us start from a new beginning and speak about what follows from it. All goods are either outside or in the soul, and of these those in the soul are more desirable; this distinction we make even in our popular discussions. For prudence, virtue, and pleasure are in the soul, and some or all of these seem to all to be the end. But of the contents of the soul some are states or faculties, others activities and movements.

Let this then be assumed, and also that virtue is the best state or condition or faculty of all things that have a use and work. This is clear by induction; for in all cases we lay this down: e.g. a garment has an excellence, for it has a work and use, and the best state of the garment is its excellence. Similarly a vessel, house, or anything else has an excellence; therefore so also has the soul, for it has a work. And let us assume that the better state has the better work; and as the states are to one another, so let us assume the corresponding works to be to one another. And the work of anything is its end; it is clear, therefore, from this that the work is better than the state; for the end is best, as being end: for we assume the best, the final stage, to be the end for the sake of which all exists. That the work, then, is better than the state or condition is plain.

But 'work' has two senses; for some things have a work beyond mere employment, as architecture has a house and not the act of building, medicine health and not the act of curing and restoring to health; while the work of other things is just their employment, e.g. of vision seeing and of mathematical science contemplation. Hence, necessarily, in those whose work is their employment the employment is more valuable than the state.

Having made these distinctions, we say that the work of a thing is also the work of its excellence, only not in the same sense, e.g. a shoe is the work both of the art of cobbling and of the action of cobbling. If, then, the art of cobbling and the good cobbler have an excellence, their work is a good shoe: and similarly with everything else.

Further, let the work of the soul be to produce living, this consisting in employment and being awake – for slumber is a sort of inactivity and rest. Therefore, since the work must be one and the same both for the soul and for its excellence, the work of the excellence of the soul would be a good life. This, then, is the complete good, which (as we saw) is happiness. And it is clear from our assumptions (for these were that happiness is the best of things, and ends and the best goods are in the soul; and it is itself either a state or an activity), since the activity is better than the state, and the best activity than the best state, and virtue is the best state, that the activity of the virtue of the soul is the best thing. But happiness, we saw, is the best of things; therefore happiness is the activity of a good soul. But since happiness was something complete, and living is either complete or incomplete and so also virtue – one virtue being a whole, the other a part – and the activity of what is incomplete is itself incomplete, happiness must be the activity of a complete life in accordance with complete virtue.

And that we have rightly stated its genus and definition common opinions prove. For to do well and to live well is held to be identical with being happy, but each of these – living and doing – is an employment, an activity; for the practical life is one of using or employing, e.g. the smith produces a bridle, the good horseman uses it.

We find confirmation also in the common opinion that we cannot ascribe happiness to a single day, or to a child, or to each of the ages of life; and therefore Solon's advice holds good, never to felicitate a man when living, but only when his life is ended. For nothing incomplete is happy, not being whole.

Further, praise is given to virtue because of its actions, and encomia are bestowed on actions. And we crown the actual conquerors, not those who have the power to conquer but do not actually conquer. Further, our judging the character of a man by his acts is a confirmation. Further, why is happiness not praised? Surely because other things are praised owing to this, either by their having reference to it or by their being parts of it. Therefore felicitation, praise, and encomium differ; for encomium is discourse relative to the particular act, praise declares the general nature of the man, but felicitation is for the end. This clears up the difficulty sometimes raised – why for half their lives the good are no better than the bad, for all are alike when asleep; the cause is that sleep is an inactivity, not an activity of the soul. Therefore, even if there is some other part of the soul, e.g. the vegetative, its excellence is not a part of entire virtue, any more than the excellence of the body is; for in sleep the vegetative part is more active, while the perceptive and the desiderative are incomplete in sleep. But as far as they do to some extent partake of movement, even the dreams of the good are better than those of the bad, except so far as they are caused by disease or bodily defect.

After this we must consider the soul. For virtue belongs to the soul and essentially so. But since we are looking for human virtue, let it be assumed that the parts of the soul partaking of reason are two, but that they partake not in the same way, but the one by its natural tendency to command, the other by its natural tendency to obey and listen; if there is a part without reason in some other sense, let it be disregarded. It makes no difference whether the soul is divisible or indivisible, so long as it has different faculties, namely those mentioned above, just as in the curved we have unseparated the concave and the convex, or, again, the straight and the white, yet the straight is not white except incidentally and is not the same in essence.

We also neglect any other part of the soul that there may be, e.g. the vegetative, for the above-mentioned parts are peculiar to the human soul; therefore the virtues of the nutritive part, that concerned with growth, are not those of man. For, if we speak of him *qua* man, he must have the power of reasoning, a governing principle, moral action; but reason governs not reason, but desire and the passions; he must then have these parts. And just as general good condition of the body is compounded of the partial excellences, so also the excellence of the soul, *qua* end.

But of virtue or excellence there are two species, the moral and the intellectual. For we praise not only the just but also the intelligent and the wise. For we assumed that what is praiseworthy is either the virtue or its act, and these are not activities, but have activities. But since the intellectual virtues involve reason, they belong to that rational part of the soul which governs the soul by its possession of reason, while the moral belong to the part which is irrational but by its nature obedient to the part possessing reason; for we do not describe the character of a man by saying that he is wise or clever, but by saying that he is gentle or bold.

Let us, then, take another starting-point for the succeeding inquiry. Every substance is by nature a sort of principle; therefore each can produce many similar to itself, as man man, animals in general animals, and plants plants. But in addition to this *man* alone of animals is also the source of certain actions; for no other animal would be said to act. Such principles, which are primary sources of movements, are called principles in the strict sense, and most properly such as have necessary results; God is doubtless a principle of this kind. The strict sense of 'principle' is not to be found among principles without movement, e.g. those of mathematics, though by analogy we use the name there also. For there, too, if the principle should change, practically all that is proved from it would alter; but its consequences do not change themselves, one being destroyed by another, except by destroying the assumption and, by its refutation, proving something. But man is the source of a kind of movement, for action is movement. But since, as elsewhere, the source or principle is the cause of all that exists or arises through it, we must take the same view as in demonstrations. For if, supposing the triangle to have its angles equal to two right angles, the quadrilateral must have them equal to four right angles, it is clear that the property of the triangle is the cause of this last. And if the triangle should change, then so must the quadrilateral, having six right angles if the triangle has three, and eight if it has four: but if the former does not change but remains as it was before, so must the quadrilateral.

The necessity of what we are endeavouring to show is clear from the *Analytics*; at present we can neither omit it nor give an accurate account, but only say this much.

Supposing there were no further cause for the triangle's having the above property, then the triangle would be a sort of principle or cause of all that comes later. So that if anything existent may have the opposite to its actual qualities, so of necessity may its principles. For what results from the necessary is necessary; but the results of the contingent might be the opposite of what they are; what depends on men themselves forms a great portion of contingent matters, and men themselves are the sources of such contingent results. So that it is clear that all the acts of which man is the principle and controller may either happen or not happen, and that their happening or not happening – those at least of whose existence or non-existence he has the control – depends on him. But of what it depends on him to do or not to do, he is himself the cause; and what he is the cause of depends on him. And since virtue and vice and the acts that spring from them are respectively praised or blamed – for we do not praise or blame for what is due to necessity, or chance, or nature, but only for what we ourselves are causes of; for what another is the cause of, for that he bears the blame or praise – it is clear that virtue and vice have to do with matters where the man himself is the cause and source of his acts. We must then ascertain of what actions he is himself the source and cause. Now, we all admit that of acts that are voluntary and done from the choice of each man he is the cause, but of involuntary acts he is not himself the cause; and all that he does from choice he clearly does voluntarily. It is clear then that virtue and vice have to do with voluntary acts.

7 We must then ascertain what is the voluntary and the involuntary, and what is choice, since by these virtue and vice are defined. First we must consider the voluntary and involuntary. Of three things it would seem to be one, agreement with either desire, or choice, or thought – that is, the voluntary would agree, the involuntary would be contrary to one of these. But again, desire is divided into three sorts, wish, anger, and appetite. We have, then, to distinguish these, and first to consider the case of agreement with appetite.

Now all that is in agreement with appetite would seem to be voluntary; for all the involuntary seems to be forced, and what is forced is painful, and so is all that men do and suffer from compulsion – as Evenus says, 'all to which we are compelled is unpleasant'. So that if an act is painful it is forced on us, and if forced it is painful. But all that is contrary to appetite is painful – for appetite is for the pleasant – and therefore forced and involuntary; what then agrees with appetite is voluntary; for these two are opposites. Further, all wickedness makes one more unjust, and incontinence seems to be wickedness, the incontinent being the sort of man that acts in accordance with his appetite and contrary to his reason, and shows his incontinence when he acts in accordance with his appetite; but to act unjustly is voluntary, so that the incontinent will act unjustly by acting according to his appetite; he will then act voluntarily, and what is done according to appetite is voluntary.

From these considerations, then, the act done from appetite would seem voluntary, but from the following the opposite. What a man does voluntarily he wishes, and what he wishes to do he does voluntarily; and no one wishes what he thinks to be bad. But surely the man who acts incontinently does not do what he wishes, for to act incontinently is to act through appetite contrary to what the man thinks best. The result will be that the same man acts at the same time both voluntarily and involuntarily; but this is impossible. Further, the continent will do a just act, and more so than incontinence; for continence is a virtue, and virtue makes men more just. Now one acts continently whenever he acts against his appetite in accordance with his reason. So that if to act justly is voluntary as to act unjustly is – for both these seem to be voluntary, and if the one is, so must the other be – but action contrary to appetite is involuntary, then the same man will at the same time do the same thing voluntarily and involuntarily.

The same argument may be applied to anger; for there is thought to be a continence and incontinence of anger just as there is of appetite; and what is contrary to our anger is painful, and the repression is forced, so that if the forced is involuntary, all acts done out of anger would be voluntary. Heraclitus, too, seems to be regarding the strength of anger when he says that the restraint of it is painful – 'It is hard,' he says, 'to fight with anger; for it gives its life for what it desires.' But if it is impossible for a man voluntarily and involuntarily to do the same thing at the same time, and in regard to the same part of the act, then what is done from wish is more voluntary than that which is done from appetite or anger; and a proof of this is that we do many things voluntarily without anger or desire.

It remains then to consider whether to act from wish and to act voluntarily are identical. But this too seems impossible. For we assumed and all admit that wickedness makes men more unjust, and incontinence seems a kind of wickedness. But the opposite will result from the hypothesis above; for no one wishes what he thinks bad, but does it when he becomes incontinent. If, then, to commit injustice is voluntary, and the voluntary is what agrees with wish, then when a man becomes incontinent he will be no longer committing injustice, but will be more just than before he became incontinent. But this is impossible. That the voluntary then is not action in accordance with desire, nor the involuntary action in opposition to it, is clear.

8 But again, that action in accordance with, or in opposition to, choice is not the true description of the voluntary and involuntary is clear from the following considerations: it has been shown that the act in agreement with wish was not involuntary, but rather that all that one wishes is voluntary, though it has also been shown that one may do voluntarily what one does not wish. But we do many things from wish suddenly, but no one chooses an act suddenly.

But if, as we saw, the voluntary must be one of these three – action according either to desire, choice, or thought, and it is not two of these, the remaining alternative is that the voluntary consists in action with some kind of thought. Advancing a little further, let us close our delimitation of the voluntary and the involuntary. To act on compulsion or not on compulsion seems connected with these terms; for we say that the enforced is involuntary, and all the involuntary is enforced: so that first we must consider the action done on compulsion, its nature and its relation to the voluntary and the involuntary. Now the enforced and the necessary, force and necessity, seem opposed to the voluntary and to persuasion in the case of acts done. Generally, we speak of enforced action and necessity even in the case of inanimate things; for we say that a stone moves upwards and fire downwards on compulsion and by force. But when they move according to their natural internal tendency, we do not say it is by force; nor do we call it voluntary either; there is no name for this antithesis; but when they move contrary to this tendency, then we say they move by force. So, too, among things living and among animals we often see things acting and being acted upon by force, when something from without moves them contrary to their own internal tendency. Now in the inanimate the moving principle is simple, but in the animated there is more than one principle; for desire and reason do not always agree. And so with the other animals the action on compulsion is simple (just as in the inanimate), for they have not desire and reason opposing one another, but live by desire; but man has both, that is at a certain age, the age to which we attribute the power of action; for we do not use this term of the child, nor of the brute, but only of the man who has come to act from reason.

So the compulsory act seems always painful, and no one acts from force and yet with pleasure. Hence there arises much dispute about the continent and incontinent, for each of them acts with two tendencies mutually opposed, so that (as the expression goes) the continent forcibly drags himself from the pleasant appetites (for he feels pain in dragging himself away against the resistance of desire), while the incontinent forcibly drags himself contrary to his reason. But still the latter seems less to be in pain; for appetite is for the pleasant, and this he follows with delight; so that the incontinent rather acts voluntarily and not from force, because he acts without pain. But persuasion is opposed to force and necessity, and the continent goes towards what he is persuaded of, and so proceeds not from force but voluntarily. But appetite leads without persuading, being devoid of reason. We have, then, shown that these alone seem to act from force and involuntarily, and why they seem to, viz. from a certain likeness to the enforced action, in virtue of which we attribute enforced action also to the inanimate.

Yet if we add the addition made in our definition, there also the statement becomes untrue. For it is only when something *external* moves a thing, or brings it to rest against its own internal tendency, that we say this happens by force; otherwise we do not say that it happens by force. But in the continent and the incontinent it is the present *internal* tendency that leads them, for they have both tendencies. So that neither acts on compulsion nor by force, but, as far at least as the above goes, voluntarily. For the external moving principle, that hinders or moves in opposition to the internal tendency, is what we call necessity, e.g. when we strike some one with the hand of one whose wish and appetite alike resist; but when the principle is from within, there is no force. Further, there is both pleasure and pain in both; for the continent feels pain now in acting against his appetite, but has the pleasure of hope, i.e. that he will be presently benefited, or even the pleasure of being actually at present benefited because he is in health; while the incontinent is pleased at getting through his incontinency what he desires, but has a pain of expectation, thinking that he is doing ill. So that to say that both act from compulsion is not without reason, the one sometimes acting involuntarily owing to his desire, the other owing to his reason; these two, being separated, are thrust out by one another. Whence men apply the language to the soul as a whole, because we see something like the above in the case of the elements of the soul. Now of the parts of the soul this may be said; but the soul as a whole, whether in the continent or the incontinent, acts voluntarily, and neither acts on compulsion, but one of the elements in them does, since by nature we have both. For reason is in them by nature, because if growth is permitted and not maimed, it will be there; and appetite, because it accompanies and is present in us from birth. But these are practically the two marks by which we define the natural – it is either that which is found with us all as soon as we are born, or that which comes to us if growth is allowed to proceed regularly, e.g. grey hair, old age, and so on. So that each acts, in a way, contrary to nature, and yet, *tout court*, according to nature – not the same nature. The puzzles then about the continent and incontinent are these – do both, or one of them, act on compulsion, so that they act involuntarily or else at the same time both on compulsion and voluntarily; that is, if the compulsory is involuntary, both voluntarily and involuntarily? And it is tolerably clear from the above how these puzzles are to be met.

In another way, too, men are said to act by force and compulsion without any disagreement between reason and desire in them, viz. when they do what they consider both painful and bad, but they are threatened with stripes, imprisonment, or death, if they do not do it. Such acts they say they did on compulsion. Or shall we deny this, and say that all do the act itself voluntarily? for they had the power to abstain from doing it, and to submit to the suffering. Again perhaps one might say that some such acts were voluntary and some not. For whatever of the acts that a man does without wishing them he has the power to do or abstain from doing, these he always does voluntarily and not by force; but those in which he has not this power, he does by force in a sense (but not *tout court*), because he does not choose the very thing he does, but the purpose for which it is done, since there is a difference, too, in this. For if a man were to murder another that he might not catch him at blind man's buff he would be laughed at if he were to say that he acted by force, and on compulsion; there ought to be some greater and more painful evil that he would suffer if he did not commit the murder. For then he will act on compulsion, and either by force, or at least not by nature, when he does something evil for the sake of good, or release from a greater evil; then he will at least act involuntarily, for such acts are not subject to his control. Hence, many regard love, anger in some cases, and natural conditions, as involuntary, as being too strong for nature; we feel indulgence for them as things capable of overpowering nature. A man would more seem to act from force and involuntarily, if he acted to escape violent than if to escape gentle pain, and generally if to escape pain than if to get pleasure. For that which depends on him – and all turns on this – is what his nature is able to bear; what it is not, what is not under the control of his natural desire or reason, that does not depend on him. Therefore those who are inspired and prophesy, though their act is one of thought, we still say have it not in their own power either to say what they said, or to do what they did. And so of acts done through appetite. So that some thoughts and passions do not depend on us, nor the acts following such thoughts and reasonings, but, as Philolaus said, some arguments are too strong for us.

So that if the voluntary and involuntary had to be considered in reference to the presence of force as well as from other points of view, let this be our final distinction.

9 Since we have finished this subject, and we have found the voluntary not to be defined either by desire or by choice, it remains to define it as that which depends on thought. The voluntary, then, seems opposed to the involuntary, and to act with knowledge of the person acted on, instrument and tendency – for sometimes one knows the object, e.g. as father, but not that the tendency of the act is to kill, not to save, as in the case of Pelias's daughters; or knows the object to be a drink but takes it to be a philtre or wine when it was really hemlock – seems opposed to action in ignorance of the person, instrument, or thing, if, that is, the action is essentially the effect of ignorance. All that is done owing to ignorance, whether of person, instrument, or thing, is involuntary; the opposite therefore is voluntary. All, then, that a man does – it being in his power to abstain from doing it – not in ignorance and owing to himself must needs be voluntary; voluntariness is this. But all that he does in ignorance and owing to his ignorance, he does involuntarily. But since science or knowledge is of two sorts, one the possession, the other the use of knowledge, the man who has but does not use knowledge may in a sense be justly called ignorant, but in another sense not justly, e.g. if he has not used his knowledge owing to carelessness. Similarly, one might be blamed for not having the knowledge, if it were something easy or necessary and he does not have it because of carelessness or pleasure or pain. This, then, we must add to our definition.

Such, then, is the completion of our distinction of the voluntary and the involuntary.

10 Let us next speak about choice, first raising various difficulties about it. For one might doubt to what genus it belongs and in which to place it, and whether the voluntary and the chosen are or are not the same. Now some insist that choice is either opinion or desire, and the inquirer might well think that it was one or the other, for both are found accompanying it. Now that it is not desire is plain; for then it would be either wish, appetite, or anger, for none desires without having experienced one of these. But anger and appetite belong also to the brutes while choice does not; further, even those who are capable of both the former often choose without either anger or appetite; and when they are under the influence of those passions they do not choose but remain unmoved by them. Further, anger and appetite always involve pain, but we often choose without pain. But neither are wish and choice the same; for we often wish for what we know is impossible, e.g. to rule all mankind or to be immortal, but no one chooses such things unless ignorant of the impossibility, nor even what is possible, generally, if he does not think it in his power to do or to abstain from doing it. So that this is clear, that the object of choice must be one of the things in our own power.

Similarly, choice is not an opinion nor, generally, what one thinks; for the object of choice was something in one's power and many things may be thought that are not, e.g. that the diagonal is commensurable; and further, choice is not true or false. Nor yet is choice identical with our opinion about things which it is in our own power to do, as when we think that we ought to do or not to do something. This argument applies to wish as well as to opinion. For no one chooses an end, but the means to an end, e.g. no one chooses to be in health, but to walk or to sit for the purpose of keeping well; no one chooses to be happy but to make money or run risks for the purpose of being happy. And in general, in choosing we show both what we choose and for what we choose it, the latter being that for which we choose something else, the former that which we choose for something else. But it is the end that we specially *wish for*, and we *think* we ought to be healthy and happy. So that it is clear through this that choice is different both from opinion and from wish; for wish and opinion are specially of the end, but choice is not.

It is clear, then, that choice is not wish, or opinion, or judgement simply. But in what does it differ from these? How is it related to the voluntary? The answer to these questions will also make it clear what choice is. Of possible things, then, there are some such that we can deliberate about them, while about others we cannot. For some things are possible, but the production of them is not in our power, some being due to nature, others to other causes; and about these none would attempt to deliberate except in ignorance. But about others, not only existence and non-existence is possible, but also human deliberation; these are things the doing or not doing of which is in our own power. Therefore, we do not deliberate about the affairs of the Indians nor how the circle may be squared; for the first are not in *our* power, the second is wholly beyond the power of action; but we do not even deliberate about all things that may be done and that are in our power (by which it is clear that choice is not opinion simply), though the matters of choice and action belong to the class of things in our own power. One might then raise the problem – why do doctors deliberate about matters within their science, but not grammarians? The reason is that error may occur in two ways (either in reasoning or in perception when we are engaged in the very act), and in medicine one may go wrong in both ways, but in grammar one can do so only in respect of the perception and action, and if they inquired about this there would be no end to their inquiries. Since then choice is neither opinion nor wish singly nor yet both (for no one chooses suddenly, though he thinks he ought to act, and wishes, suddenly), it must be compounded of both, for both are found in a man choosing. But we must ask – how compounded out of these? The very name is some indication. For choice is not simply taking but taking one thing before another; and this is impossible without consideration and deliberation; therefore choice arises out of deliberative opinion.

Now about the end no one deliberates (this being fixed for all), but about that which tends to it – whether this or that tends to it, and – supposing this or that resolved on – how it is to be brought about. All consider this till they have brought the commencement of the production to a point in their own power. If then, no one deliberately chooses without some preparation, without some consideration whether it is better or worse to do so and so, and if one considers all that are in one's power of the means to the end which are capable of existing or not existing, it is clear that choice is a considered desire for something in one's own power; for we all consider what we choose, but we do not choose all that we consider. I call it considered when consideration is the source and cause of the desire, and the man desires because of the consideration. That is why in the other animals choice does not exist, nor in man at every age or in every condition; for there is not consideration or judgement of the ground of an act. It is quite possible that many animals have an opinion whether a thing is to be

1226b

done or not; only thinking with consideration is impossible to them. For the deliberative part of the soul is that which has in view a certain kind of cause. For the *purpose* is one of the causes, since that owing to which a thing comes about is a cause; and the purpose of a thing's existence or production we call its cause, e.g. of walking, the fetching of things, if this is the purpose for which one walks. Therefore, those who have no aim fixed have no inclination to deliberate. So that since, if a man of himself and not through ignorance does or abstains from that which is in his power to do or abstain from, he acts or abstains voluntarily, but we do many such things without deliberation or premeditation, it follows that all that has been deliberately chosen is voluntary, but not all the voluntary is deliberately chosen, and that all that is according to choice is voluntary, but not all that is voluntary is according to choice. And at the same time it is clear from this that those legislators define well who enact that some states of feeling are to be considered voluntary, some involuntary, and some premeditated; for if they are not thoroughly accurate, at least they approximate to the truth. But about this we will speak in our investigation of justice; meanwhile, it is clear that choice is not simply wish or simply opinion, but opinion and desire together when following as a conclusion from deliberation.

But since in deliberating one always deliberates for the sake of some end, and he who deliberates has always an aim by reference to which he judges what is expedient, no one deliberates about the end; this is the starting-point and assumption, like the assumptions in theoretical science (we have spoken about this shortly in the beginning of this work and minutely in the *Analytics*). Every one's inquiry, whether made with or without art, is about what tends to the end, e.g. whether they shall go to war or not, when this is what they are deliberating about. But the cause or object will come first, e.g. wealth, pleasure, or anything else of the sort that happens to be our object. For the man deliberating deliberates if he has considered, from the point of view of the end, what conduces to bringing the end within his own action, or what he at present can do towards the object. By nature the object or end is always something good, and men deliberate about the particular questions, e.g. the doctor whether he is to give a drug, or the general where he is to pitch his camp. To them the absolutely best end is good. But contrary to nature and by perversion not the good but the apparent good is the end. And the reason is that some things cannot be used for anything but what their nature determines, e.g. sight; for one can see nothing but what is visible, nor hear anything but what is audible. But science enables us to do also what it is not the science of; for the same science is not of health and of disease alike, but naturally it is of the former, and unnaturally of the latter. And similarly wish is of the good naturally, but also of the bad unnaturally, and by nature one wishes the good, but unnaturally and through perversion the bad as well.

But further, the corruption and perversion of a thing does not tend to anything at random but to the contrary or the intermediate between it and the contrary. For out of this province one cannot go, since error too leads not to anything at random but to the contrary of truth where there is a contrary, and to that contrary which is according to the appropriate science contrary. Therefore, the error and the resulting choice must deviate from the mean towards the opposite – and the opposite of the mean is excess or defect. And the cause is pleasantness or painfulness; for we are so constituted that the pleasant appears good to the soul and the more pleasant better, while the painful appears bad and the more painful worse. So that from this also it is clear that virtue and vice have to do with pleasures and pains; for they have to do with objects of choice, and choice has to do with the good and bad or what seems such, and pleasure and pain naturally seem such.

It follows then, since moral virtue is itself a mean and wholly concerned with pleasures and pains, and vice lies in excess or defect and is concerned with the same matters as virtue, that moral virtue is a habit tending to choose the mean in relation to us in things pleasant and painful in regard to which, according as one is pleased or pained, men are said to have a definite sort of character; for one is not said to have a special sort of character merely for liking what is sweet or what is bitter.

11 These distinctions having been made, let us say whether virtue makes the choice correct and the end right so that a man chooses

for the right end, or whether (as some say) it makes the reason so. But what does this is continence, for this preserves the reason. But virtue and continence differ. We must speak later about them, since those who think that virtue makes the reason right, do so for this reason – namely, that continence is of this nature and continence is one of the things we praise. Now that we have discussed preliminary questions let us state our view. It is possible for the aim to be right, but for a man to go wrong in the means to that aim; and again the aim may be mistaken, while the means leading to it are right; or both may be mistaken. Does then virtue make the aim, or the means to that aim? We say the aim, because this is not attained by inference or reasoning. Let us assume this as starting-point. For the doctor does not ask whether one ought to be in health or not, but whether one ought to walk or not; nor does the trainer ask whether one ought to be in good condition or not, but whether one should wrestle or not. And similarly no art asks questions about the end; for as in theoretical sciences the assumptions are our starting-points, so in the productive the end is starting-point and assumed. E.g. we reason that since this body is to be made healthy, therefore so and so must be found in it if health is to be had – just as in geometry we argue, if the angles of the triangle are equal to two right angles, then so and so must be the case. The end aimed at is, then, the starting-point of our thought, the end of our thought the starting-point of action. If, then, of all correctness either reason or virtue is the cause, if reason is not the cause, then the end (but not the means) must owe its rightness to virtue. But the end is the object of the action; for all choice is of some thing and for the sake of some object. The object, then, is the mean, and virtue is the cause of this by choosing it. Still choice is not of this but of the things done for the sake of this. To hit on these things – I mean what ought to be done for the sake of the object – belongs to another faculty; but of the rightness of the end of the choice the cause is virtue. And therefore it is from a man's choice that we judge his character – that is from the object for the sake of which he acts, not from the act itself. Similarly, vice makes the choice to be for the sake of the opposite object. If, then, a man, having it in his power to do the honourable and abstain from the base, does the opposite, it is clear that this man is not good. Hence, it follows that both vice and virtue are voluntary; for there is no necessity to do what is wicked. And that is why vice is blamable and virtue praiseworthy. For the involuntary if base or bad is not blamable, if good is not praiseworthy, but only the voluntary. Further, we praise and blame all men with regard to their choice rather than their acts (though activity is more desirable than virtue), because men may do bad acts under compulsion, but no one chooses them under compulsion. Further, it is only because it is not easy to see the nature of a man's choice that we are forced to judge of his character by his acts. The activity then is more desirable, but the choice more praiseworthy. And this both follows from our assumptions and is in agreement with observation.

Book VIII

chapter 3

3 About each virtue by itself we have already spoken; now, since we have distinguished their natures separately, we must also describe clearly the excellence that arises out of the combination of them, what we have already called nobility and goodness. That he who truly deserves this denomination must have the separate virtues is clear; it cannot be otherwise with other things either, for no one is healthy in his entire body and yet healthy in no part of it, but the most numerous and important parts, if not all, must be in the same condition as the whole. Now goodness and nobility-and-goodness differ not only in name but also in themselves. For all goods have ends which are to be chosen for their own sake. Of these, we call noble those which, existing all of them for their own sake, are praised. For these are those which are the source of praised acts and are themselves praised, such as justice itself and just acts; also temperate acts, for temperance is praised, but health is not praised, for its effect is not; nor vigorous action, for vigour is not. These are good but not praised. Induction makes this clear about the rest, too. A good man, then, is one for whom the natural goods are good. For the goods men fight for and think the greatest – honour, wealth, bodily excellences, good fortune, and power – are naturally good, but may be to some hurtful because of their dispositions. For neither the imprudent nor the unjust nor the intemperate would get any good from the employment of them, any more than an invalid from the food of a healthy man, or one weak and maimed from the equipment of one in health and sound in all limbs. A man is noble and good because those goods which are noble are possessed by him for themselves, and because he practises the noble and for its own sake, the noble being the virtues and the acts that proceed from virtue.

There is also what we may call the 'civic' disposition, such as the Laconians have, and others like them might have; its nature would be something like this – there are some who think one should have virtue, but only for the sake of the natural goods, and so such men are good (for the natural goods are good for them), but they have not nobility and goodness. For it is not true of them that they acquire the noble for itself, that they purpose acts good and noble at once – more than this, that what is not noble by nature but good by nature is noble to them; for objects are noble when a man's motives for acting and choosing them are noble. Wherefore to the noble and good man the naturally good is noble – for what is just is noble, justice is proportion to merit, and the perfect man merits these things; or what is fitting is noble, and to the perfect man these things, wealth, high birth, and power, are fitting. So that to the perfect man things profitable are also noble; but to the many the profitable and the noble do not coincide, for things absolutely good are not good for them as they are for the good man; to the 'noble and good' man they are also noble, for he does many noble deeds by reason of them. But the man who thinks he ought to have the virtues for the sake of external goods does deeds that are noble only *per accidens*. 'Nobility and goodness', then, is complete virtue.

About pleasure, too, we have spoken, what it is and in what sense good; we have said that the absolutely pleasant is also noble, and the absolutely good pleasant. But pleasure only arises in action; therefore the truly happy man will also live most pleasantly: that this should be so is no idle demand of man.

But since the doctor has a standard by reference to which he distinguishes the healthy from the unhealthy body, and with reference to which each thing up to a certain point ought to be done and is wholesome, while if less or more is done health is the result no longer, so in regard to actions and choice of what is naturally good but not praiseworthy, the good man should have a standard both of disposition and of choice, and similarly in regard to avoidance of excess or deficiency of wealth and good fortune, the standard being – as above said – 'as reason directs'; this corresponds to saying in regard to diet that the standard should be medical science and its principles. But this, though true, is not clear. One must, then, here as elsewhere, live with reference to the ruling principle and with reference to the formed habit and the activity of the ruling principle, as the slave must live with reference to that of the master, and each of us by the rule proper to him. But since man is by nature composed of a ruling and a subject part, each of us should live according to the governing element within himself – but this is ambiguous, for medical science governs in one sense, health in another, the former existing for the latter. And so it is with the theoretic faculty; for God is not a ruler issuing commands, but is the end with a view to which prudence issues its commands (the word 'end' is ambiguous, and has been distinguished elsewhere), for God of course needs nothing. What choice, then, or possession of the natural goods – whether bodily goods, wealth, friends, or other things – will most produce the contemplation of God, that choice or possession is best; and this is the noblest standard. But any that through deficiency or excess hinders one from the contemplation and service of God is bad. Man possesses this in his soul, and this is the best standard for the soul – to perceive the irrational part of the soul, as such, as little as possible.

So much, then, for the standard of perfection and the object of the absolute goods.

DE ANIMA

DE ANIMA

Book III

chapters 9-11

9 THE soul of animals is characterized by two faculties, (a) the **432a** 15 faculty of discrimination which is the work of thought and sense, and (b) the faculty of originating local movement. Sense and mind we have now sufficiently examined. Let us next consider what it is in the soul which originates movement. Is it a single part of the soul separate either spatially or in definition? Or is it the soul as a whole? If it is a part, is that part different from those 20 usually distinguished or already mentioned by us, or is it one of them? The problem at once presents itself, in what sense we are to speak of parts of the soul, or how many we should distinguish. For in a sense there is an infinity of parts: it is not enough to 25 distinguish, with some thinkers, the calculative, the passionate, and the appetitive, or with others the rational and the irrational; for if we take the dividing lines followed by these thinkers we shall find parts far more distinctly separated from one another than these, namely those we have just mentioned: (1) the nutritive, which belongs both to plants and to all animals, and (2) the 30 sensitive, which cannot easily be classed as either irrational or rational; further (3) the imaginative, which is, in its being, **432b** different from all, while it is very hard to say with which of the others it is the same or not the same, supposing we determine to posit *separate* parts in the soul; and lastly (4) the desiderative, which would seem to be distinct both in definition and in power from all hitherto enumerated.

It is absurd to break up the last-mentioned faculty: as these 5 thinkers do, for wish is found in the calculative part and appetite and passion in the irrational; and if the soul is tripartite desire will be found in all three parts. Turning our attention to the present object of discussion, let us ask what that is which originates local movement of the animal.

The movement of growth and decay, being found in all living things, must be attributed to the faculty of reproduction and nutrition, which is common to all. Inspiration and expiration, sleep and waking, we must consider later; these too present much difficulty. At present we must consider local movement, asking what it is that originates forward movement in the animal.

That it is not the nutritive faculty is obvious; for this kind of movement is always for an end and is accompanied either by imagination or by desire; for no animal moves, except when moved by force, unless it has an impulse towards or away from an object. Further, if it were the nutritive faculty, even plants would have been capable of originating such movement and would have possessed the organs necessary to carry it out. Similarly it cannot be the sensitive faculty either; for there are many animals which have sensibility but remain fast and immovable throughout their lives.

If then Nature never makes anything without a purpose and never leaves out what is necessary (except in the case of mutilated or imperfect growths; and that here we have neither mutilation nor imperfection may be argued from the facts that such animals (a) can reproduce their species and (b) rise to completeness of nature and decay to an end), it follows that, had they been capable of originating forward movement, they would have possessed the organs necessary for that purpose. Further, neither can the calculative faculty or what is called 'mind' be the cause of such movement; for mind as speculative never thinks what is practicable, it never says anything about an object to be avoided or pursued, while this movement is always in something which is avoiding or pursuing an object. No, not even when it is aware of such an object does it at once enjoin pursuit or avoidance of it; e.g. the mind often thinks of something terrifying or pleasant without enjoining the emotion of fear. It is the heart that is moved (or in the case of a pleasant object some other part). Further, even when the mind does command and thought bids us pursue or avoid something, sometimes no movement is produced; we act in accordance with appetite, as in the case of moral weakness.

Book III.9

And, generally, we observe that the possessor of medical knowledge is not necessarily healing, which shows that something else is required to produce action in accordance with knowledge; the knowledge alone is not the cause. Lastly, desire too is incompetent to account fully for movement; for those who successfully resist temptation have desire – i.e. appetite – and yet follow mind and refuse to enact that for which they have desire.

These two at all events appear to be sources of movement: desire and mind (if one may venture to regard imagination as a kind of thinking; for many men follow their imaginations contrary to knowledge, and in all animals other than man there is no thinking or calculation but only imagination).

Both of these then are capable of originating local movement, mind and desire: (1) mind, that is, which calculates means to an end, i.e. mind practical (it differs from mind speculative in the character of its end); while (2) desire is in every form of it relative to an end: for that which is the object of desire is the stimulant of mind practical; and that which is last in the process of thinking is the beginning of the action. It follows that there is a justification for regarding these two as the sources of movement, i.e. desire and practical thought; for the object of desire starts a movement and as a result of that thought gives rise to movement, the object of desire being to it a source of stimulation. So too when imagination originates movement, it necessarily involves desire.

That which moves therefore is a single faculty and the faculty of desire; for if there had been two sources of movement – mind and desire – they would have produced movement in virtue of some common character. As it is, mind is never found producing movement without desire (for wish is a form of desire; and when movement is produced according to calculation it is also according to wish), but desire can originate movement contrary to calculation, for appetite is a form of desire. Now mind is always right, but desire and imagination may be either right or wrong. That is why, though in any case it is the object of desire which originates movement, this object may be either the real or the apparent good. To produce movement the object must be more than this: it must be good that can be brought into being by action;

and only what can be otherwise than as it is can thus be brought into being. That then such a power in the soul as has been described, i.e. that called desire, originates movement is clear.

Those who distinguish parts in the soul, if they distinguish and divide in accordance with differences of power, find themselves with a very large number of parts, a nutritive, a sensitive, an intellective, a deliberative, and now a desiderative part; for these are more different from one another than the faculties of appetite and passion.

Since desires run counter to one another, which happens when a principle of reason and an appetite are contrary and is possible only in beings with a sense of time (for while mind bids us hold back because of what is future, appetite is influenced by what is just at hand: a pleasant object which is just at hand presents itself as both pleasant and good, without qualification in either case, because of failure to see what is in the future), it follows that while that which originates movement must be specifically one, viz. the faculty of desire as such (or rather furthest back of all the object of that faculty; for it is it that itself remaining unmoved originates the movement by being apprehended in thought or imagination), the things that originate movement are numerically many.

All movement involves three factors, (1) that which originates the movement, (2) that by means of which it originates it, and (3) that which is moved. The expression 'that which originates the movement' is ambiguous: it may mean either (a) something which itself is unmoved or (b) that which at once moves and is moved. Here that which moves without itself being moved is the realizable good, that which at once moves and is moved is the faculty of desire (for that which is influenced by desire so far as it is actually so influenced is set in movement, and desire in the sense of actual desire *is* a kind of movement), while that which is in motion is the animal. The instrument which desire employs to produce movement is no longer psychical but bodily: hence the examination of it falls within the province of the functions common to body and soul. To state the matter summarily at present, that which is the instrument in the production of movement is to be found where a beginning and an end coincide as e.g. in a ball and socket joint; for there the convex and the concave sides are

Book III.10

respectively an end and a beginning (that is why while the one remains at rest, the other is moved): they are separate in definition but not separable spatially. For everything is moved by pushing and pulling. Hence just as in the case of a wheel, so here there must be a point which remains at rest, and from that point the movement must originate.

To sum up, then, and repeat what I have said, inasmuch as an animal is capable of desire, it is capable of self-movement; it is not capable of desire without possessing imagination; and all imagination is either (1) calculative or (2) sensitive. In the latter all animals, and not only man, partake.

11 We must consider also in the case of imperfect animals, sc. those which have no sense but touch, what it is that in them originates movement. Can they have imagination or not? or appetite? Clearly they have feelings of pleasure and pain, and if they have these they must have appetite. But how can they have imagination? Must not we say that, as their movements are indefinite, they have imagination and appetite, but indefinitely?

Sensitive imagination, as we have said, is found in all animals, deliberative imagination only in those that are calculative: for whether this or that shall be enacted is already a task requiring calculation; and there must be a single standard to measure by, for that is pursued which is *greater*. It follows that what acts in this way must be able to make a unity out of several images.

This is the reason why imagination is held not to involve opinion, in that it does not involve opinion based on inference, though opinion involves imagination. Hence desire contains no deliberative element. Sometimes it overpowers wish and sets it in movement: at times wish acts thus upon desire, like one sphere imparting its movement to another, or desire acts thus upon desire, i.e. in the condition of moral weakness (though by *nature* the higher faculty is *always* more authoritative and gives rise to movement). Thus *three* modes of movement are possible.

The faculty of knowing is never moved but remains at rest. Since the one premiss or judgement is universal and the other deals with the particular (for the first tells us that such and such a kind of man should do such and such a kind of act, and the second that *this* is an act of the kind meant, and I a person of the type intended), it is the latter opinion that really originates movement, not the universal; or rather it is both, but the one does so while it remains in a state more like rest, while the other partakes in movement.

DE MOTU ANIMALIUM

DE MOTU ANIMALIUM

chapters 6–11

6 Now whether the soul is moved or not, and how it is moved if **700b** it be moved, has been stated before in our treatise concerning it. 5 And since all inanimate things are moved by some other thing – and the manner of the movement of the first and eternally moved, and how the first mover moves it, has been determined before in our *Metaphysics*, it remains to inquire how the soul moves the body, and what is the origin of movement in a living creature. 10 For, if we except the movement of the universe, things with life are the causes of the movement of all else, that is of all that are not moved by one another by mutual impact. And so all their movements have a term or limit, inasmuch as the movements of things with life have such. For all living things both move and 15 are moved with some object, so that this is the term of all their movement, the end, that is, in view. Now we see that the living creature is moved by intellect, imagination, choice, wish, and appetite. And all these are reducible to mind and desire. For both imagination and sensation are on common ground with mind, 20 since all three are faculties of judgement though differing according to distinctions stated elsewhere. Wish, however, anger and appetite, are all three forms of desire, while choice belongs to intellect and desire jointly. Therefore the object of desire and of intellect first initiates movement – not, that is, every object of intellect, only the end in the domain of conduct. Accordingly among goods that which moves is a practical end, not the good 25 in its whole extent. For it initiates movement only so far as something else is for its sake, or so far as it is the object of that which is for the sake of something else. And we must suppose that a seeming good may take the room of actual good, and so may the pleasant, which is itself a seeming good. From these considerations it is clear that in one regard that which is eternally 30 moved by the eternal mover is moved in the same way as every

living creature, in another regard differently, and so while it is moved eternally, the movement of living creatures has a term. Now the eternal beautiful, and the truly and primarily good (which is not at one time good, at another time not good), is too divine and precious to be relative to anything else. The prime mover then moves, itself being unmoved, whereas desire and its faculty are moved and so move. But it is not necessary for the last in the chain of things moved to move something else; wherefore it is plainly reasonable that motion in place should be the last of what happens in things that are moved, since the living creature is moved and goes forward by reason of desire or choice, when some alteration has been set going on the occasion of sensation or imagination.

But how is it that thought is sometimes followed by action, sometimes not; sometimes by movement, sometimes not? What happens seems parallel to the case of thinking and inferring about the immovable objects of science. There the end is the truth seen (for, when one thinks of the two premisses, one thinks of and puts together the conclusion), but here the two premisses result in a conclusion which is an action – for example, one thinks that every man ought to walk and that one is a man oneself: straightway one walks; or that no man should walk now and that one is a man: straightway one remains at rest. And one so acts in the two cases provided that there is nothing to compel or to prevent. Again, I ought to make a good, a house is good: straightway I make a house. I need a covering, a coat is a covering: I need a coat. What I need I ought to make, I need a coat: I ought to make a coat. And the conclusion – 'I ought to make a coat' – is an action. And the action goes back to the beginning or first step. If there is to be a coat, one must first have B, and if B then A, so one gets A to begin with. Now that the action is the conclusion is clear. But the premisses of action are of two kinds, of the good and of the possible.

And as sometimes happens in asking questions, so here the mind does not stop to consider at all an obvious minor premise; for example if walking is good for man, one does not dwell upon the minor 'I am a man'. That is why what we do without reflection, we do quickly. For when a man actualizes himself in relation to his object either by perceiving, or imagining or thinking of it, what he desires he does at once. For the actualizing of desire is a substitute for inquiry or reflection. I want to drink, says appetite; this is drink, says sense or imagination or mind: straightway I drink. In this way living creatures are impelled to move and to act, and desire is the last or immediate cause of movement, and desire arises through perception or through imagination and thought. And things that desire to act make things or do things, some because of appetite or anger, others because of desire or wish.

The movements of animals may be compared with those of automatic puppets, which are set going on the occasion of a tiny movement – the levers are released, and strike the twisted strings against one another – or with the toy wagon. For the child mounts on it and moves it straight forward, and then again it is moved in a circle owing to its wheels being of unequal diameter (the smaller acts like a centre on the same principle as the cylinders). Animals have parts of a similar kind, their organs, the sinewy tendons to wit and the bones; the bones are like the wooden levers in the automaton, and the iron; the tendons are like the strings, for when these are tightened or released movement begins. However, in the automata and the toy wagon there is no change of quality, though if the inner wheels became smaller and greater by turns there would be the same circular movement set up. In an animal the same part has the power of becoming now larger and now smaller, and changing its form, as the parts increase by warmth and again contract by cold and change their quality. This change of quality is caused by imaginations and sensations and by ideas. For sensations actually are changes of quality of a certain sort, while imagination and thinking have the same effect as the actual objects. For in a measure the form thought of be it of hot or cold or pleasant or fearful is like what the actual objects would be, and so we shudder and are frightened at the mere thought. Now all these are affections, i.e. changes of quality, and with those changes some parts of the body enlarge, others grow smaller. And it is not hard to see that a small change occurring at the centre makes great and numerous changes at the circumference, just as by shifting the rudder a hair's breadth you get a wide deviation at the prow. And further, when by reason of heat or cold or some kindred affection a change is set up in the region of the heart, even in an imperceptibly small part of the heart, it produces a vast difference in the periphery of the body, – blushing, let us say, or turning white, goose-skin and shivers and their opposites.

But to return, the object we pursue or avoid in the field of action is, as has been explained, the origin of movement, and upon the thought and imagination of this there necessarily follows a change in the temperature of the body. For what is painful we avoid, what is pleasing we pursue. We are, however, unconscious of what happens in the minute parts; still anything painful or pleasing is generally speaking accompanied by a definite change of temperature in the body. One may see this by considering the affections. Blind courage and panic fears, erotic emotions, and the rest of the corporeal affections, pleasant and painful, are all accompanied by a change of temperature, some in a particular member, others in the body generally. And memories and expectations, using as it were the reflected images of these pleasures and pains, are, now more and now less, causes of the same changes of temperature. So now we see the reason of nature's handiwork in the inward parts, and in the centres of movement of the organic members; they change from solid to moist, and from moist to solid, from soft to hard and vice versa. And since these things happen in this way, and since, also, the passive and active have the character we have many times described, as often as it comes to pass that one is active and the other passive, and neither of them falls short of the elements of its essence, straightway one acts and the other responds. And on this account thinking that one ought to go and going are virtually simultaneous, unless there be something else to hinder action. The organic parts are suitably prepared by the affections, these again by desire, and desire by imagination. Imagination in its turn depends either upon thinking or sense-perception. And the simultaneity and speed are due to the natural correspondence of the active and passive.

However, that which first moves the animal organism must be situate in a definite origin. Now we have said that a joint is the beginning of one part of a limb, the end of another. And so nature employs it sometimes as one, sometimes as two. When movement arises from a joint, one of the extreme points must remain at rest, and the other be moved (for as we explained above the mover must support itself against a point at rest). Accordingly, in the case of the elbow-joint, the last point of the forearm is moved but does not move anything, while, in the flexion, one point of the elbow, which lies in the whole forearm that is being moved, is moved, but there must also be a point which is unmoved; and this is our meaning when we speak of a point which is in potency one, but which becomes two in actual exercise. Now if the arm were the living animal, somewhere in its elbow-joint would be the soul's origin of movement. Since, however, it is possible for a lifeless thing to be so related to the hand as the forearm is to the upper (for example, when a man moves a stick in his hand), it is evident that the soul could not lie in either of the two extreme points, neither, that is, in the last point of the stick which is moved, nor in the other origin of movement. For the stick too has an end and an origin by reference to the hand. Accordingly, this example shows that the origin of movement which derives from the soul is not in the stick; and if not, then not in the hand; for a precisely similar relation obtains between the hand and the wrist, as between the wrist and the elbow. In this matter it makes no difference whether the part is a continuous part of the body or not; the stick may be looked at as a detached part of the whole. It follows then of necessity that the origin cannot lie in any individual origin which is the end of another member, even though there may lie another part outside the one in question. For example, relatively to the end point of the stick the hand is the origin, but the origin of the hand's movement is in the wrist. And so if the true origin is not in the hand, because there is still something higher up, neither is the true origin in the wrist, for once more if the elbow is at rest the whole part below it can be moved as a continuous whole.

9 Now since the left and the right sides are symmetrical, and these opposites are moved simultaneously, it cannot be that the left is moved by the right remaining stationary, nor vice versa; the origin must always be in what lies above both. Therefore, the

origin of movement of the moving soul must be in that which lies in the middle, for of both extremes the middle is the limiting point; and this is similarly related to the movements from above and the ones from below, those for example from the head and those from the spine (in animals that have a spine).

And this is a reasonable arrangement. For the sensorium is in our opinion in the centre too; and so, if the region of the origin of movement is altered in structure through sense-perception and thus changes, it carries with it the parts that depend upon it and they too are extended or contracted, and in this way the movement of the creature necessarily follows. And the middle of the body must needs be in potency one but in action more than one; for the limbs are moved simultaneously from the original seat of movement, and when one is at rest the other is moved. For example, in the line BAC, B is moved, and A is the mover.

There must, however, be a point at rest if one is to move, the other to be moved. A then being one in potency must be two in action, and so be a definite spatial magnitude not a mathematical point. Again, C may be moved simultaneously with B. Both the origins then in A must move and be moved, and so there must be something other than them which moves but is not moved. For otherwise, when the movement begins, the extremes, i.e. the origins, in A would rest upon one another, like two men putting themselves back to back and so moving their legs. There must then be some one thing which moves both. This something is the soul, distinct from the spatial magnitude just described and yet located therein.

Although from the point of view of the definition of movement — a definition which gives the cause — desire is the middle term or cause, and desire moves being moved, still in the material animated body there must be some material which itself moves being moved. Now that which is moved, but whose nature is not to initiate movement, is capable of being passive to an external force, while that which initiates movement must needs possess a kind of force and power. Now it is clear that all animals do both possess connatural spirit and derive power from this. (How this connatural spirit is maintained in the body is explained in other passages of our works.) And this spirit appears to stand to the origin in the soul in a relation like that between the point in a joint which moves being moved and the unmoved. Now since the origin is for some animals in the heart, in the rest in a part analogous with the heart, we further see the reason for the connatural spirit being situate where it actually is found. The question whether the spirit remains always the same or constantly changes and is renewed, like the cognate question about the rest of the parts of the body, is better postponed. At all events we see that it is well disposed to excite movement and to exert power; and the functions of movement are thrusting and pulling. Accordingly, the organ of movement must be capable of expanding and contracting; and this is precisely the characteristic of spirit. It contracts and expands naturally, and so is able to pull and to thrust from one and the same cause, exhibiting gravity compared with the fiery element, and levity by comparison with the opposites of fire. Now that which is to initiate movement without change of structure must be of the kind described, for the elementary bodies prevail over one another in a compound body by dint of disproportion; the light is overcome and kept down by the heavier, and the heavy kept up by the lighter.

We have now explained what the part is which is moved when the soul originates movement in the body, and what is the reason for this. And the animal organism must be conceived after the similitude of a well-governed commonwealth. When order is once established in it there is no more need of a separate monarch to preside over each several task. The individuals each play their assigned part as it is ordered, and one thing follows another in its accustomed order. So in animals there is the same orderliness – nature taking the place of custom – and each part naturally doing its own work as nature has composed them. There is no need then of a soul in each part, but it resides in a kind of central governing place of the body, and the remaining parts live by continuity of natural structure, and each part does its own work naturally.

So much then for the voluntary movements of animal bodies, and the reasons for them. These bodies, however, display in certain members involuntary movements too, but most often non-voluntary movements. By involuntary I mean movements of the heart and of the privy member; for often upon an image arising and not at the bidding of reason these parts are moved. By non-voluntary I mean sleep and waking and respiration, and other similar movements. For neither imagination nor desire is properly mistress of any of these; but since the animal body must undergo natural changes of quality, and when the parts are so altered some must increase and others decrease, the body must straightway be moved and change with the changes that nature makes dependent upon one another. Now the causes of the movements are natural changes of temperature, both those coming from outside the body, and those taking place within it. So the involuntary movements which occur in spite of reason in the aforesaid parts occur when a change of quality supervenes. For thought and imagination, as we said above, produce the conditions that bring about the affections, since they produce the images or forms of the things that bring them about. And the two parts aforesaid display this motion more conspicuously than the rest, because each is in a sense a separate vital organism, the reason being that each contains vital moisture. In the case of the heart the cause is plain, for the heart is the seat of the senses, while an indication that the generative organ too is vital is that there flows from it the seminal potency, itself a kind of organism. Again, it is a reasonable arrangement that the movements arise in the origin upon movements in the parts, and in the parts upon the movements in the origin, and so reach one another. Conceive A to be the origin. The movements then arrive at the origin from each letter in the diagram we have drawn, and flow back again from the origin which is moved and changes (for the origin is potentially multiple), the movement of B going to B, that of C to C, the

11

movement of both to both; but from B to C the movements flow by dint of going from B to A as to an origin, and then from A to C as from an origin.

Moreover a movement contrary to reason sometimes does and sometimes does not arise in the organs on the occasion of the same thoughts; the reason is that sometimes the matter which is passive to the impressions is there in sufficient quantity and of the right quality and sometimes not.

NOTES

NICOMACHEAN ETHICS

Book I

Chapter 1 (*page* 41)
The first sentence is best taken as affirming a conceptual connection between *choice* etc. on the one hand and *good* on the other. This is not to deny that different activities have different aims: 1097a15-22, *E.E.* 1218a31. On the question whether (we ought to say that) men aim at the good or what they *think* good, see III.4, *M.A.* 700b29. Can one infer that something is good from the fact that it is sought by all? See 1153b25 note, and passages cited there.
On the relation of activity to product, compare *E.E.* 1219a9-18.

Chapter 2 (*pages* 41-42)
It is difficult to acquit Aristotle of fallacy in the first sentence. That every purposive activity aims at some end desired for its own sake does not imply that there is some end desired for its own sake at which every purposive activity aims. That there is - in a sense - *one* thing (*eudaimonia* or 'happiness') at which all men ultimately aim is argued for differently in I.7.1097a25-b21.
On the relation between ethics and political philosophy, see 1102a5-26, 1141b23-1142a10, and X.9 (which serves as a transition to Aristotle's *Politics*); and *Politics* VII.1-2.

Chapter 3 (*pages* 42-43)
On the degree of precision to be expected in this enquiry, see 1098a26-b8, 1104a1-10, 1107a28-32, 1137b11-32, 1180b7-23. Rules of conduct are not like mathematical axioms from which conclusions can be deduced, but like medical generalisations. To apply them to particular situations requires knowledge of the complex facts of the case and a good judgement based on experience. Compare 1109b14-23, 1141b14-22, 1142a11-20, 1143b11-14.
The aim of the present investigation is practical (1103b26-31, 1179a33-b4, *E.E.* 1216b3-25) and will benefit a student only if he is of good character (1095b4-8, 1179b20-1180a1). Though the *Ethics* certainly contains recommendations and advice the larger

part is philosophical argument and analysis – concerned indeed with practical concepts, but not designed to *inculcate* a special morality or to *stimulate* the student to try to do better. It will however serve to give the legislator a real understanding of his task and so help him to succeed at it.

Chapter 4 (*pages* 43–44)

1095 a 18   The word '*eudaimonia*' is used by everyone to refer to whatever life is most desirable and satisfying: it would be absurd to say that one did not want *eudaimonia*. But people differ as to what sort of life is in fact best. This is not a dispute about the means to achieve a future goal but a disagreement as to what is the best way to live – what constitutes *eudaimonia*. The word 'happiness' has not got quite the same force as '*eudaimonia*', and it is important in reading a translation of the *Ethics* not to forget this. In particular, *eudaimonia* is not a state of feeling or enjoyment or content, and *eudaimonia* is not something that a man might contemplate sacrificing for some greater good.

1095 b 2   Aristotle's remarks about starting-points are in accord with his philosophical method not only in ethics but in general. The contrast between fact and reason can of course be drawn at different levels; and it is not obvious whether Aristotle here contrasts recognition of what to do in particular circumstances with knowledge of general rules of conduct, or knowledge of general rules with understanding of the fundamental purpose and justification of such rules.

Chapter 5 (*pages* 44–45)

Compare E.E. I.4–5. It is to be noted that Aristotle does not reject – or consider – the suggestion that the best life to lead is the most enjoyable. The life of pleasure which he dismisses as suitable for animals and not distinctively human (1095 b 20, E.E. 1215 b 35, compare 1097 b 33–1098 a 3) is the life of *bodily* pleasures. He will in due course argue that the life of fine action is enjoyable, and the life of philosophic contemplation supremely so; but this will not be his basic reason for recommending them. Roughly: it is not its being pleasantest that makes a certain life the best one for a man to lead, it is its being the best one for him to lead that explains its being pleasantest. Here, as on some other important points, Aristotle is closer to Bishop Butler than to Jeremy Bentham.

Nicomachean Ethics, Book I.6

Chapter 6 (*pages* 45–47)

In this important chapter Aristotle is primarily concerned to deny that goodness is a single property common to all good things: 'good' has a great variety of different uses, though they are not unconnected. He is further concerned to show that if there *were* a Platonic Form of Good it would not be what we are looking for – a specification of the best life for man. Compare *E.E.* I.8.

1096a23 The argument is usually taken to be that 'good' must have different senses since items in different categories can all be called good. Perhaps however Aristotle is making the following point. If asked why you call something good ('how do you mean "good"?') you will sometimes mention qualities the thing has, sometimes its size, and so on. Thus the criteria for calling various things good vary, and vary even in category; goodness is not, therefore, a single common quality like yellow. Compare *Topics* 107a3–17.

1096b27 Two suggestions as to how the uses of 'good' are connected. Perhaps different goods are so called through being related in various ways to one thing, or perhaps through being related in the same way to different things. It is tempting to assign the latter explanation to the attributive uses of 'good' in which it works like 'efficient' (a good knife does *its* job successfully, a good chair does *its* – different – job successfully), and to invoke the former explanation for the predicative use of 'good' in which e.g. knowledge, virtue, pleasure may be called good – each being good as contributing in its own way to the one final end *eudaimonia*. On *eudaimonia* as 'the first principle and cause of goods', see I.12 and *E.E.* 1219b13.

Chapter 7 (*pages* 47–50)

The first four paragraphs develop the idea of a most final end and show that *eudaimonia* is that end. The crucial facts about the concept *eudaimonia* are that we never (say that we) pursue it for the sake of anything else (though we pursue other things for its sake), and that we regard *eudaimonia* as self-sufficient and as including everything desirable in itself (with 1097b17 compare 1172b33). A man's idea of *eudaimonia* would be a life containing in full measure all the things he regards as intrinsically worthwhile. He desires each of these 'for the sake of *eudaimonia*' not in the sense that he hopes to reach *eudaimonia* subsequently as a result of achieving them, but in the sense that he expects to be living a life of *eudaimonia* in living a life which contains them. They will be ingredients in, not instrumental means to, his ideal life.

This account of the logical role of the term '*eudaimonia*' may lead one to say: 'there is one thing all men pursue, namely *eudaimonia*'. But this may be misleading, since different people would no doubt give different specifications of their ideal life. So in passing on at 1097b22 to the question 'what is *eudaimonia*?' Aristotle is assuming something not guaranteed by the preceding discussion. He is assuming that the life all men aim at – or ought to aim at – is at least broadly the same. He will argue in I.8 that the formula he reaches ('activity of soul in accordance with virtue', 1098a16) does satisfy various common views about *eudaimonia*; and indeed the formula is so general that it might accommodate almost any human ideal. The fact remains that there is a great step from saying that each man uses the term '*eudaimonia*' for the life he most wants or envies to saying that there is one kind of life that every man, just because he is a man, would find most worth leading.

In seeking to determine what *eudaimonia* is by considering the function of man Aristotle follows Plato (*Republic* I.352d–354a). They are not assuming that man was made for a purpose, but only that he has certain distinctive powers which mark him off from other animals. A distinctively human life will exploit these powers, and the best human life will be the one that exploits them most effectively. However, even if such a 'function argument' can establish something (very general) about the criteria for being *a good man*, it is not clear that it thereby establishes anything about *the good for man*. It is not self-evident that the most desirable and enviable life for a man to lead is the life a good man leads.

One would have expected the conclusion of the argument at 1098a17 to run: 'and if there is more than one virtue, in accordance with all of them' (cp. *E.E.* 1219a35–39). Aristotle's actual words 'in accordance with the best and most complete' (compare 1099a30) seem to point forward to his elevation of theoretical reason above practical reason in X.7–8. But *this* rests on considerations other than those expounded in the function argument. Theoretical reason is no more distinctive of man vis-à-vis other animals than practical reason is; it is 'higher' because more godlike. It might indeed be argued that just because theoretical reason is shared with god it is *only* practical reason that is distinctively human, so that the good *human life* should be primarily a matter of rational *action*.

Nicomachean Ethics, Book I.7

Aristotle seeks to counter such a line of thought in X.7 (1177b26–1178a8).

Chapter 8 (*pages 51–52*)

1098b10 At the beginning of chapter 13 Aristotle will return to the account of *eudaimonia* that was the conclusion of the function argument, and he will proceed to discuss its constituents – first and briefly 'soul', then at great length 'virtue'. In the present chapter he is concerned to show that the conclusion of his argument accords with ordinary views about *eudaimonia*.

1099a7 On the connection between virtuous action and pleasure, see 1104b3–8, 1117a33–b16 (with note on 1117b15).

1099a31 As regards health, money, and other such 'goods', Aristotle points out that some are necessary conditions of virtuous action; others he just accepts – following popular opinion – as requisite for the truly blessed life. See 1099b27, 1100b22–1101a16, 1153b18, IX.9, 1177a30, 1178a24. Many people confuse the essential constituents of the good life with factors that are only necessary conditions: *E.E.* I.2.

1099a13 For 'pleasant by nature' compare 1148a24, b15, 1154b16.

Chapter 9 (*pages 53–54*)

On the importance of upbringing and habituation, see II.1 and 1179b20–1180a5. If natural endowment and various forms of training determine a man's character, can a man of bad character be properly blamed for what he does? Aristotle comes closest to attacking this problem in III.5 (1114a3–31).

Chapter 12 (*page 57*)

On praise, encomium, and felicitation (calling someone happy or blessed), see *E.E.* 1219b8–16 and *Rhetoric* 1367b28–36.

Chapter 13 (*pages 57–60*)

Aristotle here gives an abbreviated or popular version of his psychological doctrines, which are expounded more fully in the *De Anima*. He refers to three 'parts' or powers of the human soul: the nutritive, the desiring or desiderative, and the thinking faculty. Plants too can nourish themselves and reproduce; and animals other than man have desire. It is the power to think that distinguishes man from other living things. In virtue of this power man can display two distinct types of excellence: excellence in thinking itself ('intellectual virtue'),

NOTES

and excellence of character ('moral virtue') – this being the condition in which desires are in accordance with reason. For subdivisions of desire, see 1111b11 note. Intellectual excellence will be differentiated into practical wisdom and theoretical wisdom (1139a1–17), and a necessary connection will be established between practical wisdom and excellence of character (1144b30–1145a2).

Aristotle does not think of the soul as an immaterial substance dwelling in the body. The soul is the *form* or *actuality* of the body: to study an animal's soul and its 'parts' is to study the animal's life and the animal's various powers and activities as a living thing. There is one important exception to Aristotle's decidedly psychophysical approach, in that he holds that the exercise of pure theoretical thought does not involve any physiological process, and that pure reason is not the actuality of the body or any part of the body. See *De Anima* I.4, II.1–3.

BOOK II

Chapter 1 (pages 61–62)

1103a19 Aristotle returns to the distinction – and the relation – between innate and acquired dispositions at VI.13 and (in connection with the problem of responsibility) at III.5.1114a3–b25.

1103a31 Aristotle rightly insists that the way to acquire skills or virtues is to practise; reading a book won't do (1179b4). This point must be distinguished from the purely conceptual point that virtues are actualised or exercised in appropriate performances. A neuro-surgeon might be able to bring it about that a man previously mean became generous; but nobody could bring it about that a generous man went through life hoarding his money. (Could a man be generous though lacking funds? See 1178a28–b3).

On the difference between acts done in acquiring virtue and acts done by the already vituous, see II.4.

Chapter 2 (pages 62–63)

The first paragraph repeats points made in I.3, the second foreshadows the account of virtue as a mean in II.6, and the third continues the theme of II.1 and leads naturally on to chapters 3 and 4.

Chapter 3 (pages 63–65)

1104b5 On the connection between virtue and pleasure, see

Nicomachean Ethics, Book II.3

1099a7 note. That the good man's life is necessarily enjoyable – since he is not accounted truly good unless he finds it enjoyable – does not of course entail that it is more enjoyable than anyone else's. Compare X.5 and (for the pleasure of pure thought) 1177a22–27.

Chapter 4 (pages 65–66)

The ascription to someone of either a skill or a virtue requires more than that he should have done something right. The possibility that he did it by luck or under instruction must be excluded. The ascription of a virtue on the basis of what is done requires also that the motive be good.

1105a28 'It is enough that they should have a certain character'. This seems confused, since for the appraisal of the performer this is *not* enough (as Aristotle has just pointed out). It is indeed enough for the appraisal of the product, but this is true also in the case of action: we can settle without reference to the agent's character or state of mind whether what he did was the kind thing to do (1105b5–9).

1105a32 'He must... choose them for their own sakes'. Compare 1135b19–25, 1144a13–20. Doing a kind act for an ulterior motive is not a display or proof of kindness. Aristotle's requirement here does not conflict with his repeated statement that the good man does what he does 'because it is fine' (1115b12 note), or with the idea that men act for the sake of *eudaimonia*. For kindness is a *form of* 'fineness', and *eudaimonia* is not a consequence of good actions but a life consisting of them.

Must acts be deliberately chosen if they are to qualify as displays of virtue? See 1111b5 note.

The possession of a 'firm and unchangeable' disposition is perhaps relevant to the ascription of skills as well as of virtues, in that the way to show that the correct performance was not just a fluke is to repeat it successfully. Still skill can be quickly lost or forgotten whereas virtue cannot (1100b12–17, 1140b29).

Chapter 5 (pages 66–67)

The word '*hexis*', here translated 'state of character' really has a wider meaning: Aristotle freely applies it to *bodily* states or conditions, and also to *intellectual* excellences. No doubt he here has in mind states or traits of character; but even so his account at 1105b25–28 seems unduly narrow.

The word '*pathos*', here translated 'passion', also has a very wide meaning, and it is elsewhere often rendered by 'emotion' or 'feeling'. In the *Ethics* it is usually emotions (and associated desires and aversions) that Aristotle has in mind. For the way in which emotions involve physical reaction, thought, desire, and feeling, see *De Anima* 403a3-b2 and *Rhetoric* II. 1-11.

Chapter 6 (*pages 67–69*)

On the 'doctrine of the mean', see Introduction, page 22.

1106a31 'relatively to us'. This does not mean that a man is the only or best judge of what is best for him to do, but that what *is* best for him to do depends on his individual circumstances, powers, etc.

1106b6 'concerned with passions and actions'. Does Aristotle think that *some* virtues are to do with 'passions', *others* with actions; or that every virtue has to do with both? In one sense certainly the latter. For in any area what marks the virtuous man off from the merely self-controlled or 'continent' is that his desires and emotions lead him to do what he does; he does not have to fight rebel passions, his actions are in accordance with his reason and also in harmony with his desires. Nevertheless some excellences seem definable primarily by reference to distinct emotions, other by reference to types of action: good temper relates to the emotion of anger, generosity to the activity of giving money. Again, a different *pathos* distinguishes good temper from courage (anger, fear); but the difference between 'liberality' and 'magnificence' rests on a criterion of another kind (1107b18: the scale of the expenditure).

1106b31 'only in one way'. But the correct 'mean' is often a range. On the right size for a city Aristotle says: 'the proper number is presumably not a single number, but anything that falls between certain fixed points' (1170b32). Compare 1173a23-28. In any case small errors are forgiveable; we are not talking about mathematics but about complicated and variable human affairs where the final decision rests with perception and judgement.

1106b36 'concerned with choice'. See 1111b5 note. We cannot of course choose to be angry (1106a2), but our proneness to anger affects our choices.

1107a1 Perhaps better to translate: 'determined by a *logos*, that *logos* namely by which the man ...'; or (with a different reading) 'determined by a *logos* and in the way in which the man ...'. See 1138b18-34, 1144b21-28.

Nicomachean Ethics, Book II.7

Chapter 7 (pages 69-72)

1107a29 'the individual facts'. Or rather 'individual cases', i.e. the particular excellences he is now to discuss. When he says that we may take these cases 'from our table' he obviously points to a list on the lecture-room wall.

The virtues of courage and temperance (1107a33–b8) are discussed in detail in III. 6–11; the virtues listed in 1107b8–1108b6 are treated in book IV (except that there is no further talk of righteous indignation, envy, and spite); and justice is the subject of book V.

1107b22 'Pride then seems to be a sort of crown of the virtues; for it makes them greater, and it is not found without them. Therefore it is hard to be truly proud; for it is impossible without nobility and goodness of character' (1124a1–4).

1108a32 'Shame should not be described as a virtue; for it is more like a feeling than a state of character' (1128b10). Yet fear too is a feeling – but there is a related virtue, courage.

Aristotle also makes the point that 'the sense of disgrace is not even characteristic of a good man (*sc.* still less is it a virtue), since it is consequent on bad actions' (1128b21). It would be paradoxical to offer as proof that one is a good man the fact that one is suitably ashamed when one has behaved badly (1128b26).

1108b7 On kinds of justice, V.1–2; how justice is a mean, 1133b32–1134a13; the rational virtues, VI.

Book III

III.1–5 (on responsibility and the psychology of action) should be studied alongside V.8, *E.E.* II.6–11, *De Anima* III.9–11, and *De Motu Animalium* 6–11. See Introduction, page 24.

Chapter 1 (pages 75-78)

1110a11 It is not happy to say that actions done under pressure 'are mixed, but are more like voluntary actions'. The agent can clearly be held responsible for what he does in such circumstances, though he may escape some or all of the blame that would have attached to him if he had acted so when not subject to such pressure. No doubt he acts *reluctantly*, not *willingly*; and it is perhaps because the word translated 'voluntary' carries the suggestion of willingness that Aristotle is hesitant to apply it to cases of action under pressure.

NOTES

Aristotle does not consider in connection with force or pressure a question he does raise about ignorance of fact. Suppose a man has knowingly and culpably got himself into a situation in which he is exposed to force or to pressure: can he *then* plead these as excuses?

1110b9–15 This passage and 1111a24–b3 foreshadow the fuller discussion of responsibility in III.5.

1110b18–24 Compare 1111a20. That a man is not subsequently sorry about something he did in ignorance of fact is significant for appraisal of his character, but it has no bearing on the question whether he can be blamed for what he did. That Oedipus is glad to find he killed his father does not of course imply that he killed his father gladly – nor did he kill him reluctantly either; for he did not know that *that* (killing his father) was what he was doing.

1110b28 'Ignorance' of what in general one ought to do is proof of badness and exposes the agent to censure. Aristotle does not have in mind a person who has never been shown or taught how to behave, but one so corrupt that he fails to feel the force of moral ideals and principles. To the claim that such a man may be *naturally bad* and so should not be blamed Aristotle replies in III.5.

1111a26 Are animals capable of voluntary action? Aristotle oscillates: 1111b8, 1139a20, *E.E.* 1222b20, 1224a29. They can move from desire but not from 'choice'. Not possessing the power of thought, they cannot deliberate; and being unable to consider the future, they cannot aim at a good other than immediate pleasure – they are incapable of *wish* as opposed to *appetite* (cp. *De An.* 433b7).

Chapter 2 (*pages 78–80*)

1111b5 Why does choice discriminate characters better than actions do? Because intentions can misfire (cp. 1178a34–b2), and because for character-appraisal we need to know not only what a man did but why (II.4, *E.E.* 1228a3). Yet in the end we have to judge intentions and motives from overt performances: 1178a28–34, *E.E.* 1228a16.

Are *chosen* actions more important for character discrimination than *voluntary* actions? *Choice* enters into the definition of moral virtue (1106b36); and compare II.4, 1135b25, 1136a4. Yet how one behaves in emergencies – when there is no time for deliberation and 'choice' – can be particularly revealing: 1117a18. (It would of course be a mistake to suppose that doing something intentionally or with an intention or from a motive requires that one should have deliberated and – in Aristotle's sense – *chosen* to do it.)

Nicomachean Ethics, Book III.2

1111b11 For Aristotle's division of desire into appetite, '*thumos*', and wish compare *E.E.* II.7, *De An.* 432b3-7, *M.A.* 700b22. Appetite and wish are desires for the pleasant and the good respectively, and the clash between them is characteristic of the continent and incontinent. On *thumos*, see 1149a25-b3. In Platonic psychology *thumos* covers many desires and motives connected with a man's self-esteem, ambition, aggressiveness, etc. It plays a minor role in the *Ethics*, the notions of anger and desire for revenge being predominant.

1112a15 On choice and deliberation, compare 1113a10-12, 1139a31-b5, *E.E.* 1226b5-9, 1227a4-5.

Chapter 3 (*pages* 80-82)
On deliberation see Introduction, page 26.

Chapter 4 (*pages* 82-83)
Aristotle is wrestling here with a genuine problem about the characterisation of people's aims and the description of their actions (cp. Plato's *Gorgias* 467-8). But he fails to distinguish clearly between two contrasts: (a) the contrast between *really F* and *apparently F*, and (b) the contrast between *F to* (or *for*) *most* (or *normal*) *people* and *F to* (or *for*) *some* (or an *abnormal*) *person*. Often indeed the normal is the criterion for the real; but a gruel diet is *really* good for an invalid though not for the normal person (1129b1-6). For the same unclarity in the discussion of the pleasant see 1173b20-25, 1176a10-24.

Aristotle is not helped here by the fact that the word translated 'object of wish' can but need not have a gerundive force: it may refer either to what is actually wished for or to what ought to be – is worth being – wished for.

Chapter 5 (*pages* 83-86)
See Introduction, page 27.

The argument at 1113b3-14 to show that states of character are themselves 'voluntary' must be sharply distinguished from the argument to the same conclusion at 1114a14-31. For while the latter relies on the fact that the acts the doing of which *made me into* a good (or bad) man were voluntary, the former appeals to the fact that the acts the doing of which *constitutes* my being a good (or bad) man are voluntary.

To be the manifestation of a virtue an action must be done from

NOTES

the appropriate motive (II.4 and 1137a4-26). But I cannot choose to have – or, therefore, to act from – a particular motive. So *are* the acts that constitute my being a good man really 'in my power'?

On the voluntariness of states of character and of actions see also the curious discussion in III.12.

Chapter 6 (*pages 86–87*)

Is courage a matter of feeling or not feeling appropriate fear, or a matter of facing dangers even when afraid? Aristotle seems to touch on both.

Chapter 7 (*pages 87–89*)

1115b12   'for honour's sake', 'for a noble end' (b23), 'because it is noble' (1116a11, 15, b3 etc.) The word '*kalon*' often comes to mean little more than 'good', but it carries a suggestion of aesthetic beauty or splendour. The good man does what he does 'because it is fine' and 'for its own sake' and 'for the sake of *eudaimonia*' (1105a32 note).

Chapter 8 (*pages 89–91*)

Aristotle here distinguishes five types of courage which deviate from the central or normal type defined in chapter 6. This is a procedure characteristic of his philosophising. Sometimes he sees himself as distinguishing different senses of a word (all being related to a central sense), sometimes he adopts a less linguistic approach. In any case he certainly anticipates recent work on families of meaning and on family resemblances.

1117a18   Compare 1150b23 and 1111b5 note.

Chapter 9 (*pages 91–92*)

1117b15   See 1099a7 note. The 'end' in question is not e.g. defeating the enemy, but doing what is fine. The soldier does not in the least *enjoy* his weariness and wounds, but he does undergo them *gladly* – because, and only because, he knows that he is doing something fine and honourable.

Chapter 10 (*pages 92–94*)

1117b24   In saying that courage and temperance seem to be the virtues of the irrational parts Aristotle is reverting to the Platonic way of speaking, according to which appetite and *thumos* are the two irrational parts or faculties of the soul, the third part being the reasoning one. Compare *De An.* 432a25.

Book V

Chapter 1 (pages 99–101)

1129a26 As usual the term Aristotle is concerned with is not straightforwardly ambiguous, but has a number of related senses or uses. Compare 1130a32, 1096b26.

1129b3 On this distinction, see 1137a26, 1152b27, E.E. 1248b26; and III.4 note.

1129b25 How does this form of justice – obedience to the law – differ from moral virtue in general? 'In relation to our neighbour'. But does not moral virtue necessarily involve our neighbours? And does not a good man often do things *not* required by law? And is *motive* as crucial for attributing justice as it is for attributing moral virtue to a man?

Chapter 2 (pages 101–103)

1130b29 See *Politics* III.2–3: only in the best state are good citizens also necessarily good men; and even in this state it is not every good citizen but only the good ruler-citizen who is necessarily a good man – for only he *must* possess practical wisdom in order to fulfil his role in the state.

1130b30 Aristotle distinguishes three sorts of 'particular justice':

(i) *distributive*, the basic principle being geometrical proportion, e.g. to each according to his effort (what ought to be the criterion – effort, need, status, etc. – is a fundamental political question);

(ii) *rectificatory*, the basis being arithmetical proportion. It redresses the effects of civil or criminal wrong and restores the *status quo ante*;

(iii) *justice in exchange*, based on proportionate reciprocity. An example would be the calculation of exchange-value by reference to the hours of work put into the products in question: if x hours produce a coat and y hours a pound of flour, y coats should exchange for x pounds of flour. Compare Karl Marx, who quotes Aristotle, in *Das Kapital* c. 1.

Chapters 3–5 deal respectively with the three forms of particular justice and end with the passage translated in the text. Chapter 6 distinguishes the *political* justice that holds between citizens from the justice found in other associations (e.g. the associations of master and slave or father and children).

NOTES

Chapter 7 (*pages* 104–105)

1134b33 Aristotle's example – the right hand is naturally stronger – does not make clear how we are to discover what laws express *natural* justice, given that we cannot find unanimity or rely on majority opinion.

Chapter 8 (*pages* 105–107)

To be studied along with III.1–5.

1135a33–b2 A valuable addition to the III.1 analysis. See also *M.A.* 703b4–9.

1135b21 Is the nature (or degree) of the passion relevant? Surely, whether I have been carried away by a natural or by a monstrous passion, what I do *will* be an act of injustice but will *not* show me to be an unjust man. The nature or degree of the passion is relevant only to the question whether or to what extent I should be blamed for what I do; if the passion was natural and excusable I shall not be blamed (even though I remain liable for damages).

1136a5–9 Here Aristotle recognises involuntary acts that are nevertheless not excused. Contrast 1109b32, and see Introduction, page 25.

Chapter 9 (*pages* 107–110)

1136a10–1137a4 A characteristically acute examination of some conceptual puzzles (carried further in c.11): can a man be treated unjustly *voluntarily*? In an unjust distribution is the distributor or the recipient guilty of injustice?

1137a4–26 Compare II.4, III.5. Aristotle does not seem to distinguish clearly between:

(a) it is not easy to do the right thing, because it is not easy to apply general rules to particular circumstances; and
(b) it is not easy to act with justice, because this is not simply a matter of doing such-and-such a thing but requires that one do it from a certain motive and character.

Chapter 10 (*pages* 110–111)

On equity, see also *Rhetoric* 1374a18–b23. Compare I.3 note.

Chapter 11 (not printed in this volume) argues three points:

(a) a man cannot treat himself unjustly;
(b) acting unjustly is in itself worse than being unjustly treated;

(c) metaphorically one can speak of justice as between the rational and irrational parts of the soul.

BOOK VI

Chapter 1 (pages 113–114)

1138b34 Compare *E.E.* 1222b8, 1249a21 note.

1139a6 Aristotle does not make sufficiently clear the difference between two contrasts: (a) that between thinking concerned with necessary and invariable matters and thinking concerned with contingent matters that might be otherwise – a contrast of *objects* of thought; and (b) that between thinking simply in order to discover the truth and thinking with a view to doing something – a contrast of *aims*. There is a connection: no one deliberates about what cannot be otherwise (1112a21). Nevertheless we may think only 'theoretically' about contingent matters. Notice that the part or aspect of the mind here (1139a12) labelled 'deliberative' or 'calculative' is later (1140b26) characterised as the part 'that forms opinions' – a phrase that does *not* possess the *practical* nuance.

For further distinctions, see 1139b1 ('practical' *versus* 'productive' thinking) and 1143a8 (thinking about what someone else could or should do *versus* thinking what to do oneself).

Chapter 2 (pages 114–115)

1139a19 Of the three 'things in the soul' none is by itself sufficient to originate action or animal movement generally. What is needed is a combination of desire on the one hand with a power of apprehension on the other – the power to conceive or perceive or imagine something capable of being desired. See *De An.* III.10, *M.A.* cc. 6–7.

1139b1 Aristotle distinguishes between acting and making, between practical thinking (which may display practical wisdom) and productive thinking (which may display skill). Compare VI.4 and 1140b6: 'while making has an end other than itself, action cannot; for good action itself is its end'. But he fails to examine this distinction closely enough. Does not an action often consist in taking steps to bring about some change or outcome? May not the same performance be appraised in either of two ways, morally or technically? If a doctor helps at an accident, the *kindness* of his action does not depend on whether his efforts to revive the victim are successful;

NOTES

but nevertheless his kind action is doing something to bring something else about, and as such it may be skilful or the reverse. (See 1176b7 and 1177b1–26 with notes.)

Aristotle's failure to examine this distinction carefully enough may explain why his account of deliberation in III.3 takes over an analysis originally developed for productive technique rather than for action, and why he does not examine the relation between it and the other type of deliberation that comes to the fore in VI and VII.

Chapter 3 (*pages* 115–116)

Knowledge as defined in this chapter ('scientific knowledge') is demonstrative and has to be accompanied by the *nous* ('intuitive reason') of chapter 6 (cp. 1142a25, 1143b1) which provides starting-points, both universals and necessary truths, for demonstration. The combination of both, directed to the noblest objects, is *sophia*, 'philosophic wisdom' (1141a19, b3). *Posterior Analytics* is concerned with demonstrative knowledge; its last chapter, II.19, deals with the acquisition of starting-points.

Chapter 5 (*pages* 116–118)

1140b11 On the necessary connection between practical wisdom and the excellence of character that 'makes the end right' (1144a8, a20, 1145a5), see Introduction, page 29.

1140b17 Is Aristotle's really *bad* man a man with no principles or 'end', or a man with the wrong ones? Is his really *self-indulgent* man a man with extreme desires controlled by no rule, or a man who follows the rule 'satisfy your immediate desires'? See 1144a35, 1146b22, 1148a17, 1151a13, a23, 1152a5, a24.

Chapter 7 (*pages* 118–120)

1141b18 On the crucial importance of experience, see 1142a15, 1143b11, 1180b18, 1181a19.

On the practical syllogism, see Introduction, page 30. Aristotle's example here is not very felicitous. 'Chicken is wholesome' is less general than 'light meats are wholesome', but it is still general; it is no help unless we also know that *this* is a chicken. Contrast the example at 1142a23 ('this water...').

1141b20 The text of the manuscripts says: 'the man who knows that chicken is light and wholesome...'.

Nicomachean Ethics, Book VI.8

Chapter 8 (*pages* 120-121)

1142a11 'What has been said' refers back to the point made at the end of the previous chapter, that practical wisdom has to do with particulars. The intervening passage is perhaps misplaced.

1142a25 Compare 1143a25-b14. The *phronimos* has to decide what to do in particular and often complicated circumstances. So he must be able to seize the relevant facts, weigh them up, consider alternatives, and reach the right decision. That requires experience, an eye (1143b14) for what is and what is not essential, a 'sense' of what is fitting (1109b23, 1113a1, 1142a27).

Chapter 9 (*pages* (121-123))

1142b19 The words 'if he is clever' translate a conjectural emendation of a difficult Greek text. The words translated 'the incontinent man and the bad man' could be rendered 'the incontinent man – or rather, the bad man'. The incontinent man does *not* achieve the good he wishes for.

1142b23 Does Aristotle refer to the taking of wrong means to right ends, or to the reaching of correct conclusions by erroneous reasoning?

Chapter 11 (*pages* 124-125)

1143a35 'Intuitive reason' (*nous*) in its strict sense is to be *contrasted* with the grasp of particular facts (as above, 1142a25). Here Aristotle speaks of 'intuitive reason ... in both directions' in order to stress a similarity, the *immediacy* of apprehension that is involved both in knowledge of unprovable starting-points for theoretical demonstrations and in recognition of particular facts to do with action.

Chapter 12 (*pages* 125-127)

1143b34 On the relation of practical wisdom to philosophic wisdom, and on the place of action and of theoretical activity in the happy life, see 1144a5, 1145a9, X.7 and 8, *E.E.* 1249b14 note, and Introduction, page 29.

Chapter 13 (*pages* 127-128)

1145a1 Is the notion that you cannot have one excellence of character unless you have all the others a relic of the Socratic view that *any* virtue presupposes knowledge of the good, and knowledge of the good guarantees *every* virtue? Aristotle does not of course think that knowledge by itself – without desire – can guarantee virtue or indeed generate action of any kind. But *phronesis* (practical wisdom) is so defined as to imply moral virtue, the excellence of the desiring faculty, and *vice versa*. The conclusion that the various excellences of character are inseparable from one another is paradoxical at the ordinary level; but see Introduction 23.

Book VII

Aristotle's discussion of *akrasia* in VII.1-10 should be read in conjunction with *E.E.* II.7-8.

Chapter 1 (*pages* 129-130)

1145b3 On Aristotle's philosophical method, and on the translation 'observed facts', see Introduction, page 15.

Chapter 2 (*pages* 130-132)

1145b21 A better rendering would be: 'what *kind* of right judgement has the man who acts *akratically*'. *Akrasia* is doing wrong when *in some sense* you know better. The question is, in what sense? What is the nature and content of this 'knowledge' that you somehow have and yet go against?

Chapter 3 (*pages* 132-135)

1146b31 Here begins a series of logical points about 'know', followed (from 1147a24) by a fuller and more psychological account of the *akratic* situation. See Introduction, page 31.
1147a28 On 'immediately', see *M.A.* 702a15 note.
1147b15 A plausible textual emendation would give the meaning: 'for it is not what is thought to be knowledge proper that the affection of incontinence overcomes..., but perceptual knowledge'.

Chapter 4 (*pages* 135-137)

In this and the following chapters Aristotle distinguishes the central or unqualified type of *akrasia* from special types and sub-types (themselves distinguished and classified by a variety of criteria), and from certain states that are sufficiently like *akrasia* to need being mentioned and separated off from it. Compare the treatment of courage and temperance in III.6-12.

It is important to keep distinct:

(a) the general problem of *akrasia*;

(b) detailed questions about the ordinary use of the word *'akratic'*, with or without additions ('over money', 'with regard to anger', etc.);
(c) questions about the relative blameworthiness of various sorts of *akrasia* or of *akrasia* displayed in various areas.

1147b24   'For 'necessary' as opposed to 'worthy of choice in itself', see 1176b3. Why should excessive pursuit of things naturally good and choiceworthy be let off so much more lightly than excessive pursuit of 'necessary' pleasures (cp. 1148a4, b2)? At the end of IV.2 Aristotle says that vulgarity (in expenditure) and niggardliness are indeed faults ('vices'), 'yet they do not bring *disgrace* because they are neither harmful to one's neighbour nor very unseemly'. In IV.3, speaking of certain forms of humility and vanity, he says that such people are not thought *bad* because they do not do harm. That *akrasia* in respect of anger is less disgraceful than *akrasia* in respect of the appetites is argued at length in VII.6.

1148a25   The 'intermediate' objects referred to here are presumably the 'necessary' ones of 1147b24. Those 'contrary' to the ones naturally choiceworthy are objects of the perverse and shameful desires discussed in chapter 5. On 'naturally good', compare *E.E.* VIII.3.

Chapter 7 (*pages* 140–142)

1150a11   For the relevance of the *average* – what most people are like – to our habits of classifying and describing see 1118b23, 1150b1, b12, 1151a5, 1152a27. However, in his accounts of excellences of character Aristotle seems to be speaking of (e.g.) *perfect* generosity: the generous man *always* gives appropriately. These two approaches are not inconsistent. The difference between them makes itself felt over the question whether the moral virtues are inseparable from one another (1144b32). The Socratic answer – that they are not – may be right for *perfect* virtues; but as we actually describe men there is no doubt that one may be e.g. courageous but rather mean.

1150a22   The root meaning of the word translated 'self-indulgent' is *incorrigible*. Aristotle remarks that it is appropriate so to label one who, unable to repent, is *incurable*.

1150b19   For this distinction, compare 1151a1, 1152a18, a28. Does the account at the end of chapter 3 fit either (or both) of these types of *akrasia*?

NOTES

Chapter 9 (pages 143–145)

The first paragraph takes up a problem stated at 1146a16–21. Aristotle is trying to analyse and find a clear way of describing the case of a man who mistakenly thinks he ought to behave in a certain way and does so in spite of counter-temptations (or, alternatively, fails to do it because of counter-temptations). Is this man to be called continent (or, alternatively, incontinent, i.e. *akratic*); and what rule or principle should he be described as sticking to (or, alternatively, not sticking to): is it a correct or an incorrect rule? Compare the problem discussed in III.4.

Aristotle's answer seems to imply that both the continent and the incontinent necessarily have the right *basic* aim or end or principle. He does not seem to provide for a man with quite the wrong principles who then does (or, alternatively, fails to do) what he thinks they require, when tempted not to do that. Perhaps he thinks that nobody has 'quite the wrong principles' – the really bad man has *no* principles; or perhaps he thinks that the bad man's principle is to go for his own present pleasure and that no possibility of *akrasia* arises in the presence of that principle. See 1140b17 note.

Chapter 10 (pages 145–146)

1152a12 For the distinction between cleverness and practical wisdom, see 1144a23–b4.

1152a15 'asleep or drunk', compare 1147a13, b7.

1152a17 'The end to which he does it' must refer to the immediate aim or point of what he does, 'his purpose' to the end he in general and normally (i.e. when not subject to *akrasia*) wishes for and aims at.

Chapter 11 (pages 146–147)

1152b9 An alternative reading has the meaning 'since the same thing is not good and a pleasure'. This gives better support to the claim that no pleasure is a good even incidentally than does the contention that the good and pleasure are not the same.

1152b13 The formula here suggested (the elements of which are to be found in Plato's *Philebus*, 31–34 and 54) is corrected at 1153a13.

Chapter 12 (pages 147–149)

Here and elsewhere in his discussions of pleasure Aristotle uses a variety of contrasts whose meaning and inter-relations need investigation. Something may be pleasant in itself, by nature, without

Nicomachean Ethics, Book VII.12

qualification, really; or it may only be pleasant incidentally, for a certain person or at a certain time, apparently. Also a pleasure may be unmixed (with 'pain') or mixed. See, for example, 1154b15–20, 1173b20–25, 1176a10–29, 1176b25; and compare III.4 note.

1153a9 That enjoyment is not a *genesis* ('process' or 'coming into being') nor a *kinesis* ('movement' or 'change') is argued in book X (1173a29–b20, 1174a13–b14).

Chapter 13 (pages 149–150)

1153b2 Or: 'other pain is bad in some respect [i.e. *not* without qualification bad] in that it is an impediment to us'.

1153b5 Compare 1173a5–13. The words 'that pleasure is contrary both to pain and to good' are not in the text. Neither Speusippus' suggestion nor Aristotle's riposte is entirely clear.

1153b25 Compare 1172b9–15, 1172b35–1173a5, 1175a10–17, *Metaphysics* Λ. 7 and 9. The Aristotelian universe focuses on god. God is pure eternal thought. The heavenly bodies imitate this as closely as they can – by unceasing regular movement. Animals and plants are driven by the same deep impulse, and they strive above all to carry on and perpetuate their species: 'an animal producing an animal, a plant a plant, in order that, as far as its nature allows, it may partake in the eternal and divine. That is the goal towards which all things strive, that for the sake of which they do whatsoever their nature renders possible' (*De An.* 415a28–b2). Man, possessing reason, can imitate god in another way also, by engaging in pure thought. See 1177b26–31, 1178b25–28.

1154a1 The argument is obscure. A conjectural emendation would give: 'if pleasure is not a good and activity is not a pleasure'; the first part being taken up in a2–5, the second part in a5–7.

Chapter 14 (pages 150–152)

1154a23 The error is the supposition that bodily pleasures (rather than those of contemplation) constitute the good. For the explanation see 1153b33–1154a1, 1154a26–31, b5–15.

1154b21 For 'not simple', see 1177b28, 1178a20. It is not clear whether Aristotle means that a man is a compound of matter and form (body and soul) or that a man's soul is not just reason but has other 'parts' or faculties. These two points are of course connected, since Aristotle holds that psychological powers and activities other than pure reason necessarily involve bodily organs and functions. Compare *De An.* 403a3–b19, 408b1–29.

NOTES

Book IX

In VIII and IX Aristotle distinguishes and discusses various forms of friendship and association, examining the purposes they serve and the obligations they involve. The chapters from IX printed here are those most likely to interest the student of moral philosophy.

Chapter 4 (*pages 153–155*)

The criteria of inter-personal friendship derive from the relationship of a good man to himself, and they are *not* satisfied by the *bad* man's relation to himself.

1166a17   Compare a22, 1168b35, 1178a2.

Chapter 8 (*pages 155–157*)

At 1166a34 Aristotle postponed the question whether a man can be his own friend, can love himself – though the answer was indicated at 1166a35: 'insofar as he is two or more'. (Compare the question whether a man can treat himself unjustly, V.11 note). In this chapter Aristotle asks whether the good man should love himself more than he loves anyone else. The criteria listed in chapter 4 suggest that he should – since he is his own best friend (1168b1–10). Yet self-love is condemned as characteristic of a bad man, and it is contrasted with a good man's motive for action: *he* acts not for himself but for another, and because it is a fine thing to do (1168a29–35).

Having set up the puzzle Aristotle indicates at 1168b14 the nature of his solution. With his clear account of two forms of self-love compare Bishop Butler's masterly discussion of self-love and love of others in *Sermon* XI.

Chapter 9 (*pages 157–160*)

Will the happy man need friends? Having outlined two views, Aristotle points out that the fact that the happy man will not need friends for their usefulness or to give him pleasure does not imply that he will not need them at all. He then gives three arguments to show that he will: 1169b28–1170a4, 1170a4–13, 1170a13–b19.

Central to this last, very complex argument is the appeal at 1170b5–7 to the idea, put forward in chapter 4, that a good man is related to his friend as he is to himself. Two comments:

(a) If A is related to A as A is related to his friend, A is related to A's existence as A is related to his friend's existence; but A desires for

Nicomachean Ethics, Book IX.9

its own sake *A*'s existence; therefore *A* desires for its own sake his friend's existence. There is an ambiguity in this conclusion. It might mean (roughly): (i) if *B* is *A*'s friend, *A* desires that *B* should (continue to) exist; *or* (ii) *A* desires that there should exist (and continue to exist) some person to be his friend. The conclusion Aristotle wants is (ii); but perhaps his premisses give only (i).

(b) Aristotle does not recognise the difference between one's 'consciousness' of one's own activities and one's 'consciousness' of one's friend's activities.

Book X

Chapter 1 (*page* 161)

1172a34 Compare 1179a17–22. Aristotle seems to have in mind *both* a contrast between what people say and what they do (words are less convincing than deeds) *and* a contrast between theories and facts (theory must not fly in the face of facts). 'Arguments' is not here a very helpful rendering of '*logoi*'.

Chapter 2 (*pages* 161–163)

1172b14 See I.1 note.

1172b23 For the argument about addition see 1097b16–20, Plato's *Philebus* 20–22 and 67a, and G.E. Moore's *Principia Ethica* pp. 27–29 (where the principle that the value of a whole is the sum of the values of its parts is questioned).

1173a4 See 1153b25 note. The words translated 'natural good' have been suspected by some commentators, and perhaps we should read simply: '. . . there is something superior to ourselves'. Compare 1153b32: 'all things have by nature something divine in them'.

Chapter 3 (*pages* 163–165)

1173a13 It looks as if someone had confused the question 'what things are good?' with the question 'what forms of goodness are there?'.

1173a15 The connection between *good* and limit or definiteness, and between *bad* and lack of limit, had a long history in Greek thought, and it was exploited by Plato in the *Philebus* (24e–25a, 31a) in discussion of pleasure and the good. Aristotle's three arguments here bring out the crudity of the argument that if you can speak of more or less *X*, *X* cannot be the good.

1173a29   Plato, *Philebus* 53c–54d.
1173b7   Plato, *Philebus* 31e–32b, 42cd.
1173b20–31   See VII.12 note. The third reply suggested here represents Aristotle's central view, developed in chapters 4 and 5.

Chapter 4 (*pages* 165–168)

1174a15   See 1153a9 note. In this and the following chapter 'complete' and 'completed' might mislead; 'perfect' and 'perfected' would be safer.
1174b33   Compare 1175a19–21. Aristotle's famous formula – 'a supervening end' – suggests two theses: (a) enjoying is necessarily enjoying doing (or thinking or feeling . . .) something; (b) the pursuit of pleasure presupposes primary desires for particular objects.

Chapter 5 (*pages* 168–170)

1176a26   This points back to I (1098a17 and 1099a30) and forward to X.7 and 8. Just as there are activities (and hence excellences) distinctive of man, so there are enjoyments distinctive of man. That these are more enjoyable than any others available to a man – this the good man (the proper arbiter) tells us (1176b25).

Chapter 6 (*pages* 170–172)

1176b7   This view of virtuous actions, consistent with what Aristotle has said in previous books, seems to be challenged in the next chapter, where he contrasts philosophical contemplation with practical activities on the ground that from the latter we gain something apart from the action itself. See 1177b1–26 note.
1176b19   For the claim that those who dispute the philosopher's grading of his enjoyments are incompetent to judge because they have never experienced them, see Plato's *Republic* IX.582a–c, 584e–585a. Compare Mill's *Utilitarianism*, chapter 2, paragraphs 5–8.

Chapter 7 (*pages* 172–174)

1177a12   See last paragraph of note on I.7. Aristotle now takes for granted that contemplation of eternal truths is the highest activity of man, and he proceeds to show how this activity, performed excellently, satisfies agreed criteria for *eudaimonia*. For the criteria, see I.8. On 'philosophic wisdom' see VI.6–7.

It is slightly odd that Aristotle *identifies* the reason that is our 'natural ruler and guide' with the reason that contemplates things noble and divine. The description seems to fit *practical* reason or wisdom; it is this that rules, is architechtonic, is epitactic. The contemplative reason or 'philosophic wisdom' that he is talking about in this chapter is surely different.

1177a21   Aristotle may mean that we tire (or he tires) more quickly of fighting or gardening than of philosophising. Or he may mean that doing things is necessarily intermittent: once you have given a contribution or saved the man's life you cannot go on performing the same action, whereas you can in principle go on contemplating a truth indefinitely.

1177a26   Why should this be expected?

1177a30   That the exercise of moral virtues requires material equipment (as well as other people) is emphasised in the next chapter. See 1099a31 note.

1177b1–26   See 1176b7 note. Aristotle's point is, presumably, that good action often consists in taking steps to bring about a desirable change in the world. But is this a reason for denying that the good man performs the action – and 'loves' to perform it – for its own sake? See 1139b1 note. It is clear that a proper understanding of these matters will not be reached without careful attention to the different descriptions that may be given of what the agent does.

The excellences most important in war are not those most important in peace: *Politics* VII.15.

1177b28   On our 'composite nature', see 1154b21 note. In what follows Aristotle strives to explain how the question what *human* happiness consists in can be given the answer: the exercise of *divine* reason. See end of note on I.7, and compare 1168b28–1169a3.

Chapter 8 (*pages* 174–177)

1178a22   Aristotle frequently says or implies that *nous* is a power *not* necessarily connected with bodily functions and therefore is separable and capable of operating apart from the body. 'It remains, then, that *nous* alone enters in from outside and that it alone is divine; for activity of the body has no part in *its* activity' (*G.A.* 736b27). He nevertheless holds that thinking involves the use of images (*De An.* III.7–8), and that having images involves bodily processes. The mysterious doctrine of 'active reason' (*De An.* III.5) may possibly be relevant to this puzzle.

1178b24   Aristotle seems to be appealing to the fact that animals other than men are not described as 'happy'. But this need not be because they are incapable of theoretical thinking; it might be because they are incapable of practical thinking.

NOTES

1179a24 This argument exploits a popular notion of gods and of piety which Aristotle does not share. See 1153 b 25 note.

Chapter 9 (*pages* 177–181)

1179b20 Compare I.9 and *E.E.* VIII.2. For the importance of early habituation, see Plato's *Republic* 401 b – 402 a.

1180a6 A reference to Plato's recommendation (and practice) in his *Laws*. A law should contain a reasoned explanation why such-and-such is being forbidden. The good man will keep the law because he understands and accepts this explanation. The part of the law that lays down penalties for breaches is necessary to secure the compliance of those inaccessible to reason.

1181 b 15 The programme here outlined corresponds pretty well to what Aristotle actually does in the *Politics*.

EUDEMIAN ETHICS

Book I

The materials in this book correspond closely to those in *E.N.* I.1–7, but they are differently organised. The concepts of a final end, of *eudaimonia*, and of the good for man are introduced in a different order. The critique of Plato's Idea of Good is subordinate to the elucidation of 'the good itself'; it leads into the identification of the good itself with the end of human action and the object of the master-art.

E.E. II.1 (to 1220 a 12) contains the function argument (*E.N.* I.7), the appeal to common opinions (*E.N.* I.8), and a brief discussion of the soul (*E.N.* I.13).

Chapter 1 (*pages* 185–186)

1214 a 32 The word '*phronesis*', translated 'practical wisdom' in the *Nicomachean Ethics*, is rendered by 'prudence' in the *Eudemian Ethics* (or sometimes by 'wisdom'). The meaning of the word in *E.E.* has been a matter of dispute: does it already, as in *E.N.*, stand for decidedly *practical* wisdom, or does it still cover, as for Plato, knowledge of changeless truths?

Eudemian Ethics, Book I.2

Chapter 2 (*page* 186)

The sensible idea, referred to at 1214b4, that the best life may have several distinct aims or ingredients seems to be immediately set aside in the first sentence of this chapter. But too much should not be made of this. The *main* point of chapter 2 is to distinguish *elements in* from *necessary conditions of* happiness, a distinction drawn more sharply here than anywhere in *E.N.* (but see 1099a31 note).

Chapter 3 (*pages* 186–187)

1215a1 Compare the brusqueness of 1095b20. Contrast Aristotle's usual attitude to what people think: *E.E.* 1216b26–35, *E.N.* 1098b9 –12, 1145b2–7. See Introduction, page 15.

Chapter 5 (*pages* 188–190)

1216b20 Knowing *what* an excellence is is different from knowing *what to do* to acquire it (*E.N.* 1103b26–31); and *knowing* what to do to acquire it is different from *doing* it (*E.N.* 1105b12–18, 1179a35–b16).

Chapter 8 (*pages* 192–195)

The phrase 'the good itself' or 'the good *per se*' translates a phrase often used by both Plato and Aristotle as a semi-technical term referring to the Form of Good. Here however Aristotle is arguing that neither a Platonic Form nor a universal could be the good itself that we are seeking. The features that distinguish the good itself – being best, the primary or original good, the cause of other things being good – belong to *the end of all human action* (1218b7–12).

For the detailed criticisms of the Platonic Form of Good, compare *E.N.* I.6.

Book II

Chapter 1 (*pages* 197–200)

1219a1 The word *'ergon'* here translated 'work' is rendered by 'function' in *E.N.* I.7 (and by 'product' in the different context of *E.N.* I.1).

1219a39 'Complete virtue' here means *all* the virtues or excellences, or at least all the distinctively human ones. Compare 1220a2– 4, and see last paragraph of note on I.7.

E.E. II.1.1220a13–II.5 correspond roughly to *E.N.* II, though

NOTES

the *final* definition of moral virtue is postponed until after the analysis of voluntary action, choice, etc. in *E.E.* II.6-10.

Chapters 7-9 (*pages* 201-207)

In analysing the concept *voluntary* Aristotle proceeds by elimination: voluntary action cannot be identified with action in accordance with desire (chapter 7) nor with action in accordance with choice (beginning of chapter 8), so it must be action in accordance with thought (1224a7, beginning of chapter 9). The demonstration that it cannot be action in accordance with desire is fallacious. Distinguishing three kinds of desire, Aristotle easily shows that voluntary action cannot be identified with action in accordance with *any one* of them. But this does not prove that it cannot be *action in accordance with desire*. That no one form of desire is such that an action is voluntary if and only if it flows from *that* form of desire does not exclude the possibility that an action is voluntary if and only if it flows from *some* form of desire.

The notion of accordance with desire is in fact smuggled into Aristotle's final account in chapter 9, which proves to differ not at all from the account in *E.N.* III.1 ('not forced and not through ignorance'). For while Chapter 9 speaks primarily of the knowledge the agent must have if his action is to be voluntary ('not through ignorance'), Aristotle slips in that the thing must be *in his power to do or not do*, must be done *owing to himself* (1225b8-9, 1226b30-32). This clearly means *not forced*, force (and duress) having been the main topic of chapter 8. But 'not forced' means that the starting-point was in the agent, was in fact his desire (1224b11-15, *E.N.* 1110a1 and 1111a22-24). Indirectly and implicitly, therefore, Aristotle redeems the fallacious argument of chapter 7 by letting desire back into his account of voluntary action. For the necessity of both a discriminating and a desiderative component in action, compare *De An.* III.10, *M.A.* c.6.

Chapter 10 (*pages* 207-211)

1227b8 With this, the final Eudemian definition, compare and contrast the Nicomachean formula (1106b36).

Aristotle does not explain why some preferences, tendencies, etc. are, and some are not, regarded as matters of *character*.

E.E. III is on individual excellences of character (*E.N.* III.6-IV).
E.E. IV-VI are the 'common books', i.e. they are *E.N.* V-VII.
E.E. VII is on friendship (*E.N.* VIII-IX).

Book VIII

The three chapters of this book (sometimes counted as VII.13–15) are of considerable interest, since nothing in *E.N.* corresponds at all closely to them. Unfortunately the text is very corrupt. Chapter 1: virtues are not forms of knowledge; the latter can be misused. Chapter 2: are some men lucky? Aristotle distinguishes between the luckiness of an unforeseeable and improbable event and the luckiness of being an intelligent and well-disposed person.

Chapter 3 (*pages 215–217*)

Aristotle distinguishes between things like honour and wealth that are 'naturally good' (and are indeed good for the good man but not for everyone) and excellences (and acts exhibiting them) which he calls 'noble' or 'fine' – these being praised for their own sake. The man who is good and noble practises and possesses for its own sake that which is noble; and for him natural goods are good and even in a way noble. The man who is good but not noble practises virtues *for the sake of* the natural goods; he thus does deeds that are noble only *per accidens*. The basic elements of this discussion are to be found in *E.N.*, though not put together in quite the same way.

1249a21 On the 'standard', compare *E.N.* 1138b18–34. Notice the restriction to natural goods (1249a25, b16). The answer given at 1249b18 ('what will most produce the contemplation of God') is not, therefore, put forward as an answer to the question what makes certain dispositions virtues or what makes certain acts noble or fine.

1249b14 Compare *E.N.* 1145a9. Neither passage implies that the promotion of *theoria* is the one and only point and purpose of morality or the one and only justification for praising and blaming certain kinds of conduct. Aristotle nowhere tries to show that we can or should 'derive' moral principles or conceptions of virtue from the unique and supreme value of theoretical activity. Rather he assumes an independent (though lesser) value for good *action*, and takes over without fundamental criticism or explanation contemporary views as to what sorts of action *are* good.

A difficulty remains. If the noble – which is desirable for its own sake – includes not only 'the contemplation of God' but also ordinary good conduct, why should promotion of the former be given as *the* standard by reference to which one should seek to acquire natural goods? Surely any decision about what amount of money to get or keep should be determined not only by the question what would be best for promoting contemplation but also the question what would be best for promoting generous and wise practical activity.

DE ANIMA

Book III

The chapters printed here are indispensable for the study of Aristotle's psychology of action.

Chapter 9 (*pages 221–223*)

432a 25   Here and at 432b 5 Aristotle is referring to Plato's *Republic* IV and IX. Plato distinguishes three parts or forms of soul, the 'calculative', 'passionate', and 'appetitive'; and he treats each part as having its own desires. Aristotle complains that there are psychological functions that Plato's tripartite division omits to mention, and also that it is at fault in 'breaking up' the faculty of desire.

433a 6   Aristotle here argues that desire is not a sufficient explanation of action. He fails to mention that one who 'follows mind' contrary to appetite does so because he has another desire stronger than the appetite. See next chapter.

Chapter 10 (*pages 223–225*)

Animal movement is caused by desire, and desire is evoked by the apprehension of some object of desire (433 a 17–20, b 10–12, b 27–29). This apprehension may be due to sense-perception or imagination or thought. The desire may be for something immediately pleasant or for something pleasant later or good. It is not clear that Aristotle sufficiently distinguishes two contrasts: (a) desire for the pleasant now *versus* desire for the pleasant later or in the long run ('possible only in beings with a sense of time', 433 b 7); (b) desire for the pleasant *versus* desire for the good (*wish*). Does he think that wanting something in the future – not as a mere animal reaction – necessarily involves thinking it *good* and wanting it as such?

De Anima, Book III.10

433 b 13 For the basic factors in *all* movement, see *Physics* VIII. 5.256 b 14.

433 b 20 M.A. 8-10 contain Aristotle's account of the physiological processes involved in animal movement.

Chapter 11 (*pages 225–226*)

434 a 10 The text and meaning of this sentence are disputed.

434 a 17 For the form of practical syllogism given here, compare *E.N.* 1147 a 4-7. For the idea that it is the particular premiss that primarily or directly originates movement, perhaps compare *E.N.* 1147 b 10 ('what determines our actions').

DE MOTU ANIMALIUM

Chapters 6 and 7 (to 701 a 38) contain an account of the psychology of action closely similar to that in *De An*. III.7-9. They are followed by an account of the physiological processes involved. This contains many difficulties of text and interpretation. In particular it remains obscure what relation Aristotle supposes to hold between the psychological and the physiological stories that he tells.

Chapter 6 (*pages 229–230*)

700 b 9 On the first unmoved mover, see *Metaphysics* Λ.6-7 and *Physics* VIII.

700 b 20 'Faculties of judgement' – or, rather, of discrimination or discernment. It is not that they issue verdicts, but that they all pick objects out (while desire is an attitude to objects so picked out).

700 b 28 Compare *De An*. 433 a 28 and *E.N.* III.4.

700 b 35 An attractive emendation gives the meaning: 'too precious for there to be anything prior to it'.

'The prime mover' here means not god (the 'first mover' of 700 b 8), but the good aimed at in action (cp. *De An*. 433 b 11-18). It, like Aristotle's god (700 b 30), causes movement by being an object of desire, not by itself moving.

701 a 5 The word translated 'alteration' is Aristotle's term for change of *quality*. See 701 b 10ff for details of the physiological

NOTES

processes involving alteration which distinguish animals from puppets.

Chapter 7 (*pages* 230–232)

701 a 10 Compare *E.N.* 1147a25–31.

701 a 12 More literally: 'from the two premisses the conclusion becomes the action', an obscure remark. Compare a20 ('the conclusion ... is an action') and a22 ('the action is the conclusion'). Aristotle fails to distinguish as sharply as he should between two different claims: (i) the conclusion of a certain form of thinking specifies and prescribes an action (the conclusion being *entailed* by the premisses); and (ii) the outcome of a certain kind of combination of desire and cognition is an action of a certain sort (this being *caused* by the antecedent desire and cognition). The distinction is, of course, the less important for him, in that when considering the logic of the practical syllogism – (i) – he is not concerned with 'imperatival logic' in the abstract, but only with the case where the thinker actually wants what is indicated in the major premiss and really sees, recognises, etc. the item or state of affairs mentioned in the minor.

While the examples about walking are like those in *E.N.* VI and VII (the major premiss being a general rule specifying the sort of thing to be done), the train of thought at a21 corresponds to the account of deliberation in *E.N.* III.3 (the major specifying something to be brought about by causal processes, and the minor saying how it can be done). The chapter also contains some much looser examples of practical thinking (e.g. a17: 'I need a covering, a coat is a covering, so I need a coat').

701 a 19 Most manuscripts read 'I need a coat: I make a coat.' But the reading 'I need a coat: I ought to make a coat' seems to suit better what follows.

701 a 20 Or, more literally: 'And one acts from a starting-point. If there is to be a coat, there must be such-and-such first; and if such-and-such, so-and-so; and *this* one does at once.'

701 a 24 'of the good and of the possible'. Does this refer to two types of deliberation (end of note on 701a12); or does Aristotle mean that the major always sets something up as *desirable* while the minor always shows how it is *possible* to achieve that desirable objective (whether achieving it is a matter of bringing something about or a matter of following a rule or principle)?

701 a 25 In argument (asking and answering questions) we often omit to state premisses that are obvious.

De Motu Animalium, Chapter 7

701a37 Since appetite, anger, and wish are the three specific forms of desire, it seems likely that the words 'desire or' should be cut out. Otherwise the distinction Aristotle is clearly intending to make gets destroyed.

701b17 On the question whether sense-perception is in fact alteration, a kind of *being changed*, or rather a kind of *activity*, see *De An.* II.5.

On the role of imagination and thought, compare 701b35, 703b18.

701b29 The heart is, for Aristotle, the central organ in which resides 'the principle of life and the source of all motion and sensation' (*De Partibus Animalium* 665a11). See chapters 9–10 below.

Chapter 8 (*pages 232–233*)

702a12 For accounts of *acting on* and *being acted upon*, see *G.C.* I.7 and *Met.* Θ.5.

702a15 'Straightway' or 'at once': 701a14, 15, 22, 30, 33, *E.N.* 1147a28. But also 'virtually simultaneous' (a16) and 'simultaneity and *speed*' (a20), for which last compare 701a28. If there is a wavering here it may be connected with the distinction, referred to in the note on 701a12, between logical necessity and causal necessity.

702a19 On the relation of imagination to thought and sense-perception, see 701a36, *De An.* 433b28–29.

702a23, a27 Aristotle is referring to *M.A.* 1. The general drift of what follows is clear, but the details are sometimes obscure. The Greek word (*archē*) rendered by 'origin' can refer to a temporal beginning, to a spatial starting-point, or to a ruling principle.

Chapter 10 (*pages 234–236*)

703a5 Compare *De An.* 433b16–19.

703a11 On the difficult but important doctrine of 'connate spirit' (*symphūton pneuma*), see Appendix B in A. L. Peck's *Generation of Animals* (Loeb Classical Library).

Chapter 11 (*pages 236–237*)

703b5 With this classification of movements compare and contrast *E.N.* III.1 and V.8.1135a33–b2.

703b30 See diagram at 702b28.

READING LIST

While the following list is obviously far from exhaustive, I have included a fairly wide range of reading to serve the various purposes of different readers.

Translations of Aristotle

Good alternative translations of *E.N.*, *E.E.*, and *M.A.* are to be found in the Loeb Library. For an alternative version of *De Anima*, see D. W. Hamlyn's volume in the Clarendon Aristotle series (1968).

General Books

D. J. Allan	*The Philosophy of Aristotle* (Oxford, 1970)
M. Grene	*A Portrait of Aristotle* (London, 1963)
G. E. R. Lloyd	*Aristotle: the Growth and Structure of his Thought* (Cambridge, 1968)
W. D. Ross	*Aristotle* (London, 1949)
A. E. Taylor	*Aristotle* (London, 1943)
A. W. H. Adkins	*Merit and Responsibility* (Oxford, 1960)
T. Ando	*Aristotle's Theory of Practical Cognition* (The Hague, 1971)
P. Aubenque	*La Prudence chez Aristote* (Paris, 1963)
R.-A. Gauthier	*La Morale d'Aristote* (Paris, 1963)
R.-A. Gauthier and J. Y. Jolif	*Aristote, Éthique à Nicomaque* (Introduction, Traduction, et Commentaire) (Louvain, 1958–9)
W. F. R. Hardie	*Aristotle's Ethical Theory* (Oxford, 1968)
P. M. Huby	*Greek Ethics* (London, 1967)
R. D. Milo	*Aristotle on Practical Knowledge and Weakness of Will* (The Hague, 1966)

J. D. Monan	*Moral Knowledge and its Methodology in Aristotle* (Oxford, 1968)
J. M. E. Moravcsik (ed.)	*Aristotle* (New York, 1967; London, 1968)
J. J. Walsh	*Aristotle's Conception of Moral Weakness* (New York, 1963)
J. J. Walsh and H. H. Shapiro (ed.)	*Aristotle's Ethics: Issues and Interpretations* (Belmont, 1967)

Works on Specific Topics

(a) *Eudaimonia* and the Good for Man (*E.N.* I)

H. A. Prichard	'The Meaning of *Agathon* in the *Ethics* of Aristotle' (*Philosophy*, 1935; *Moral Obligation*, 1949, chap. 3; and in *Aristotle*, ed. Moravcsik, New York, 1967)
J. L. Austin	'*Agathon* and *Eudaimonia* in the *Ethics* of Aristotle' (in *Aristotle*, ed. Moravcsik, New York, 1967; *Philosophical Papers*, 2nd ed., Oxford, 1970, chap. 1)
P. Glassen	'A Fallacy in Aristotle's Argument about the Good' (*Philosophical Quarterly*, 1957)
B. A. O. Williams	'Aristotle on the Good: a Formal Sketch' (*Philosophical Quarterly*, 1962)
W. F. R. Hardie	'The Final Good in Aristotle's *Ethics*' (*Philosophy*, 1965; and in *Aristotle*, ed. Moravcsik, New York, 1967)
C. W. Kirwan	'Logic and the Good in Aristotle' (*Philosophical Quarterly*, 1967)
F. Siegler	'Reason, Happiness, and Goodness' (in *Aristotle's Ethics*, ed. Walsh and Shapiro, Belmont, 1967)
P. T. Geach	'Good and Evil' (*Analysis*, 1956; and in *Theories of Ethics*, ed. Foot, Oxford, 1967)

READING LIST

R. M. Hare	'Geach: Good and Evil' (*Analysis*, 1957; and in *Theories of Ethics*, ed. Foot, Oxford, 1967)
G. H. von Wright	'The Good of Man' (*The Varieties of Goodness*, London, 1963, chap. 5)
L. A. Kosman	'Predicating the Good' (*Phronesis*, 1968)
J. L. Ackrill	'Aristotle on "Good" and the Categories' (in *Islamic Philosophy and the Classical Tradition: Essays Presented to Richard Walzer*, ed. Stern, Oxford, 1973)

(b) Moral Virtue (*E.N.* II)

H. W. B. Joseph	'Aristotle's Definition of Moral Virtue' (*Essays in Ancient and Modern Philosophy*, Oxford, 1935, chap. 6)
W. F. R. Hardie	'Aristotle's Doctrine that Virtue is a Mean' (*Aristotelian Society Proceedings*, 1964/65; *Aristotle's Ethical Theory*, Oxford, 1968, chap. VII)
D. J. Allan	'Individual and State in the *Ethics* and *Politics*' (in *La Politique d'Aristote*, Entretiens sur l'Antiquité classique, vol. XI, Geneva, 1965)
G. H. von Wright	'Virtue' (*The Varieties of Goodness*, London, 1963, chap. VII)
M. Ringböm	'Aristotle's Notion of Virtue' (*Ajatus*, XXIX, 1967)
W. W. Fortenbaugh	'Aristotle: Emotion and Moral Virtue' (*Arethusa*, 2.2, 1969)

(c) Action and Responsibility (*E.N.* III.1-5, V.8)

R. Jackson	'Rationalism and Intellectualism in the Ethics of Aristotle' (*Mind*, 1942)

READING LIST

D. J. Furley	'Aristotle and Epicurus on Voluntary Action' (*Two Studies in the Greek Atomists*, Princeton, 1967, Study II, chaps. 2 and 4)
F. A. Siegler	'Voluntary and Involuntary' (*Monist*, 1968)
J. L. Austin	'A Plea for Excuses' (*Aristotelian Society Proceedings*, 1956/57; *Philosophical Papers*, Oxford, 1961, chap. 6; and in *The Philosophy of Action*, ed. White, Oxford, 1968)
G. E. M. Anscombe	*Intention* (Oxford, 1957)
E. D'Arcy	*Human Acts* (Oxford, 1963)
H. A. L. Hart	*Punishment and Responsibility* (Oxford, 1968)
A. R. White (ed.)	*The Philosophy of Action* (Oxford, 1968)

(d) Practical Wisdom and the Practical Syllogism (*E.N.* VI)

L. H. G. Greenwood	*Aristotle: Nicomachean Ethics Book VI* (Cambridge, 1909)
D. J. Allan	'Aristotle's Account of the Origin of Moral Principles' (*Actes du XIe. Congrès international de Philosophie*, vol. XII, 1953)
D. J. Allan	'The Practical Syllogism' (in *Autour d'Aristote*, Louvain, 1955)
M. Mothersill	'Anscombe's Account of the Practical Syllogism' (*Philosophical Review*, 1962)
G. H. von Wright	'Practical Inference' (*Philosophical Review*, 1963)
G. E. M. Anscombe	'Thought and Action in Aristotle' (in *New Essays on Plato and Aristotle*, ed. Bambrough, London, 1965)
S. G. Etheridge	'Aristotle's Practical Syllogism and Necessity' (*Philologus*, 1968)

(e) *Akrasia (E.N.* VII.1–10)

R. Robinson	'Aristotle on Acrasia' (in *Essays in Greek Philosophy*, Oxford, 1969)
G. Matthews	'Weakness of Will' (*Mind*, 1966)
A. Kenny	'The Practical Syllogism and Incontinence' (*Phronesis*, 1966)
G. Santas	'Aristotle on Practical Inference, the Explanation of Action, and Akrasia' (*Phronesis*, 1969)
D. Davidson	'How is Weakness of the Will Possible?' (in *Moral Concepts*, ed. Feinberg, Oxford, 1969)

(f) Pleasure (*E.N.* VII.11–14, X.1–5)

A.-J. Festugière	*Aristote: Le Plaisir* (Paris, 1946)
J. L. Ackrill	'Aristotle's Distinction between *Energeia* and *Kinesis*' (in *New Essays on Plato and Aristotle*, ed. Bambrough, London, 1965)
J. O. Urmson	'Aristotle on Pleasure' (in *Aristotle*, ed. Moravcsik, New York, 1967)
T. Penner	'Verbs and the Identity of Actions' (in *Ryle*, ed. Wood and Pitcher, New York, 1970; London, 1971)
G. E. L. Owen	'Aristotelian Pleasures' (*Aristotelian Society Proceedings*, 1971/72)
G. Ryle	'Pleasure' (*Dilemmas*, Cambridge, 1954, chap. 4)
C. C. W. Taylor	'Pleasure' (*Analysis*, 1963)
J. C. B. Gosling	'Pleasure and Enjoyment' (in *The Business of Reason*, ed. Macintosh and Coval, London, 1969)
J. C. B. Gosling	*Pleasure and Desire*, Oxford, 1969

READING LIST

(g) Method

The following papers are all to be found in *Aristote et les Problèmes de Methode*, ed. Mansion, Louvain, 1961:

D. J. Allan	'Quasi-mathematical Method in the *Eudemian Ethics*'
J. D. Monan	'Two Methodological Aspects of Moral Knowledge in the *Nicomachean Ethics*'
G. E. L. Owen	'*Tithenai ta Phainomena*' (reprinted in *Aristotle*, ed. Moravcsik, New York, 1967)

INDEX

action, 24–8, 41, 62, 65 f., 75–86, 99, 105–7, 109 f., 114, 117, 126, 173, 175, 187, 191 f., 198, 200–10, 230, 250 f.
activity, 20 f., 33, 41, 49–51, 55, 61 f., 148, 152, 158 f., 165–176, 197 f., 213
appetite, 26, 75–9, 94, 96, 131, 134, 136, 139 f., 169, 201–13, 221–5, 229–31, 251, 270

character formation, 61–6, 84, 161, 177–80, 185, 246
choice, 26 f., 65, 69, 78–80, 82, 114, 132, 142–4, 161–3, 171, 186, 188 f., 201–13, 229 f., 241, 250
compulsion (force), 75–8, 105–7, 201–6, 213

deliberation, 26–8, 80–2, 114, 121–3, 146, 208–10, 225, 255 f.
desire, 26–8, 41, 78, 114, 188, 201–13, 221–225, 229–31, 234–6, 251, 270

ends, 26 f., 41–5, 48 f., 81 f., 85 f., 88, 146, 148, 186, 190, 192, 194, 210, 212, 215–7, 223, 229 f., 241
external goods, 52, 149, 157 f., 174–6, 245

function (work), 20 f., 49 f., 57, 67 f., 169, 197 f.

god (the divine), 45, 57, 152 f., 173 f., 191–193, 200, 217, 230, 261, 269
good, 18–21, 41–50, 82 f., 85, 100, 146–50, 153, 156–63, 169 f., 191–5, 210 f., 215–7, 229, 241, 243, 269

happiness (*eudaimonia*), 18–21, 24, 43–5, 48–57, 100, 149, 157–60, 170–7, 185–98, 242–4

ignorance, 25, 75–8, 84, 105–7, 109, 130, 134, 207 f., 250

incontinence (*akrasia*), 31–3, 129–46, 203–5, 258–60
involuntary, 24–8, 75–8, 83–6, 96, 105–8, 156, 201–10, 236, 249–52, 268

logos, 62, 69, 96 f., 113, 128, 134, 142–4, 156, 178 f., 216

mean, doctrine of, 21–3, 63, 67–74, 88, 95, 103, 113, 136 f., 141, 211, 216
method and aim of ethics, 15–7, 42–4, 50 f., 62, 129, 132, 150 f., 155, 161 f., 176 f., 186 f., 190 f., 241 f.

pleasure, 33 f., 51 f., 57, 63–5, 74, 76, 92–6, 132, 135–7, 140–3, 146–52, 159, 161–70, 188, 202, 204, 211, 232, 242, 261

reason (intellect), 80, 114 f., 118–21, 124 f., 127, 153, 156 f., 172–6, 199, 222 f., 229, 255, 264 f.

soul, 49 f., 58 f., 66, 113 f., 197–9, 221, 229, 234 f., 245 f.
syllogism, practical, 30, 124, 127, 133 f., 139, 212, 225 f., 230 f., 272

temperance, 92–7, 131, 136, 140, 144 f., 148

virtue, intellectual, 59–61, 113–28, 199 f.
virtue, moral, 21–4, 29, 45, 60–74, 78, 83–6, 101, 113 f., 126–8, 131, 156 f., 159, 161, 174–6, 190, 197, 199–201, 211 f., 216, 247 f., 259

wisdom, philosophic, 115, 118 f., 125–8, 172–4
wisdom, practical, 28 f., 116–28, 130 f., 145, 174
wish, 79, 82 f., 108, 190, 201–9, 221, 229, 251, 270